LETTERS ON 'CAPITAL'

KARL MARX &
FREDERICK ENGELS

LETTERS
ON
'CAPITAL'

Translated by Andrew Drummond

NEW PARK PUBLICATIONS

Published by New Park Publications Limited
21b Old Town, Clapham, London SW4 0JT

First published in German as
Briefe Uber Das Kapital
Dietz Verlag, Berlin, 1954

This edition: 1983

Translation and Foreword
Copyright © New Park Publications Limited 1983

British Library Cataloguing in Publication Data
Marx, Karl
   Letters on 'Capital'
   1. Marx, Karl. Kapital, Das
   I. Title   II. Engels, Friedrich
   III. Drummond A.   IV. Briefe über Das
   Kapital. *English*
   335.4   HB501.M37

ISBN 0 86151 007 0
ISBN 0 86151 008 9 Pbk

Set up Printed and Bound by Trade Union Labour

Distributed in the United States by
Labor Publications Inc., GPO Box 33023
Detroit, Michigan 48216

Printed in Great Britain by
Astmoor Litho Limited (TU)
21-22 Arkwright Road, Astmoor, Runcorn, Cheshire

Translator's Note

All the following letters were first collected together in German in the East German volume *Marx, Engels: Briefe Über Das Kapital* in 1954. The German volume itself was based on a 1948 Russian volume. Several of the letters have previously appeared in English in the Progress Publishers edition *Marx, Engels: Selected Correspondence* (Moscow 1975), but all the letters in the present volume are in a new translation.

The bulk of the letters were written in German, but several are in English or French, particularly those written to Russians. Those that were written in English have been left untouched (for example, letters 155 and 161), even though the grammar is often surprising, in order to preserve the original lively and internationalist flavour of the correspondence. For the same reason, Latin, French or Russian words or phrases within German or English letters have been left as given and translated only in footnotes.

Contents

1852

1853

1857

1858

1859

1860

1862

1863

1864

1865

1866

1867

1869

1870

1871

1872

1873

1875

1876

1877

1878

1878

1880

1881

Contents

1885

1886

1887

1888

1889

1890

1891

1892

1893

1894

Contents

1895

Introduction

In considering the significance of the correspondence between Marx and Engels, Lenin made the following remarks:

> If one were to attempt to define in a single word the focus, so to speak, of the whole correspondence, the central point at which the whole body of ideas expressed and discussed converges – that word would be *dialectics*. The application of materialist dialectics to the reshaping of all political economy from its foundations up, its application to history, natural science, philosophy and to the policy and tactics of the working class – that was what interested Marx and Engels most of all, that was where they contributed what was most essential and new, and that was what constituted the masterly advance they made in the history of revolutionary thought. (Lenin, *Collected Works*, Vol.19, p.554)

What Lenin had to say about the voluminous correspondence between Marx and Engels (which has recently begun to appear in the collected edition of their works) applies equally to their correspondence which was specifically concerned with *Capital* and the economic writings generally, correspondence which is made available in English for the first time with the appearance of this volume.

But before considering this point in greater detail we must first be clear about the driving force which lay behind Marx's revolutionary transformation of the science of political economy. As is made abundantly clear in the 234 letters collected here, Marx was above all inspired throughout his long and difficult labours by one aim: to provide for the working class a scientific outlook which could guide it in its struggle and lead it to final victory against its historical enemy, the bourgeoisie. It was this which led Marx, with the greatest possible scientific scrupulousness, to expose the limitations of even the greatest efforts by bourgeois ideologists in the field of political economy (Smith, Ricardo) not to say the representatives of what Marx contemptuously dubbed the 'vulgar school' in economics, who increasingly apologised for the capitalist system and presented it as the best possible system in the best of all possible worlds. Marx's ultimate aim is summed up in one of his letters of 1864, before the first volume of *Capital* appeared, when he writes:

> . . . I have been ill for the whole of this year (carbuncles and furuncles) – Without that, my work, *Capital*, on political economy would have been published already. Now I hope to finish it in a couple of months and to deal a theoretical blow to the bourgeoisie from which they will never recover. (61)*

And while in Germany to arrange for the publication of the first volume of his work (the only part to be published during his lifetime) Marx, writing to Becker, said: 'It is assuredly the most frightening missile which has ever been launched at the heads of the bourgeoisie (including landowners).' (70) In other words, Marx did not take up the study of political economy out of any idle interest; his purpose in exposing the shallowness of the bourgeois apologists for the capitalist system, his merciless criticism of all those who presented the system of capitalist property relations as one in accordance with the laws of nature, was always profoundly revolutionary, part of the task to which Marx devoted his entire life: the liberation of the working class and the establishment of socialism.

Throughout both his and Engels's letters – which span the years from 1845 to Engels's death in 1895 – runs a constant theme: the tremendous hardship under which Marx laboured while writing *Capital*. He complains continually that his scientific work is disrupted by the need to make even a minimum of money for his family to survive; he has to engage in 'continual scribbling' (18) for the bourgeois press in order to live; apologising for not having answered one of his numerous correspondents Marx says:

---

* Numbers in brackets refer to the number of the letter concerned.

I was continually hovering between life and death. So I had to use *every* moment available for work in order that I could finish the work for which I have sacrificed health, happiness and family . . . The so-called 'practical' men and their wisdom make me laugh. If one wished to be an ox, then one could naturally turn one's back on the horrors of humanity and only look after one's own interests. But I would have considered myself really *unpractical* if I had snuffed it without completing my book, at least in manuscript. (71)

Because of poverty Marx was forced often to prepare newspaper articles; to study in the British Museum by day and prepare his manuscripts throughout the night. As Marx wrily observed to Engels: 'Hence the shift-system, as the English manufacturing swine have applied it to the *same* people [the workers] between 1848 and 1850, has been applied to my own person by myself.' (67)

During his long theoretical struggle – in which he was sustained alone by Engels's unswerving devotion and support – Marx was able to carry through a revolution in the field of political economy 'to lay bare the law of motion of modern society' as he puts it in the Preface to *Capital*, only because of his systematic re-working of Hegelian dialectics from the standpoint of materialism. Here the letters on *Capital* and other economic writings are invaluable in further exposing all those who have pretended that Marx's *Capital* owes nothing to Hegelian dialectics. Leading the field here has of course been the Stalinist Louis Althusser – darling of the revisionists – who in a series of works throughout the 1960s and 1970s argued that Marx soon put behind him his youthful flirtation with German philosophy and by the time he wrote *Capital* was a fully fledged 'scientist' who had dispensed almost entirely with any concern for dialectics. But contrary to these assertions it was his critical assimilation of all that was positive in classical German philosophy that alone enabled Marx to grasp the movement of capitalism *as a whole*, to present it conceptually in its birth, development and death. As these letters show, Engels often pressed Marx to publish the results of his scientific work but they were pressures which Marx nearly always resisted, and for good reason, as he explains to his friend and collaborator as follows:

I cannot make up my mind to send anything off before I have the whole thing lying in front of me. Whatever shortcomings they may have, the advantage of my works is that they form an artistic whole, and I can only achieve that by my practice of never having them printed before I have them *complete* in front of me. The Jakob Grimm method is impossible for this and works better for books which are not formed dialectically. (64)

Writing to Conrad Schmidt in the early 1890s Engels is explicit about the role which the concrete critical assimilation and transformation of Hegelian dialectics had played in his work and that of Marx. Engels says:

> . . . The inversion of Hegel's dialectics is based on its pretensions to being a 'self-development of thought' and so the dialectic of things is only its reflection, whereas the dialectic in our heads is in fact only the reflection of the real development which takes place in the natural and human-historical world, in accordance with dialectical forms. Just compare Marx's study of the development from commodity into capital with Hegel's development from being to essence [in the *Short Logic*], and you will see a very good parallel; here the concrete development resulting from the facts, there the abstract construction in which the most brilliant thoughts and very often important negations, such as that of quality into quantity and vice versa, are presented as an apparent self-development of one concept from another, negations of which one could have easily invented a dozen others . . . (210)

Here two points are clear. First the central role which Hegelian dialectics played in the entire theoretical work of Marx and Engels, not least in their work for *Capital*. And second, the fact that in its idealist form this dialectic was of no use; it had to be reworked, appropriated from the standpoint of materialism, 'stood on its head, or rather its feet' as Marx puts it. This last point gives the lie to all those revisionists who, from the time of Bernstein onwards, have accused Marx and especially Engels of 'foisting' the categories of Hegelian dialectics onto the material and social world. But as these letters once again make abundantly clear there is no basis whatsoever to these charges. One of the early sections of these letters deals with Marx's settlement of accounts with the anarchist Proudhon. It was Proudhon who did precisely what Marx and Engels have been falsely charged with − that is taking certain 'dialectical phrases' from Hegel and on their basis constructing an 'analysis' of bourgeois society. The letter to Annenkov written by Marx at the end of 1846 should be studied carefully from this point of view. (4) For here Marx not only demolishes the pretensions of Proudhon's 'philosophy' contained in his book *Philosophie de la Misère* (The Philosophy of Poverty) but Marx at the same time outlines his conception of history, historical materialism. Marx accused Proudhon of living off the 'crumbs of German philosophy' (4) just as he later accused another opponent who thought that a few empty phrases could replace the detailed analysis of empirical material: 'he is an ass who thinks he can judge empirical things with a few abstract phrases'. (41)

Marx's reference here to empirical material reminds us of the enormous amount of such material which he painstakingly analysed throughout his entire work for *Capital*. Here again is involved a refutation of the stance of Althusser and his followers who in their peculiarly haughty manner have denounced as 'ideological' any concern with empirical material. (See Althusser's *Reading Capital*.) But this was certainly never Marx's position. As he said in the Preface to one of his earliest works, *The Economic and Philosophical Manuscripts of 1844*:

> It is hardly necessary to assure the reader conversant with political economy that my results have been attained by means of a wholly empirical analysis based on a conscientious critical study of political economy. (Marx Engels *Collected Works*, Vol.3, p.231)

Of course this in no sense renders Marx an empiricist. Empiricism is the philosophy which believes that an adequate theory of knowledge – indeed the only true theory of knowledge – is one limited to that derived from direct experience. For such a theory the role of the mind is confined to codifying, arranging, processing, such empirical data, and doing so invariably by means of the canons furnished by formal logic. Marx rejected such a theory. As a materialist he started from the premise that sensations were a product of an objective world which existed prior to and independently of consciousness. But this in no sense meant that he turned his back on empirical material in favour of empty and idle speculation, à la Proudhon. Quite the contrary: Marx set out to *explain* the appearances of bourgeois society, to establish the *nature* and *necessity* of such appearances, and thereby to prove, theoretically, that such appearances were not eternal, not 'natural', as bourgeois 'science' held, but were transient, destined to be 'smashed up' in the struggle of classes as Marx at one point puts it. It was necessary for Marx to establish the interconnections of all the at first sight unconnected aspects of bourgeois economy and for this it was necessary to reject the narrow outlook of empiricism in favour of dialectics. That is why Lenin places this question, that of dialectics, at the centre of the entire correspondence.

We can put the matter this way: it is of course true, as Lenin said, that there are three 'sources and component parts of Marxism', namely English classical political economy (Adam Smith and David Ricardo) French social theory and classical German philosophy. Although it would be wrong to counterpose rigidly these three elements against each other, there is no doubt that Marx's critical reworking of Hegelian idealist dialectics was decisive. For Marx 'philosophy was the head and the working class the heart' of the revolution. Although Marx had great respect for English classical political economy, especially in the shape of Ricardo (and this respect is evident throughout much of this correspondence) he at the same time recognised the severe limitations of this school. For not only did it see in capitalism the final form of society but it was at the same time a school whose work was severely vitiated by its narrow empirical outlook, an outlook derived from the philosophy of John Locke. (See letter 125 where Ricardo's a-historical outlook is dealt with.) Hegel's philosophy was by comparison much richer in content. Not only is philosophy, in its tendency, and certainly in its classical period of development, much wider in its scope than any one particular science, but Hegel had the advantages over a figure such as Ricardo not only of an encyclopaedic mind but also a great sense of history. His philosophy cannot be written off as idealist merely, but as an idealism which, however paradoxically, came close to the standpoint of dialectical materialism. It was, according to Engels, materialism turned inside out. For although Hegel, as an idealist, believed that the categories of thought were manifestations of the movement of the Absolute Idea (God) these categories were in fact invested with a real content, the content of history. Speaking of aspects of German history Marx remarks: (99)

> But what would old Hegel say if he learned, on the one hand, that the world 'Allgemeine' in German and Nordic means only 'common land' and that the word 'Sundre, Besondre' only meant the particular owner who had split away from the common land. Then, dammit, all the logical categories would proceed from 'our intercourse'.

In other words the categories of dialectical logic were not, as Hegel believed, the product of some unfolding Absolute Mind, but rather the (indirect) product of the social relations of production ('our intercourse'). So Marx and Engels would have no truck with the mechanical materialists of the Lange School who failed to understand why Marx and Hegel took 'dead dogs' such as Hegel and Spinoza so seriously. (See 191)

Included in this volume is Marx's celebrated letter to his friend Dr Kugelmann of July 11, 1868 (113). This letter was especially recommended for study by Lenin. In it Marx shows the distance separating his work from that of both the classical economists and their 'vulgar' descendents. Marx says to Kugelmann:

> Every child knows that any nation which stopped work – I will not say for one year – but just for a couple of weeks, would die. And every child knows that the volume of products corresponding to the various needs call for various and quantitatively determined amounts of total social labour. It is self-evident that this *necessity* of the *division* of social labour in certain proportions is not at all negated by the *specific form* of social production, but can only alter its *mode of appearance*. Natural laws can never be negated. Only the form in which those laws are applied can be altered in historically different situations. And the form in which this proportional division of labour asserts itself in a social situation and in which the connection of social labour asserts itself as a *private exchange* of the individual products of labour, is precisely the exchange-value of those products.

Here is the clue to grasping the real nature of Marx's 'labour theory of value', a theory which has been so often misunderstood in reformist and revisionist circles. This theory does *not* consist of the proposition 'labour is the source of all value', as is widely believed. Labour, together with nature provides for man's needs in all epochs and under all possible social conditions. But the form taken by this universal law varies from epoch to epoch. And it is the study of this form, under the specific conditions of capitalist economy which is the decisive question. As Marx here indicates, the form taken by this law under conditions of the private exchange of the products of labour (that is commodity production) is the exchange-value of such products. This law, the law of value, is peculiar to conditions of commodity production (and therefore to capitalism where such production becomes universal and all-dominant). And 'science consists precisely in working out *how* the law of value asserts itself'. But this law asserts itself *indirectly*, in mediated form, and never *directly* as even the best of the classical economists imagined. Here again was an expression of the empiricism of this school and an indication of the vast superiority of dialectics against this narrow standpoint. For as Marx notes, again in this same letter:

The vulgar economist has not the slightest idea that the real, daily relations of exchange can *not be identical* to the amounts of value. The whole point about bourgeois society consists precisely in the fact that, a priori, there is no conscious social control of production. What is reasonable and naturally necessary is only achieved as a blindly produced average. And then the vulgar economist thinks he has made a great discovery when he insists, in opposition to the revelation of the inner connectedness, that things look different in appearance. In fact, he boasts that he clings to appearance and takes it as final. So why then do we need a science?

That is, science consists precisely in going beyond appearances, to establish the source of such appearances in the movement of the social relations of production. And it is precisely this step, the step beyond the immediate appearance of things, which is debarred by empiricism. Here again, Marx could not have taken a single step forward from bourgeois economics without the critical review of classical German philosophy with which he began in the 1840s. This is the significance of Marx's statement in a letter at the beginning of this collection:

> I thought it very important to despatch a polemical piece against the German philosophy and against previous *German socialism* of a *positive* nature *earlier*. This was necessary in order to prepare the public for my position in the *Economy*, which stands in direct opposition to the previous German science. (2)

An introduction to this collection cannot pass over in silence the role which Engels played in every aspect of Marx's work in connection with *Capital*. Mention has already been made of Engels's unstinting financial and moral support which sustained Marx through his darkest days as he fought against poverty, personal illness (his 'damned carbuncles' feature in many letters) and the tragic loss of children as a direct result of the conditions he was forced to endure. So it was quite appropriate that the very night on which Marx put the very final touches to the first volume of his great work he should write to Engels (at 2a.m.):

> So *this volume is ready*. I have only *you* to thank for making this possible! Without the sacrifices you made for me, I would have been unable to finish the monstrous labours for the 3 volumes. I embrace you, full of thanks! (79)

But Engels's part was not confined to this moral and financial sustenance, crucial though it was. These letters reveal, in more detail than was possible from the limited amount of correspondence hitherto available in English, the great part which Engels, living in Manchester, played in providing Marx with detailed information on many aspects of business and commercial practices, practices with which Engels was directly familiar. Marx continually asked Engels to give him information about the technical side of production, about the commercial practices of the Lancashire textile producers, about their relations with the banks, and all this information was vital for Marx in enriching and concretising his theoretical work. Writing to Engels soon after the finishing of the first volume and noting the fact that several Blue Books appeared as the proof copy was being checked over, Marx says: 'I was charmed to see my theoretical results fully confirmed by the facts. It was finally written, carbuncles and the daily knock of the creditor and all!' (81) And in the same letter Marx asks Engels to tell him how a businessman organises the use of any surplus value before it is put back into the prices of production; 'you must give me an answer on this point (without theory, *only practically*)'. (For a sample of the invaluable help which Engels was able to provide for Marx about the working of capitalist business see the following letters: 28, 30, 31, 47, 52, 65, 81, 91, 121.)

Once having completed his first volume Marx had an enormous struggle to make his work known to the reading public, faced as he was with either open hostility or an ignorant or frightened silence. Here again Engels worked unremittingly to bring *Capital* to the notice of potential readers, especially workers, however small the numbers concerned might be. The English 'liberal' middle class showed their real face then as they do today. The *Fortnightly Review*, a journal bringing together a number of 'progressive' radicals and positivists of the John Stuart Mill type refused a review by Engels of the first volume. Engels tried every means possible to find out why the review had been rejected (one of those associated with the journal, the positivist E.S. Beesly, claimed that the review was too complicated for the average reader). Marx and Engels considered many subterfuges in an effort to break the wall of silence and indifference that first greeted the work – including the possibility of publishing attacks on it so that it would elicit other responses. (See many letters on these matters: 89, 90, 92 provide a sample.)

As we have already noted Marx was able to see only the publication of the first volume of *Capital* in his lifetime. Engels was responsible for seeing the second and third volumes through the press; Kautsky brought out *Theories of Surplus Value* after Engels's death in a highly distorted and unsatisfactory form which attempted to hide its revolutionary implications. The problems presented to Engels by the third volume were especially daunting. The manuscript was left in a state approaching chaos. Marx had found no time to arrange the various sections, to eliminate the large amount of repetition and to sort out the various drafts of sections of the work which had been written at various points in more than a quarter of a century during which he worked at his 'economics'. In the decade following Marx's death in 1883 Engels worked without a break to complete and bring to fruition the results of Marx's theoretical labours. Engels knew that he was the only person alive capable of doing this, just as in a different period Trotsky knew that he alone held the key to the fight to continue the theoretical and political work of Lenin in his struggle against the emerging Stalinist bureaucracy in the 1920s and 1930s. Only Engels had the intimate knowledge of Marx's work to allow him to publish the manuscripts in satisfactory form and in this sense the final volume of *Capital* is truly a joint work between him and Marx. Not least of Engels's virtues was his ability to decipher Marx's notorious handwriting. Many of Engels's letters in the latter half of the 1880s express his fear that his eyesight will not last out in time for the manuscripts to be published and he devised a plan to teach others, including Kautsky, to read Marx's 'hieroglyphics' so that the work could be completed in the event of his death or the serious deterioration of his eyesight.

But even here Engels's work was not confined to ensuring the publication of the Marx manuscripts. Not only was Engels at the centre of the international movement, advising Marxists and workers throughout Europe and beyond. He also took up the theoretical struggle against those tendencies which were beginning to emerge in outline and which were to come to a head in the period following his death: the abandonment of materialist dialectics in favour of evolutionism (Kautsky) and neo-Kantianism (Bernstein and others).

Highly revealing in this connection is a letter from Engels to Bernstein immediately prior to Marx's death in which Engels points out the anti-dialectical nature of Kautsky's thinking. Drawing attention to Kautsky's changed position on the theory of population Engels says the following:

Wonderful irony: three years ago he said the population should be limited, because otherwise they would have nothing to eat; and now there is not enough population to eat up even the American produce! This is what comes of studying so-called 'questions' one after another, with no connectedness. Thereby one naturally falls victim to that dialectic which – in spite of Dühring – is objectively inherent to things themselves. (170)

It is of course precisely the anti-dialectical method of thinking (metaphysics) which insists on taking each question separately, disconnected from the concrete whole of which it is in reality an objective part.

Engels returns to these fundamental questions in the theory of knowledge, questions without which there can be no scientific study of capitalist economy, in a letter to Kautsky shortly before his death. Saying that there were certain positive features to an article by Kautsky Engels then says:

> ... what I wish to dispute are your apodictic statements in fields where you yourself are not certain and where you lay yourself open to S[chramm] who has been skilled enough to attack. This is particularly the case in the 'abstraction' which you have picked to pieces ...

And Engels goes on to reveal the essence of the difference between Marx's dialectical method of abstraction on the one hand and Rodbertus's formal abstractions on the other (Kautsky's article had been concerned with Rodbertus):

> Marx unites the available general content of things and relations in their most general expression of thought, so his abstraction only reflects the already existing content of things in a form of thought. R[odbertus], on the other hand, invents a more or less incomplete expression of thought for himself and measures things against this concept, and they are supposed to behave according to it. He looks for the true, *eternal* content of things and of social relations but their real content is essentially transient. (186)

Engels also carried out another important theoretical struggle in defence of *Capital* which is recorded in this volume. This involved the neo-Kantian and later revisionist Conrad Schmidt. One form taken by Schmidt's neo-Kantianism was his argument that Marx's law of value was a fiction, albeit a 'useful' one. Engels immediately detects the influence of Kant here. (228) Schmidt became 'so tied up with details without . . . paying attention to the interconnection as a whole, that you degrade the law of value to a fiction, a necessary fiction, somewhat in the way that Kant turned the existence of God into a postulate of the practical reason'. And Engels goes on to say:

> The identity of thinking and being, if I might express myself in a Hegelian manner, everywhere coincides with your example of the circle or the polygon. Or else the two of them, the concept of a thing and its reality, run side by side like two asymptotes, always approaching each other but never meeting. This difference between the two is the very difference which prevents the concept from being reality and prevents reality from being its own concept immediately. Because a concept has the essential nature of the concept and does not therefore prima facie coincide with reality, from which it had to be abstracted in the first place, it is nevertheless more than a fiction, unless you declare all the results of thought to be fictions because reality corresponds to them only very circuitously, and even then only approaching it asymptotically.

In this Introduction it has been possible to touch only on certain aspects of the correspondence. There is much here that will interest those wishing to develop their knowledge of Marxism. Particularly important are the letters written by Engels at the end of his life which deal with the materialist conception of history. Engels is at pains to stress that the theory of history developed by himself and Marx from the 1840s onwards has little in common with mechanical materialism. He explains with reference to a series of specific questions that while historical materialism holds unswervingly to the premise that the social relations of production determine the political, ideological, legal etc. superstructure, this relationship – between economic base and superstructure – is a truly dialectical one. That is, 'economics' is decisive, but decisive in the sense of a *tendency*. Historical materialism must not be misconstrued – as it was, deliberately so, by Stalinism – to mean that politics, state forms, ideology had no role to play in the historical process. These letters by Engels should therefore be read in conjunction with both Marx's early letter to Annenkov (4) as well as the famous statement on the fundamentals of the materialist conception of history in the Preface to the *Critique of Political Economy* (1859).

Apart from these questions on historical materialism, several of the letters deal with aspects of Indian history, notably the role of British colonialism in India. Various aspects of the Asiatic mode of production are also touched upon by both Marx and Engels, and Russia is a topic which occupied a large measure of Marx's time. His material for *Capital* was of course based largely on the development of English economy and this for the good reason that it represented the highest, most developed and therefore 'purest' form of capitalism where its laws operated with greatest force. But Marx had to turn elsewhere for materials involved in the study of landed property and here Russian development was of particular interest to him. His outstanding 'scientific conscience', as he termed it, led him to study the Russian language so that he could consult original materials. It is noteworthy that the first country to see a translation of *Capital* from the original German was Russia. Both Marx and Engels carried out a long exchange of views with all the leading figures in the Russian revolutionary movement: one of the last letters of this volume is one from Engels to Plekhanov. (227) Here is an expression of the continuity between the theoretical and political struggles of Marx and Engels on the one hand and the Russian Revolution of 1917. Marx was able, because of his theoretical genius, to see in to the future (although he was naturally unable to forsee the revolutionary struggle in all its empirical unfolding); in this respect his hand was present in the first proletarian revolution in history, an event which he had predicted in the 1840s and was one of the central themes of his correspondence with Engels and others.

This brings us back to the central point from which this Introduction began. Marx studied political economy not as an economist but as a revolutionary fighter. His aim was to arm the working class theoretically, to provide it with a theory which would enable its most conscious elements to grasp capitalism in its real development. Marx did not live to see the first successful revolution of the working class. Nor did Engels. But they both laid the indispensable theoretical groundwork for that success. Speaking of the relations of capitalist economy in a letter to Kugelmann Marx emphasises the decisive role of his struggle to uncover the law of motion of this economic formation:

> Once insight into the connectedness has been gained, all theoretical belief in the permanent necessity of existing conditions collapses before the practical collapse. (113)

Here was a classic expression of theory truly guiding practice, the practice of the socialist revolution. It is from this standpoint that this invaluable collection of letters should be studied by every revolutionary fighter in the working class.

Last but not least. The translator of the present volume, Andrew Drummond, is to be warmly congratulated on his work. His translation is throughout concise and lucid. Some of these letters have of course appeared before but many have hitherto been unavailable to the English reader. Drummond's careful and diligent work will now make them available to much wider layers of youth and workers. This is entirely to be welcomed.

G. Pilling

Karl Marx, 1818-1883

Friedrich Engels, 1820-1895

Marx's letter to Engels announcing the completion of the first volume of 'Capital', 2a.m. August 6, 1867 – see letter 79

End of Engels's letter to Danielson of October 29-31, 1891, with an excerpt from 'Eugene Onegin' – see letter 209

1845

1. Engels to Marx

What really gives me pleasure is to see how communist literature has settled down in Germany, and is now a fait accompli. A year ago it began to put down roots outside Germany, in Paris, and now it is breathing down the neck of the ordinary German. Newspapers, weeklies, monthlies and quarterlies and an increasing reserve of heavy artillery are now all in the best condition. It has all happened damned quickly! Underground propaganda has also had its successes – every time I go to Cologne, every time I enter a bar, there is new progress, new recruits. The Cologne congress has worked wonders – gradually we are uncovering isolated communist cliques which have developed quietly without our intervention. Even the *Gemeinnützige Wochenblatt*, which used to be published along with the *Rheinische Zeitung*, is now under our control. D'Ester has taken it over and will see what can be done with it. But what we require most of all is a couple of lengthy works, so that the many half-educated people who have the will, but not the means, to manage by themselves, can get a proper grasp of things. See if you can get your book on economics finished,[1] even if you yourself are not happy with it: it does not matter; the mood is right and we must strike while the iron is hot. The effect of my study on England[2] will not be inconsiderable, for the facts are too striking, but all the same I wish I had more freedom to complete a host of things which would be more conclusive and effective in the present period and given the German bourgeoisie. We German theoreticians – it is laughable, but still a sign of the times and of the dissolution of the German national mire – we cannot develop our theory because we have not been able to publish the Critique of Nonsense yet.[3] But it is high time. So see that you are finished *before* April; do as I do, set yourself a time when you positively *wish to be finished*, and arrange for early publication. If you cannot get it published there,[4] then get it done in Mannheim, Darmstadt or anywhere. But it must come out soon . . .

[1] Reference to Marx's planned but never completed *Critique of Politics and Political Economy*.
[2] Engels, *The Condition of the Working Class in England*.
[3] Marx and Engels, *The Holy Family, or Critique of Critical Criticism*.
[4] i.e. Paris.

1846

2. Marx to Leske

You received a much-delayed reply to your letter containing your thoughts on publication. With reference to your question about 'scientific methods', I answered: The book[1] is 'scientific, but not scientific in the sense that the Prussian government etc. would like'. If you can still recall your first letter, you wrote most anxiously about the Prussian official warning and the police search which had just been carried out at your place. I wrote to you at the same time that I would look around for another publisher . . .

I *received* a second letter from you, in which you revoked the agreement on publishing, and also determined the repayment of the deposit in the form of a recommendation to the relevant new publisher . . .

Now, as for the delay in replying, it was as follows:

Several capitalists in Germany had accepted for publication several texts by myself, Engels and Hess. There was then even hope of a really lengthy series of publications free from all police considerations. With the help of a friend[2] of these gentlemen, the publication of my *Critique of Political Economy etc.* was also as good as settled. This same friend stayed in Brussels until May in order to bring the manuscript of the first volume of the publication (edited by myself and with the co-operation of Engels etc.) safely across the border. And then he was supposed to write from Germany to say definitely whether the *Economy* was accepted or rejected. But no – or at best indefinite – news arrived, and after the greater part of the manuscript of the second volume of that publication was already dispatched to Germany, these gentlemen finally wrote, only a short time ago, to say that, because their capital was tied up elsewhere, the whole affair was off. A definite answer to you was thus delayed. When everything had been decided, I made an agreement with Herr Pirscher of Darmstadt, who was here, that he should deliver my letter to you.

Because of that agreement with the German capitalist publishers, I interrupted the work on the *Economy*. For I thought it very important to despatch a polemical piece against the German philosophy[3] and against previous *German socialism* of a *positive* nature *earlier*. This was necessary in order to prepare the public for my position in the *Economy*, which stands in direct opposition to previous German science. Incidentally, it is the same polemical article about which I wrote to you before in one of my letters, asking that it should be completed before the publication of the *Economy*.

Enough of that . . .

Since the almost completed manuscript of the first volume of my study has been lying here for so long, I will not have it printed without revising it once more, in content and style. It goes without saying that a writer who makes progress in six months cannot allow something which he wrote six months earlier to be printed word for word the same.

I should add that the *Physiocrats*[4] appeared in two folio volumes only at the *end of July* and will only arrive here in a few days, although its publication was already announced during my stay in Paris. Now they must be fully considered . . .

The revised first volume will be ready for printing at the *end of November*. The second volume, which is more historical, could follow quickly.

I have already told you in an earlier letter that the manuscript will be more than 20 printed sheets more than the agreed length, partly due to new material from England, partly due to the necessities arising from revision . . .

If necessary, I could give you evidence in numerous letters which I have received from Germany and France, that the public awaits this study with great excitement.

[1] i.e. the uncompleted *Critique of Politics and Political Economy*.

[2] Joseph Weydemeyer.

[3] Marx & Engels, *The German Ideology. Critique of the latest German Philosophy and its representatives Feuerbach, B. Bauer and Stirner, and of German socialism and its various prophets*.

[4] E. Daire, *Les Physiocrates*, Paris 1846.

3. Engels to Marx

I have really done Proudhon a crying injustice in the business letter. Since there was no room in that letter, I must make amends here. You see, I thought that he was guilty of a slight nonsense, a nonsense just on this side of common sense. Yesterday, the matter came up again, and was thoroughly discussed, and then I discovered that this new nonsense was really *an unlimited nonsense*. Just imagine: proletarians are supposed to *take* minor shares of stock. From this (of course we cannot start with less than 10 – 20,000 workers) we could first set up one or more workshops in one or more factories, employ some shareholders there and then sell 1. the products to the shareholders at the price of the raw material plus labour (so that there is no profit made) and 2. any surplus at the current world market-price. As long as the capital of the company is incremented by newcomers or through new savings by the old shareholders, it would be used for new workshops and factories, and so on and so forth until – *all* proletarians are employed, all productive forces in the land are bought up and thus all the capital at present in the hands of the bourgeoisie will have lost its power to command labour and make a profit! Thus capital can be negated, for one 'finds an authority before which capital, that is, the realm of interest' (a Grün-ification of the somewhat more common droit d'aubaine[1] of yesteryear) 'vanishes, as it were'. You will see in this phrase, repeated many a time by Papa Eisermann and thus learned by heart by Grün, the original Proudhonesque flourishes shining forth. These people have nothing more and nothing less in mind than to *buy up* firstly toute la belle France,[2] then perhaps the rest of the world, given proletarian thriftiness and renunciation of profit and interest on their capital. Has anyone ever dreamed up such a wonderful plan before, and would it not be much easier – if we wanted a real tour de force – to mint five-thaler pieces out of the silvery light of the moon? And these stupid workers here – the Germans, I mean – *believe* this rubbish; they, who do not have six farthings in their pockets between them to take down to the wine shop in the evening, they want to buy up la belle France with their savings. Rothschild and his friends are real bunglers compared with these tycoons. It is enough to give you a fit. Grün has so ruined these people that they find more sense in the most nonsensical phrase than in the simplest fact of applied economics. It is really outrageous that we should have to counter such barbaric nonsense. But one must be patient, and I will not let them go until I have driven Grün off the pitch and have cleared their befuddled skulls . . .

---

[1] 'Right of escheat' – a feudal law which gave the state the right to take the property of a deceased alien without heirs after his death.
[2] 'Beautiful France'.

4. Marx to Annenkov[1]   *December 28, 1846*

You would have received my reply to your letter of 1st November long ago if my bookseller had not waited until last week to deliver Proudhon's book *Philosophie de la Misère*.[2] I got through it in two days so as to be able to tell you my opinion straight away. Since I read the book very quickly, I cannot go into details; I can only discuss my general impression of it. If you wish, I could discuss details in a later letter.

Frankly, I will confess that I found the book generally very, very bad. In your letter you yourself joked about 'the crumbs of German philosophy' which M. Proudhon parades in this amorphous and presumptuous work; but you also suppose that the economic argument has not been infected by this philosophical poison. I too am very unwilling to impute the faults in the economic argument to M. Proudhon's philosophy. M. Proudhon does not present a false criticism of political economy because he is the proud propounder of a ridiculous philosophy, but rather he presents a ridiculous philosophy because he has not understood the real social conditions in their interconnection – to use a word which M. Proudhon has borrowed, like so many other things, from Fourier.

Why does M. Proudhon talk of God, of Universal Reason, of the Impersonal Reason of Humanity, which is never wrong, which has at all times been equal to itself, and of which we only need to be conscious to find Truth? Why does he use tame Hegelianism in order to appear like a wild man?

He provides a clue to this enigma himself. M. Proudhon sees a distinct chain of social developments in history; he finds that progress is given reality by history; and he finds, finally, that men, taken as individuals, did not know what they were doing, that they mistook their own motion – that is, their social development appeared at first as something indistinct, separate, independent of their individual development. He cannot explain these facts, so his hypothesis of Universal Reason in its self-realisation fits just nicely. Nothing is simpler than inventing mystical causes (i.e. phrases) whenever common sense is at a loss.

But this M. Proudhon, when he admits that he understands nothing of the historical development of mankind – and he admits it when he has recourse to fine words like 'Universal Reason', 'God' etc. – does he not implicitly and necessarily admit that he is incapable of understanding *economic developments*?

What is society, in whatever form? It is the product of the reciprocal action of men. Are men at liberty to choose this or that social form? Not in the least. Given a specific stage of development in the productive forces, you will also have a specific form of commerce and consumption. Given specific stages in the development of production, commerce and consumption, you will have a specific social organisation, a set organisation of the family, of castes or classes: in short, a specific civil society. Given a specific civil society, you will have a specific political form, which is only the official expression of civil society. This is what M. Proudhon will never understand, for he thinks he is a visionary when he works from the State to civil society, that is, from the official epitome of society to official society.

It is not necessary to add that men are not free to decide their *productive forces* – which are the basis of their entire history – for all productive forces are accumulated forces, the product of previous activity. Thus, productive forces are the result of men's practical energy; but this energy itself is determined by the conditions in which men are placed by productive forces already acquired, and by the social form which existed before them, which they did not create, which is the product of a previous generation. Because of the simple fact that each succeeding generation uses productive forces acquired by the preceding generation and used as the raw material for new production, a connectedness in human history is created; and it is all the more a history of mankind because the productive forces of men, and hence their social relations, have increased. As a necessary consequence, the social history of men is never merely the history of their individual development, whether they know it or not. Their material relations are only the necessary forms for the realisation of their material and individual activity.

M. Proudhon confuses ideas and objects. Men never renounce what they have gained; but that is not to say that they never renounce the social form in which they acquired certain productive forces. On the contrary. So as not to be deprived of the results attained and so as not to lose the fruits of civilisation, men are forced to change all their traditional social forms, from the moment that the form of their commerce no longer corresponds to the acquired productive forces – I use the word 'commerce' here in its broadest sense, just as we use the word 'Verkehr'[3] in German: for example: privilege, the institutions of guilds and corporations, the regimentation of the Middle Ages – all these were social relations which alone corresponded to the accumulated productive forces and to the preceding social form in which these institutions arose. Under the protection of the guilds and regulations, capital was accumulated, maritime commerce developed, colonies were established – and men would have lost these very fruits if they had tried to preserve the forms under whose protection these fruits ripened. There were also two thunderbolts, the revolutions of 1640 and 1688. All the old economic forms, and the social relations which corresponded to them, and the political state which was the official expression of the old civil society, were shattered in England. Thus, the economic forms in which men produce, consume and exchange, are transitory and historical. With new, acquired productive forces, men change their mode of production, they change all their economic relations, which are only the necessary relations of that determined mode of production.

This is what M. Proudhon has not understood, let alone proved. M. Proudhon, incapable of following the real motion of history, presents us with a phantasmagoria with the pretensions of being a dialectical phantasmagoria. He does not feel obliged to discuss the 17th, 18th or 19th centuries, because his History takes place in the nebulous atmosphere of the imagination and raises itself high above time and place. In a word, it is Hegelian crap, it is not a history, it is not a profane history – the history of men – but a sacred history – a history of ideas. In his vision, Man is only the instrument which the Idea or Universal Reason uses for its own development. The *evolutions* which M. Proudhon discusses are considered to be the evolutions as they occur in the mystical womb of the absolute Idea. If you draw back the curtains on this mystical language, it boils down to saying that M. Proudhon is presenting the order in which economic categories are arranged inside his head. I would not be hard pressed to prove that this arrangement is the arrangement of a very disorganised head.

M. Proudhon opens his work with a dissertation on value, which is his hobby-horse. I will not review this dissertation just now.

The series of economic evolutions in Eternal Reason begins with the *division of labour*. M. Proudhon finds the division of labour a most simple affair. But is not the caste system a kind of division of labour? And is not the guild system another division of labour? And was not the division of labour in the system of manufacture, which began in the middle of the 17th century and ended in the last part of the 18th century, also totally different from the division of labour in large scale industry – in modern industry?

M. Proudhon is so far away from reality that he even ignores the profane economists. When discussing the division of labour, he feels no need to mention the world *market*. Well! In the 14th and 15th centuries, when there were as yet no colonies, when America did not exist as far as Europe was concerned, when the Far East only existed via Constantinople, was not the division of labour utterly and completely different from that of the 17th century when the colonies were already developed?

That is not all. The entire internal organisation of nations, all their international relations – are these something other than the expression of a specific division of labour? And should they not change with a change in the division of labour?

M. Proudhon has understood the question of the division of labour so poorly that he does not even mention the separation between town and country, which, in Germany for example, took place between the 9th and 12th centuries. Thus, M. Proudhon sees this separation as an eternal law, since he recognises neither its origin nor its development. He will devote his entire book to speaking as if this creation of a specific mode of production would last until doomsday. All that M. Proudhon tells you about the division of labour is only a summary (and a very superficial and very incomplete summary at that) of what Adam Smith and a thousand and one others had said before him.

The second evolution is *machinery*. The connection between the division of labour and machinery is a complete mystery to M. Proudhon. Each mode of the division of labour had specific instruments of production. For example, from the middle of the 17th to the middle of the 18th century, men did not do everything with their bare hands. They had tools, and these tools were very complicated, such as work-benches, ships, levers etc. etc.

Thus, nothing could be more ridiculous than to present machinery as a direct consequence of the division of labour in general.

I will mention in passing that M. Proudhon, since he has not understood the historical origin of machinery, has understood their development even less. Until 1825 – the time of the first world crisis – one could say that the requirements of general consumption overtook production and that the development of machinery was the necessary consequence of market requirements. Since 1825, the invention and the use of machinery has only been the result of the war between employers and workers. And that only holds true for England. As for the European nations, they have been obliged to use machinery because of England's competitiveness both on their own territory and on the world market. Finally, in North America, the introduction of machinery was a result both of competition with other nations and of the scarcity of labour, i.e. of the discrepancy between the population and the industrial requirements of North America. You could conclude from this what kind of wisdom has been developed by M. Proudhon when he calls up the ghost of competition as a third evolution, as an antithesis to machinery!

Generally speaking, therefore, it is truly absurd to place machinery in a separate economic category apart from the division of labour, competition, credit, etc.

Machinery is no more a separate economic category than an ox that pulls a wagon. The present use of machines is one of the relations in our present economic system, but the *method* of using machines is completely different from the machines themselves. Gunpowder remains the same whether it is used to wound a man or to treat his wounds.

M. Proudhon surpasses himself, when he develops competition, monopoly, taxes or the police, balance of payments, credit, property, in that order in his head. Almost all the credit institutions were developed in England at the beginning of the 18th century before the invention of machinery. Public credit was merely a new way of increasing taxation and of satisfying the new needs created by the assumption of power by the bourgeoisie. Property, finally, forms the last category in M. Proudhon's system. In the real world, however, the division of labour and all the other categories of M. Proudhon are social relations and their totality forms what is currently called '*property*': bourgeois property outside these relations is nothing but a metaphysical or legal illusion. The property of another epoch, feudal property, developed in a series of entirely different social relations. M. Proudhon, in establishing property as an independent relation, commits more than one methodological fault – he proves conclusively that he has not grasped the thread which connects all the forms of *bourgeois* production, and that he has not understood the *historical* and *transitory* character of modes of production in a given epoch. M. Proudhon, who cannot see historical products in our social institutions, who understands neither their origins nor their development, can only make a dogmatic criticism.

And M. Proudhon is forced to have recourse to *fiction* in order to explain this development. He thinks that the division of labour, credit, machinery, etc. have all been invented in order to serve his fixed idea, his idea of Equality. His explanation is superbly naive. These things have been invented for Equality, but alas, they have turned against Equality. That is his entire reasoning. That is to say, he makes a gratuitous supposition, and because the actual development and fiction contradict each other at every turning, he concludes that there is a contradiction. He conceals the fact that the only contradiction is between his fixed preconceptions and actual motion.

Thus M. Proudhon, mainly through his lack of historical knowledge, has not seen that men, in developing their productive forces – that is, in living – develop certain relations with each other, and that the form of these relations necessarily changes with the transformation and the development of these productive forces. He has not observed that *economic categories* are only the *abstractions* of these real relations, and that they are only valid as long as these conditions exist. Hence he commits the error of bourgeois economists who consider these economic categories to be eternal laws and not historical laws which remain laws only during a certain historical development determined by productive forces. Thus, instead of considering political and economic categories as the abstractions of actual, transitory, historical social relations, M. Proudhon, by mystical inversion, only sees actual relations as the embodiments of these abstractions. These abstractions themselves are formulae which have slumbered in the bosom of the Lord God since the Creation.

But here our good M. Proudhon undergoes great intellectual convulsions. If all these categories are emanations from the heart of God, if they form the secret eternal life of men, then how does it come about, firstly, that there is any development and, secondly, that M. Proudhon is not a Conservative? He will explain these manifest contradictions with his mighty system of Antagonism.

Let us take an example and explain this system of Antagonism.

Monopoly is good, because it is an economic category and hence an emanation of God. Competition is good, because it is also an economic category. But what is *not* good is the reality of monopoly and the reality of competition. And what is worse is that monopoly and competition mutually devour each other. So what should we do? Since these two eternal thoughts of God contradict each other, it is clear that, in the bosom of God, there must also be a synthesis of these two thoughts, by which the evils of monopoly are balanced by competition, and vice versa. The struggle between these two ideas would then only result in the best aspects. So we must wrest this secret from God, then apply it, and all will end happily; we must decode the synthetic formula hidden in the night of the impersonal reason of humanity. M. Proudhon does not hesitate for a moment to present himself as the decoder.

But cast your eyes for a moment on real life. In real economic life we find not only competition and monopoly, but also their synthesis, which is not a *formula* but a *movement*. Monopoly produces competition, competition produces monopoly. However, this equation, far from easing the difficulties of the actual situation, as bourgeois economists would like, results in a more difficult and complex situation. Thus, in changing the basis upon which actual economic relations are founded, in destroying the actual *mode* of production, we destroy not only competition, monopoly and their antagonism, but also their unity, their synthesis, and their motion, which is the real balance of competition and monopoly.

Now I shall give you an example of M. Proudhon's dialectic.

Freedom and *slavery* form an antagonism. Here I do not need to speak about the good and bad sides of freedom. As for slavery, I do not need to speak about its bad side. The only thing I need to explain is the good side of slavery. We are not discussing indirect slavery, the slavery of the proletariat, but direct slavery, the enslavement of negroes in Surinam, in Brazil, in the southern states of North America.

Direct slavery is the pivot of our industry as much as machinery, credit, etc. are. Without slavery there can be no cotton, without cotton, no modern industry. It is slavery which has given value to the colonies, it is the colonies which have created world trade, it is world trade which is the necessary pre-condition for large-scale machine industry. In addition, before the slave trade arose, the colonies only yielded very few products for the old world and did not visibly change the face of the world. Thus, slavery is an economic category of the greatest significance. Without slavery, North America and its most progressive people would be transformed into a patriarchal country. Just erase North America from the face of the earth and there will be anarchy and complete decadence in commerce and modern civilisation. But to destroy slavery would be precisely to erase North America from the face of the earth. In addition, slavery, because it is an economic category, has existed in every nation since the Creation. Modern nations have only been able to disguise slavery at home and openly export it to the New World. So what does the excellent M. Proudhon do after these reflections on slavery? He looks for a synthesis of freedom and slavery, the true medium or the balance between slavery and freedom.

M. Proudhon understands very well that men make cloth, linen and silk, and claims great merit in having understood such a small matter! But what M. Proudhon has not understood is that men, according to their abilities, also produce the social relations in which they produce cloth and linen. And M. Proudhon has understood even less that men, producing social relations according to their material productivity, also produce *ideas, categories*, i.e. the abstract ideal expressions of these same social relations. So these categories are only as eternal as the relations which they express. They are historical and transitory products. For M. Proudhon, on the contrary, the prime causes are abstractions and categories. According to him, it is they, and not men, which make history. The *abstraction*, the *category in itself*, that is, separate from men and their material activity, is naturally immortal, immutable, insensible; it is only an entity of Pure Reason, which only means that the abstraction in itself is abstract – a fine tautology!

So the economic relations, taken in the form of categories, are eternal formulae for M. Proudhon, without origins, without progress.

Let us put it another way: M. Proudhon does not state openly that, for him, *bourgeois* life is an *eternal truth*; he says it in a roundabout way, in deifying the categories which express bourgeois relations in the form of thought. He sees the products of bourgeois society as spontaneous, eternal and endowed with their own separate existence, as soon as they appear before him as categories of thought. Thus he never crosses the bourgeois horizon. And because he operates with bourgeois thoughts and considers them to be eternally true, he looks for the synthesis of these thoughts and their equilibrium and does not see that their actual mode of self-balance is the only possible mode.

In reality, he is only doing what all good bourgeois do. They all tell you that competition, monopoly, etc., in principle (i.e. taken as abstract thoughts), form the only foundations of existence, but that they leave much to be desired in practice. They all want to have competition without the unhealthy consequences of competition. They all demand the impossible, that is to have the conditions of bourgeois life without the necessary consequences of these conditions. And none of them understand that the bourgeois mode of production is a historical and transitory mode, just as the feudal mode was. This error arises because, for them, Bourgeois Man is the only possible basis of any society, and because they cannot imagine a social system in which man would cease to be bourgeois.

M. Proudhon is therefore necessarily *doctrinaire*. For him the historical movement which overturns the real world is reduced to the problem of finding the golden mean, the synthesis of two bourgeois thoughts. Thus, by dint of subtlety, the clever lad discovers the hidden thought of God, the unity of two isolated thoughts, which are only two isolated thoughts because M. Proudhon has isolated them from real life and real production, which is the combination of the realities which the thoughts express. And in place of the great historical movement which is born of the conflict between the already acquired productive forces and man's social relations; and in place of terrible wars which develop between the different classes of a nation, and between different nations; and in place of the practical, violent action of the masses which alone can resolve these collisions; in the place of this vast, prolonged, complex movement, M. Proudhon puts the unsavoury movement of his mind. And so it is the wise men, those men capable of reading the most intimate thoughts of God, who make history. The common people have only to put these revelations into practice. Now you will understand why M. Proudhon is the avowed enemy of all political movements. For him, the answer to the present problem does not lie in social action but in the dialectical orbits of his mind. Because he considers categories to be driving forces, he does not have to change practical life in order to change categories. Quite the contrary. He has to change categories and the changing of real society will follow.

In his desire to reconcile contradictions, M. Proudhon does not ask himself whether the very basis of these contradictions should not be overthrown. He is the epitome of the political doctrinaire who would like to see the king *and* the House of Commons *and* the House of Lords as integral parts of one society, as eternal categories. The only difference is that he finds a new formula for balancing these powers, whose equilibrium consists precisely in the actual movement where each power is now the master, now the slave. That is how, in the 18th century, a whole host of mediocre minds were busily seeking the true formula for balancing the social classes, the aristocracy, the king, parliaments, etc., and then found the next day that there was no king, no parliament and no aristocracy. The exact balance between these antagonisms was the overthrow of all social relations forming the basis for feudal life and the antagonism of feudal life.

Since M. Proudhon places eternal ideas and the categories of Pure Reason on one side and men and their practical life (which is the application of these categories, according to him) on the other side, you find here the beginnings of *dualism* between life and thought, between body and soul – a dualism which repeats itself in many forms. You can now see that this antagonism is only the incapacity of M. Proudhon to understand the origins and profane history of the categories which he has deified.

My letter has already grown too long for me to discuss the ridiculous trial which M. Proudhon makes of communism. For the moment, you will grant me that a man who has not understood the present state of society can understand even less the movement which tends to overthrow it and the literary expressions of this revolutionary movement.

The *only point* in which I agree with M. Proudhon is his disgust at socialist airy-fairiness. I myself have plenty of enemies because of my mockery of sheep-brained, sentimental, utopian socialism. But does M. Proudhon not strangely delude himself when he opposes petty-bourgeois sentimentality – and by this I mean his declamations on the home, on conjugal love and all those banalities – to socialist sentimentality, which (with Fourier for example) is much more profound than those presumptuous platitudes of our good Proudhon? He himself senses so well the emptiness of his reasoning and his utter incapacity to talk of these matters that he hurls himself feet first into rages, exclamations, the irae hominis probi,[4] that he foams, curses, denounces, that he cries 'Infamy!' and 'Plague!', that he beats his breast and glorifies himself before God and Man as one unsullied by socialist infamies! He does not criticise socialist sentimentalities, or what he considers to be sentimentalities. He excommunicates the poor sinners, as if he were a saint or a Pope, and sings the praises of the petty bourgeoisie and of those pitiful illusions on love, the family and home sweet home. And none of this is accidental. From top to toe, M. Proudhon is a philosopher and economist of the petty-bourgeois. This petty-bourgeois, in an advanced society (and necessarily because of his position), is part socialist, part economist; that is, he is dazzled by the magnificence of the big bourgeoisie and full of sympathy for the suffering of the masses. He is at one and the same time bourgeois and proletarian. In the innermost part of his conscience he boasts of being impartial, of having found the exact balance (which claims to distinguish itself from the golden mean). This kind of petty-bourgeois deifies the contradiction, because the contradiction is the heart of his existence. He is only a social contradiction put into practice. He must justify in theory what he is in practice, and M. Proudhon claims the honour of being the scientific interpreter of the French petty bourgeoisie, which is a real enough honour since the petty bourgeoisie will be an integral part of all the social revolutions to come.

I would have liked to send you a copy of my book on political economy with this letter, but as yet I have not been able to get the work printed; the same goes for the critiques of the German philosophers and socialists which I mentioned to you in Brussels. You would never believe what difficulties such a publication meets in Germany, from the police on the one hand and booksellers (who themselves are the interested representatives of all the tendencies I attack) on the other. And as for our own party, it is not only penniless, but a large faction of the German communist party are angry because I oppose their utopias and declamations . . .

[1] This letter is in French in the original.
[2] P.J. Proudhon, *A System of Economic Contradictions, or the Philosophy of Poverty*, Paris 1846.
[3] 'Verkehr': meaning any kind of traffic, transaction, intercourse, circulation.
[4] Latin: 'the wrath of a righteous man'.

1851

5. Marx to Engels

January 7, 1851

I am writing to you today to ask you a questiuncula theoretica,[1] naturae politico-economicae,[2] naturally.

You know, to begin ab ovo,[3] that, according to the Ricardo theory, rent is nothing but the difference between production costs and the price of the basic product, or, as he also puts it, the difference between the price at which the worst piece of land can be sold in order to recoup its cost (always taking into account the profit and interest rates of the leaseholder) and the price at which the best piece of land can be sold.

As he himself presents his theory, the increase in rent arises as follows:

1. There is continual recourse to increasingly bad kinds of soil; or the same quantity of capital, successively invested in the same plot, does not bring the same return. In a word: the soil deteriorates at the same rate as people demand more of it. It becomes relatively more barren. And here Malthus finds the real basis for his theory of population, and here his pupils seek their last sheet-anchor.

2. Rent only increases if the price of corn increases (at least *according to the laws of economy*); it must fall when the price falls.

3. If the *rent of an entire country* rises, then this is only to be explained by the fact that a very large amount of relatively deteriorating land has been cultivated.

Now these three propositions contradict history everywhere.

1. There is no doubt that increasingly bad kinds of soil are cultivated as civilisation progresses. But there is just as little doubt that these worse kinds of soil are relatively good compared with the earlier good ones, as a result of progress in science and industry.

2. Since 1815, the price of corn has fallen from 90 to 50 shillings (and lower before the repeal of the Corn Laws) irregularly but continually. Rent has continually risen. That is in England. Mutatis mutandis[4] everywhere on the Continent.

3. We find in all countries, as Petty has already noted, that, when the price of corn fell, the total rent of the country rose.

The main point about all this is to balance the law of rent against progress in the fruitfulness of agriculture in general, so that historical facts can be explained and the Malthusian theory of deterioration, not only of the 'hands' but also of the soil, can be swept aside.

I think that the matter is to be explained simply as follows:

Let us say that, at a given stage in agriculture, the price of a quarter of wheat is 7 shillings and that an acre of the best quality land, giving a rent of 10 shillings, produces 20 bushels. The yield of the acre is thus = 20×7 or = 140 shillings. The production costs in this case amount to 130 shillings. So 130 shillings is the price of the product of the worst land cultivated.

Let us say now that there is a general improvement in agriculture. If we accept this, then we accept at the same time that science, industry and population are increasing. A generally increased fruitfulness of the soil, by this improvement, creates these conditions, in contrast to the accidental fruitfulness of an ideal season.

If the price of wheat now falls from 7 to 5 shillings per quarter, if the best piece of land (No.1) which previously yielded 20 bushels now yields 30 bushels, then the income is now 30×5 or 150 shillings, instead of 20×7 or 140 shillings. That is, a rent of 20 shillings instead of 10, as before. The worst piece of land, which yields no rent, must now produce 26 bushels, for according to our supposition the necessary price of the same is 130 shillings and $26 \times 5 = 130$ shillings. If the improvement is not so general – i.e. the general progress in science, which goes hand in hand with the total progress of society, population, etc. – that the worst piece of land which is under cultivation could produce 26 bushels, then the price of corn cannot fall to 5 shillings per quarter.

The 20 shillings rent expresses, as before, the difference between production costs and the price of corn from the best land, or between the production costs of the worst and those of the best land. Relatively speaking, one kind of land remains just as productive compared with the other. But the *general productiveness* has increased.

We must only assume that, if the price of corn falls from 7 to 5 shillings, consumption or demand increases proportionately, or that the productivity does not overtake the demand which can be expected at the 5-shilling price. If this assumption were to prove false, when for example the price fell from 7 to 5 shillings because of an exceptionally abundant harvest, then it must be equally true when there is a gradual and producer-effected increase in productiveness. In all cases we are dealing with the economic possibility of this hypothesis.

It then follows:

1. The rent can rise although the price of the product falls, and so Ricardo's law remains valid.

2. The law of rent, as Ricardo presents it in its simplest form (leaving aside its implementation) does not assume a decreasing productiveness of the soil, but only a *differing* productiveness of different pieces of land, *in spite of the generally increasing productiveness of the soil, in conjunction with the development of society* or a differing return from capital successively invested in the same piece of land.

3. The more general the improvement of the soil is, the more varieties of pieces of land will be included, and the rent of the whole country can increase although the price of corn in general is decreasing. Let us take, for example, the above case: it only depends on how many pieces of land there are which produce more than 26 bushels at 5 shillings without having to produce 30 bushels, that is, on how varied the quality of the soils of the land which lies between the worst and the best qualities. Here the amount of the rent of the best land is not relevant. The amount of revenue is not directly relevant at all.

You know that the best thing about rent is that it is produced by balancing the prices for the results of different production costs, but also that this law of market price is nothing more than a law of bourgeois competition. Hence, even after the abolition of bourgeois production, the problem would still remain that the soil would become relatively more barren, so that successively less would be produced by the same labour – although no longer in the same way as in the bourgeois system, where the best land yields as expensive a product as the worst. This consideration would be removed then, according to what has been said above.

I would like to hear your opinion on the matter . . .

1 Latin: 'a little theoretical question'.
2 Latin: 'of a political-economical nature'.
3 Latin: 'at the beginning'.
4 Latin: 'with the relevant changes in detail'.

6. Engels to Marx   *January 29, 1851*

. . . In any case your latest discussion on land rent is completely correct. Ricardo's theory of an infertility of the land which increases with the increase in population never seemed very enlightening to me, and I could never find evidence for his ever-increasing price of corn; but with my well-known laziness en fait de théorie,[1] I contented myself with some inner grumbling in my better self and never investigated the matter fully. It is beyond doubt that your answer is the correct one, and that you have thus gained yourself the title of the economist of land rent. If there were any justice or righteousness in the world, the entire land rent should fall to you for at least one year, and that would be the least you could claim.

I could never accept what Ricardo said in his simple statement, that land rent was the difference in productivity of the various kinds of soil, and that, in proving this statement, 1. he recognised no other moment than the yield of continually deteriorating kinds of soil, 2. he completely ignored progress in agriculture and 3. finally utterly abandoned the theory of return of deteriorating kinds of soil and instead always operated on the assumption that the capital which is successively invested in a particular field always contributed less to the profit yield. However illuminating the assumption was, the reasons given as evidence were quite foreign to this same assumption, and you will recall that I already counterposed progress in scientific agriculture to the theory of decreasing fertility, in the *Deutsch-Französische Jahrbücher*[2] – naturally, very amateurishly and not completely coherently. You have now elucidated the matter and that is another reason why you should hurry up with the completion and publication of your *Economy*. If we could get one of your articles on land rent translated and published in an English review, there would be a real sensation. Think about it, je me charge de la traduction.[3]

1 French: 'in theoretical matters'.
2 Engels, 'Outline for a Critique of Political Economy' (1844).
3 French: 'I will do the translation'.

7. Marx to Engels

. . . Meanwhile my new theory of rent has only given me that good insight for which every decent citizen strives. At any rate, I am still happy that you are happy with it. The inverse relationship between the fertility of the soil and human fertility must affect an upstanding family man like myself profoundly, all the more since my marriage is more productive than my industry.

Now I shall give you just one illustration of the theory of currency; my study of it might be characterised by Hegelians as the study of 'Being-for-Other', of the 'Object', in short of 'God'.

The theory of Mr Loyd and tutti frutti[1] from Ricardo onwards consists in the following:

Let us suppose that we have a pure metallic currency. If it was too great in quantity, then the prices would rise, and so the export of goods would decrease. Imports from abroad would then increase. Imports would thus increase against exports. And produce a bad balance of payments. A bad rate of exchange. So jingling coins would be exported and currency would contract, the price of goods would fall, imports would fall, exports would rise, money would flow in again: in short, the situation would return to the old balance.

In the opposite case it would be just the same, mutatis mutandis.[2]

The moral: since paper money must imitate the motion of metallic currency, and since an artificial regulation must replace what is normally a natural law, then the Bank of England must increase its output of paper money if bullion is coming in (e.g. through the purchase of government securities, exchequer bills, etc.), and decrease it if bullion is decreasing through a lowering of the bank rate or the sale of government securities. Now I maintain that the Bank must act in the opposite way — *increase* its lending rate if the bullion is *decreasing* and let it go its usual way if it increases, at risk of unnecessarily intensifying the crisis in trade which is developing. More of this une autre fois.[3]

What I am trying to argue here concerns the elementary basis of the matter. For I maintain that: *even with a pure metallic currency, the quantity of the currency, and its expansion and contraction, has nothing to do with the ebb and flow of pure metals, or with a favourable or unfavourable balance of payments, or with a favourable or unfavourable rate of exchange,* except in the most extreme cases which practically never arise but which are theoretically definable. Tooke maintains the same thing: but I could find no evidence adduced in his history of prices covering the period 1843 to 1847.[4]

You see, the matter is of importance. Firstly the whole basis of the theory of circulation is called into question. Secondly, we can show that the course of a crisis, however much the *credit system* contributes to it, only concerns the *currency* insofar as the insane meddling of state powers in the regulation of currency can worsen the existing crisis, as in 1847.

You should note in the following illustration that we have assumed: the influence of bullion to be connected with a boom, with prices which are not yet high but are increasing, with a surplus of capital, a surplus of exports over imports. The export of gold vice versa, mutatis mutandis. Now, this is the same assumption as that made by the people against whom the polemic is directed. They cannot deny it. In reality, there might be a thousand and one cases where gold leaves the country, although, in the country which exports it, the prices of other goods are far below those in the country which receives the gold. For example, in England from 1809 to 1811 and 1812 etc., etc. However, the *general assumption* is firstly abstractly correct, and secondly accepted by the currency experts. So we will not debate all this for the time being.

So let us suppose that *a pure metallic currency is used in England*. But that does not mean that the *credit system* has stopped: for the Bank of England would immediately be transformed into a *Deposit and Lending Bank*, although its loans would merely exist in cash form. If we do not accept this assumption, then what is described here as a *deposit in the Bank of England* would then appear as *hoarding by private persons*, and what is described as a loan from them would appear as a loan from a private person. So what is described here *in terms of a deposit in the Bank of England* is only a *paraphrase used so as not to split up the process* but so as to present it together in focus.

Case I: the influx of bullion. Here the matter is quite simple. A great deal of unused capital, and so an increase in deposits. In order to use them, the Bank would lower its lending rate. Thus an expansion of business in the country. The *circulation* would *only* increase if business increased in such a way that increased currency was necessary for its conduct. Otherwise the excess circulating currency would flow back into the Bank through the decline of exchange etc. as deposit etc. So *currency* does not act as a *cause*. Finally, its expansion is a *result* of the larger capital which is put into action, and not the other way round. (In the above case, the direct result would be a growth in deposits, i.e. in the unused capital, not in the circulation.)

Case II: here the problem really begins. *Export of bullion* is assumed. The beginning of a period of pressure. The rate of exchange – unfavourable. Then bad harvest etc. (or even an increase in the price of raw materials for industry) would necessitate an increased importation of goods. Let us suppose that the state of the books of the Bank of England at the inception of such a period is as follows:

a) Capital	£14,500,000	Government Securities	£10,000,000
Rest	3,500,000	Bills of Exchange	12,000,000
Deposits	12,000,000	Bullion or Coin	8,000,000
	£30,000,000		£30,000,000

Since, in this *assumption*, no *notes* exist, the Bank owes only 12 million pounds on *deposits*. According to their principle (which deposit and lending banks have in common, by which they only need to have a third of their liabilities in cash), their bullion of 8 million is too large by half. In order to make more profit, they *lower the interest rate,* and increase their loans, e.g. by 4 million, on the export of corn etc. The books of the Bank are now as follows:

b) Capital	£14,500,000	Government Securities	£10,000,000
Rest	3,500,000	Bills of Exchange	16,000,000
Deposits	12,000,000	Bullion or Coin	4,000,000
	£30,000,000		£30,000,000

From these figures we can deduce:

Merchants act *firstly* on the *bullion reserves of the Bank*, as soon as they have to export *gold*. This exported gold *decreases* the Bank's reserves, without having the slightest effect on the currency. Whether the 4 million is in the vaults or in a ship to Hamburg is *all the same* for currency. Finally, it appears that a significant *drain on bullion,* here of £4 million Sterling, can occur without affecting either the currency or the business of the country in the slightest. For, during the whole period, the *bullion reserve,* which was in surplus to the liabilities, is reduced to its due proportion to the same liabilities.

c) But let us assume that the circumstances which made the drain of 4 million necessary persist and give rise to a lack of corn, to an increase in the price of raw cotton etc. The Bank will become concerned for its securities. It *raises the interest rate* and limits its loans. Thus, pressure in the world trade. How does this pressure work? It is applied to the deposits in the Bank; the bullion sinks in proportion. If the deposits sink to 9 million – that is, if they decrease by 3 million, then 3 million must vanish from the bullion reserves of the Bank. So these would decline (4 million minus 3 million) to 1 million as against deposits of 9 million – a ratio which would be dangerous for the Bank. If it then wishes to keep its bullion reserves at one third of the deposits, then it must decrease its loans by 2 million.

The books then show:

Capital	£14,500,000	Government Securities	£10,000,000
Rest	3,500,000	Bills under discount	14,000,000
Deposits	9,000,000	Bullion or Coin	3,000,000
	£27,000,000		£27,000,000

It then follows that: as soon as the drain is so great that the bullion reserves have reached their due proportion against the deposits, the Bank raises its interest rate and decreases its loans. But then the *effect on deposits* starts, and as a result of their contraction, the bullion reserves contract, but in a greater proportion to the loan of bills. The currency is not affected in the least. One part of the withdrawn bullion and deposits *fills* the vacuum which is left by the contraction of the balance in domestic circulation, another part moves abroad.

d) Let us suppose that the import of corn etc. continues, and that deposits sink to 4,500,000; then the Bank would reduce its loans by another 3 million in order to maintain the necessary reserves against its liabilities, and the books are reduced as follows:

Capital	£14,500,000	Government Securities	£10,000,000
Rest	3,500,000	Bills under Discount	11,000,000
Deposits	4,500,000	Bullion or Coin	1,500,000
	£22,500,000		£22,500,000

In this case the Bank would have reduced its loan from 16 to 11 million, i.e. by 5 million. The requirements of circulation would be replaced by the withdrawn deposits. But at the same time there is a lack of capital, high prices in raw materials, decline in demand, and so in business, and so *finally* in the circulation of necessary currency. The surplus part of the same would be sent abroad as bullion for the payment of imports. The currency is affected *last of all* and it would only be decreased beyond its necessary quantity if the bullion reserves were decreased beyond the most necessary proportion to the deposits.

We must also note on the above that:

1. Instead of decreasing its loans, the Bank could thrash its public securities, which would however be unprofitable in these conditions. But the result would be the same. Instead of decreasing its own reserves and loans, it would decrease those of private persons who have invested their money in public securities.

2. Here I have supposed a drain on the Bank of 6,500,000. In 1839 there was one of 9 to 10 million

3. The process which we have supposed with a pure metallic currency can continue with paper until the Bank closes, as happened twice in Hamburg in the 18th century.

Write soon.

[1] Italian: 'all the others'.
[2] Latin: 'all other things being equal'.
[3] French: 'another time'.
[4] T. Tooke and W. Newmarch, *A History of Prices and the State of the Circulation from 1793 to 1856*, Vol. IV, London 1848.

8. Engels to Marx   *February 25, 1851*

. . . In any case, I owe you an answer on your theory of currency. The thing itself is, in my opinion, quite correct and will make a contribution to reducing the nonsensical theory of circulation to simple and clear basic facts. I have only the following to note on the explanation in your letter:

1. Let us suppose that, at the beginning of the period of pressure, the accounts of the Bank of England, as you say, stand at £12,000,000 in deposits and £8 million in bullion or coin. In order to dispose of the surplus £4 million in bullion, you let the Bank lower its lending rate. I do not think that is necessary, and as far as I recall, the lowering of the lending rate has never occurred at the start of a period of pressure. In my opinion, the pressure would have an immediate effect on the deposits and would not only bring about the balance between bullion and deposits very rapidly, but would also force the Bank to raise the lending

rate so that the bullion did not fall below one third of the deposits. In the same proportion as the pressure increases, the circulation of capital and the exchange of commodities stagnates. But the drawn bills fall due and need to be paid. So the reserve capital – the deposits – are put in motion – not qua[1] currency, you understand, but qua capital, and so the simple drain of bullion, together with the pressure, suffices to free the Bank of its surplus bullion. It is not necessary for the Bank to *lower its* lending rate in conditions where the general interest rates of the whole country rise simultaneously.

2. In a period of growing pressure, I believe, the Bank would have to raise the ratio of bullion to deposits in the same proportion as the pressure increases, in order not to be encumbered. The four surplus millions would be a stroke of luck for them, and they would hand them out as slowly as possible. Under increasing pressure, according to your suppositions, a ratio between bullion and deposits of $2/5$: 1, $1/2$: 1 or even $3/5$: 1 would not be at all extraordinary, and would be all the more simple to achieve when the bullion reserves decreased *absolutely* along with the decrease in deposits, even if they increased *relatively*. A run on the bank is just as possible here as with paper money and can be achieved in quite normal conditions of trade without shaking the credit of the bank.

3. You say that 'the currency is affected *last of all*'. Your own assumption is that it will be affected as a result of stagnation in business, so that naturally less currency is necessary, leads to the conclusion that the currency decreases at the same time as the activity of commerce and that a part of it becomes surplus in proportion to the increase in pressure. Certainly, this becomes *noticeably* reduced only at the end, under higher pressure; but on the whole this process runs from the beginning of the pressure onwards, even if it does not provide detailed evidence of this. But insofar as this superseding of one part of the currency is a *result* of the remaining commercial conditions, which is a pressure independent of the currency, and all other goods and conditions of trade were affected by it *before* currency was, and equally insofar as the decrease is noticeable in practice last of all in currency, then so far is it affected by the crisis last of all.

These notes, as you see, are limited purely to your modus illustrandi;[2] the theory itself is quite correct.

---

[1] Latin: 'as'.
[3] Latin: 'method of illustration'.

9. Marx to Engels

April 2, 1851

. . . The worst thing is that I am suddenly hindered in my studies at the library. I have got far enough to finish the whole economic crap in five weeks. And, when that is finished, I will write out the 'economy' at home and launch myself into another science at the [British] Museum. Ça commence à m'ennuyer.[1] Basically, this science has made no progress since A. Smith and D. Ricardo, however much has happened in single, and often ultra-detailed, studies.

Answer the question I asked you in my last letter . . .

[1] French: 'it is beginning to bore me'.

10. Engels to Marx

April 3, 1851

. . . As for the question which you asked in your last but one letter, it is not quite clear to me. However, I think the following will suffice.

The merchant as a firm, as a profiteer, and the same merchant as a consumer, are two quite different persons in commerce, and they are inimicably opposed. The merchant as firm is called Capital Account, either Profit or Loss Account. The merchant as guzzler, boozer, householder and child-maker is called Household Costs Account. So Capital Account debits the Household Costs Account for every farthing which moves from the commercial into the private pocket and since Household Costs Account has only a debit, and no credit, and is thus one of the worst debtors of the firm, then at the end of the year the whole debit sum of Household Costs Account is pure loss and is written off from the profit. However, the sum which was used for housekeeping, and is thus available, is regarded as a part of the profit in the balance and calculation of the rate of profit; for example, with 100,000 thaler capital, 10,000 thaler are earned, but 5,000 are eaten up; so a 10% profit is calculated and after everything has been properly accounted, the Capital Account in the next year is calculated with a debit of 105,000 thaler. The process itself is somewhat more complicated than my presentation, since Capital Account and Household Costs Account come in contact with each other rarely or only at the end of the year, and Household Costs Account usually appears as a debtor in the Cash Account which is drawn up by the broker, but it boils down to the same thing.

The matter is very simple in the case of several participants. For example: A has 50,000 thaler in the business and B also has 50,000; 10,000 thaler profit is made and each one uses up 2,500 thaler. The accounts at the end of the year – with simple book-keeping, without the imaginary accounts —— look like this:

A: Credit with 'A & B' – Capital Investment	50,000	thaler
A: " " " – Profit Share	5,000	
	55,000	
Debit with 'A & B' – in cash	2,500	
A: Credit for next year	52,500	thaler

Similarly with B. But the business always counts 10% profit. In short: merchants ignore the living costs of the participants in calculating the rate of profit, but with the circulation of capital growth through profit they allow for it . . .

I am glad that you have at last finished your *Economy*. The thing was really dragging on, and as long as you think you have an important, but unread, book in front of you, then you will never get down to writing . . .

11.   Marx to Engels   *August 14, 1851*

I will send you the Proudhon book[1] itself in a couple of days, but you should send it back to me as soon as you have read it. You see, I would like to have printed two or three sheets about the book – because of what it says about money. You should therefore give me your views in more detail than your normal hasty writing allows.

The point about Proudhon – and the whole thing is above all a polemic against communism, however much he steals from it and however much it appears to him in Cabet-Blanc's transfiguration – boils down, in my opinion, to the following reasoning:

The real enemy is capital. The pure economic affirmation of capital is interest. So-called profit is nothing more than a particular form of salary. We negate the interest by transforming it into an annuity, i.e. an annual payment on account of capital. Thus the working class – that is, the *industrial* working class is assured of hegemony for ever, and the real capitalist class is condemned to a continually dwindling existence. The different forms of interest are interest on money, house rent and land rent. Bourgeois society is upheld in this way, is justified and only deprived of its bad side.

'Liquidation sociale'[2] is merely the means to build a 'healthy' bourgeois society from the very beginning. Whether quickly or slowly is not of importance. I would like firstly to hear your opinion on the contradictions, irresoluteness and obscurities. But the true healing balsam of this new-begun society consists in the abolition of interest, that is, in the continuous transformation of interest into an annuity. When this is presented not as a means to, but as an *economic law* of the reformed bourgeois society, the result is naturally two-fold:

1. Transformation of the petty non-industrial capitalists into industrial capitalists.

2. Eternalisation of the big capitalist class, for, au fond,[3] if you strike an average in the matter, society never pays out anything except the annuity, all in all – not counting the industrial profit. If the opposite were the case, then Dr Price's accumulating interest calculations would be a reality and the whole world would not suffice to pay the interest on capital originating at the time of Christ. But, in fact, it is safe to say that, for example in England – i.e. the most peaceful bourgeois country – any capital invested in either land or estates or anywhere else has never paid interest in the last 50 or 100 years – at least in terms of price, which is what we are dealing with here. If we take for example the highest estimation of England's national wealth, say 5 thousand million. So England produces 500 million annually. The entire wealth of England is thus only = the annual labour of England multiplied by 10. So not only has the capital not paid interest, but it has not even *reproduced* itself in terms of value. And hence a simple law. Value is originally determined by the original costs of production, according to the labour time which was necessary to produce the commodity. But, once produced, the price of the product is determined by the costs which are necessary to *reproduce* it. And the costs of reproduction continually sink, and sink more rapidly as the epoch becomes more industrialised. So we have a law of continuous devaluation of the capital value itself, by which the law of rent and interest (which is normally taken to the point of absurdity) is limited. That is also the explanation of your proposition that no factory covers its costs of production. So Proudhon cannot build society anew by introducing a law which it already obeys au fond without his advice.

The means by which Proudhon hopes to achieve all this is the Bank. Here there is a confusion. The business of a bank is reduced to two main parts:

1. The *realisation* of capital. Here I just hand out *money* for *capital*, and that can happen to mere production costs, i.e. at ½ or ¼ %. 2. *Lending of capital* in the form of money, and here the interest will behave according to the quantity of capital. Proudhon considers No.2 to be as simple as No.1, and, au bout du compte,[4] he will find that, since he indicates an illusory amount of capital in the form of money, he has at best only reduced the *interest* on capital in order to raise its *price* by the same amount. So nothing has been gained except the discrediting of his bills of exchange.

I will let you enjoy the connection between customs and interest in the original text. The thing was too magnificent to be ruined by summary. Mr P[roudhon] neither explains exactly how we are to consider the role of the community in houses and land – and he should have done precisely that for the communists – nor how the workers gain ownership of the factories. In any case, he wishes to have 'des compagnies ouvrières puissantes',[5] but is really so afraid of these industrial 'guilds' that he allows society (not the State of course) the right to disband them. Like a good Frenchman, he limits the association to the bounds of the factory, because he recognises no Moses & Son and no Midlothian farmer. The French peasant and the French cobbler, tailor and merchant seem to him to be eternal facts which must be accepted. But the more I get down to this rubbish, the more I am convinced that the reform of agriculture, and so of the property crap based on it, is the alpha and the omega of the coming revolution. Without that, Father Malthus is correct.

The work is delicious on Louis Blanc etc., particularly in its insolent outpourings on Rousseau, Robespierre, God, 'fraternité' and suchlike twaddle.

Now, as for the *New York Tribune*, since I am up to my ears in the *Economy* you must help me out. Write a series of articles on Germany from 1848 onward. Lively and uninhibited. The gentlemen in the foreign department are very *insolent* . . .

[1] P.J. Proudhon, *The General Idea of Revolution in the Eighteenth Century*, Paris 1851.
[2] French: 'social liquidation'.
[3] French: 'basically'.
[4] French: 'in the end'.
[5] French: 'powerful workers' collectives'.

12. Marx to Engels

October 13, 1851

. . . By the way, you must get round to giving me your views on Proudhon, however limited they may be. They are the more of interest now that I am in the middle of setting out the *Economy*. By the way, lately I have been reading up agronomy and technology – the history of it – in the library which I continue to visit, so as to get at least some idea of that rubbish.

Qu'est-ce que fait la crise commerciale?[1] The *Economist* is full of those comfortings, regrets and statements which usually precede crises. But you can sense their fear when they try to gossip away other people's fear. If you ever get to see the book by Johnston, *Notes on North America*, 2nd vol. 1851,[2] then you will find all kinds of interesting notes on the subject. This J[ohnston] is the English Liebig, you see. An atlas on physical geography by 'Johnson' (not to be confused with the above) is perhaps to be found in one of Manchester's lending libraries. It contains the collection of all recent and other researches in this field. Costs 10 guineas. So not intended for private owners. No word from dear Harney. He still seems to be living in Scotland.

The English admit that the Americans have carried off the prize at the industrial exhibition and have beaten them roundly. 1. Gutta-percha. New material and new products. 2. Weapons. Revolvers. 3. Machines. Mowing, sowing and sewing machines. 4. Daguerrotypes applied on a large scale for the first time. 5. Shipping with their clippers. Finally, in order to prove that they too can deliver luxury goods, they have exhibited a colossal lump of Californian gold ore and next to it a golden service of virgin gold.

---

[1] French: 'how is the commercial crisis developing?'

[2] J. Johnston, *Notes on North America, Agricultural, Economical and Social*. 2 vols. Edinburgh and London 1851.

1852

. . . In your place, I would advise Messrs Democrats in general that they would be better off acquainting themselves with bourgeois literature itself before they undertake to yap at its opponents. These gentlemen should, for example, study the historical works of Thierry, Guizot, John Wade, etc. so as to enlighten themselves on the past 'History of Classes'. They should acquaint themselves with the fundamentals of political economy before trying to criticise the critique of political economy. For example, it is enough just to open Ricardo's great work[1] and find his opening words on the first page:

> The produce of the earth – all that is derived from its surface by the united application of labour, machinery and capital, is divided among *three classes* of the community; namely, the proprietor of the land, the owner of the stock or capital necessary for its cultivation, and the labourers by whose industry it is cultivated . . .[2]

H.C. Carey (of Philadelphia), the only significant North American economist, has provided the most irrefutable evidence of how little bourgeois society in the United States has developed towards making its class struggle visible and comprehensible. He attacks Ricardo, the classic representative (interpreter) of the bourgeoisie and the most stoic opponent of the proletariat, for being one whose work is supposed to have provided the arsenal for anarchists, socialists and all the enemies of the bourgeois order. He accuses not only him, but also Malthus, Mill,

Say, Torrens, Wakefield, MacCulloch, Senior, Whately, R. Jones, etc., those economic toastmasters of Europe, of tearing down the fabric of society and of promoting civil war by their proof that the economic basis of the various classes must effect a necessary and steadily growing antagonism between them. The attempts to disprove this – not, indeed, like the absurd Heinzen who blames the existence of classes on the existence of *political* privileges and *monopolies* – but by trying to represent economic conditions – rent (land ownership), *profit* (capital) and workers' wages (wage labour) – as conditions of association and harmony rather than those of struggle and antagonism. Naturally he only proves that the 'underdeveloped' situation in the US is a 'normal situation' for him.

As for me, I have not earned the honour of having discovered either the essence of classes in modern society or the struggle between them. Bourgeois historians had presented the historical development of this class struggle and bourgeois economists had presented its economic anatomy long before me. What I did that was new was to prove: 1. that the *existence of classes* is merely linked to *definite historical phases of development of production*; 2. that the class struggle necessarily leads to the dictatorship of the proletariat; 3. that this dictatorship itself forms only a transitional stage in the *removal of all classes* leading to a *classless society*. Ignorant louts, like Heinzen, who deny not only the struggle but even the existence of classes, only show that in spite of all their bloodthirsty and humanistic, self-glorifying yapping, they consider the social conditions of bourgeois rule to be the final product and the non plus ultra of history, and that they are only the servants of the bourgeoisie, in a service which is even more sickening the less these louts understand the grandeur and transient necessity of the bourgeois regime itself . . .

[1] D. Ricardo, *On the Principle of Political Economy and Taxation.*
[2] This quotation in English in original. [Marx then translates it into German in the following paragraph.]

14. Marx to Cluss   *December 7, 1852*

. . . Proudhon, in his usual industrious calling of wares, has adopted a few of my ideas and given them out as *his* 'latest discoveries'; for example, he claims that there is *no absolute science*, that everything can be explained from material conditions etc., etc. In his book on Louis Bonaparte[1] he openly admits what I had to deduce from his *Philosophie de la Misère*,[2] i.e that the petty-bourgeois is his ideal type. France, he says, consists of 3 classes: 1. Bourgeoisie; 2. Middle Class (petty-bourgeois); 3. Proletariat. The purpose of history and especially of revolution is now to dissolve classes 1 and 3 (the extremes) into class 2 (the true centre), and this is to be achieved through the Proudhon credit-operation whose final result is the abolition of interest in its various forms . . .

[1] P.J. Proudhon, *The Social Revolution in the Coup d'Etat of December 2*, Paris 1852
[2] P.J. Proudhon, *System of Economic Contradictions, or the Philosophy of Poverty*, Paris 1846.

1853

15. Marx to Engels

... I found your letter pertaining to the Hebrews and Arabs very interesting.[1] By the way, 1. a *general* relationship is to be seen in all Oriental tribes, between the settlement on the one side and the continuation of a nomadic existence on the other, from the beginning of history. 2. At the time of Mohammed, the trade route from Europe to Asia had been altered significantly, and the cities of Arabia, which played a major role in trade to India etc., were in a state of commercial decline, which was another factor. 3. As for religion, the question is resolved in the general (and therefore easily answerable) question: why does the history of the East *appear* to be a history of religions?. . .

Bernier correctly finds the basic form of most Oriental phenomena – he discusses Turkey, Persia, Hindustan – in the fact that *no private land ownership* existed. This is the real key to the Oriental heaven ...

[1] See Engels's letter to Marx of May 26, 1853, in *Selected Correspondence*, Moscow 1975, pp.73-74.

16. Engels to Marx

June 6 1853

... The absence of land ownership is in very deed the key to the whole East. Herein lies the political and religious history. But how is it that the Orientals have never had land ownership, not even of the feudal variety? I think that it mainly has to do with the climate and with the condition of the soil, especially the great stretches of desert which run from the Sahara right across Arabia, Persia, India and Tartary to the highest Asian mountains. Artificial irrigation here is the first prerequisite of land cultivation, and this is the concern either of the communities or the provinces or central government. The governments in the East have always had only three ministries: Finance (plundering at home), War (plundering at home and abroad) and Public Works (care for reproduction). The British government in India has arranged Nos.1 and 2 in a somewhat more philistine fashion and abandoned No.3 altogether, and Indian farming is being ruined. Free competition has made a complete fool of itself there. The artificial enrichment of the soil, which stopped immediately the irrigation channels fell apart, explains the otherwise curious fact that now whole stretches are desert and barren which were formerly brilliantly cultivated (Palmyra, Petra, the ruins in the Yemen, x spots in Egypt, Persia and Hindustan); it explains the fact that a single war of destruction can depopulate a country for centuries and deprive it of its entire civilisation. This includes, I think, the destruction of South Arabian trade before Mohammed, which you very rightly consider to be the main moment in the Mohammedan revolution. I do not know the history of trade in the first six centuries AD well enough to be able to judge how far the general material world situation allowed the trade route through Persia to the Black Sea and through the Persian Gulf to Syria and Asia Minor to be preferred to the route leading through the Red Sea. But, in any case, the relative safety of the caravans in the Persian and well-governed Sassanian Empire was not without importance, while the Yemen was almost continually subjugated, invaded and plundered by the Abyssinians between 200 and 600 AD. The cities of Southern Arabia, which were still flourishing in Roman times, were real deserts and ruins in the seventh century; in 500 years, the neighbouring Bedouins had acquired pure mythical, fabulous traditions concerning their origins (see the Koran and the Arabian historian Novairi), and the alphabet in which the local inscriptions were written were almost totally unknown, although *there was no other*, so that *writing* was almost de facto lost to oblivion. A quite direct, violent destruction, as only the Ethiopian invasion could explain, results in the same things, along with a superceding caused by some general trade situation. The routing of the Abyssinians occurred 40 years before Mohammed, and it was obviously the first act of the awakening Arab national feeling which was also spurred on by Persian invasions from the north, reaching almost as far as Mecca. I will deal with the history of Mohammed himself in a few days; but, up till now, it seems to have the character of a Bedouin reaction to the ruling – but degenerating – Fellahs of the cities, who were at that time also very degenerate in religion and who mingled a degenerated Judaism and Christianity with a degenerated national cult . . .

17. Marx to Engels   *June 14 1853*

. . . Carey, the American economist, has published a new book: *Slavery at Home and Abroad.*[1] By 'slavery' he means all forms of servitude, wage slavery, etc. He has sent me his book and repeatedly quoted me (from the *Tribune*), now as 'a recent English writer', now as 'correspondent of the *New York Tribune*'. I have already told you that the previous published works of this man had waxed eloquent upon the 'harmony' of the economic basis of the bourgeoisie and had blamed all mischief on excessive intervention by the State. The State was his bête noire. Now he is playing a different tune. The centralising effect of big industry is to blame for all the evil. But then England is in turn to blame for the centralising effect, since it has made itself the workshop of the world and forced all other countries back upon brutal agriculture which has been separated from manufacturing. And then the Ricardo-Malthus theory (and particularly Ricardo's theory of land rent) is responsible for the sins of England. The necessary consequence both of Ricardo's theory and of industrial centralisation is said to be communism. And, in order to avoid all this, in order to oppose centralisation with localisation and with a regionalised union of factory and agriculture in the whole country, our ultra-Free Trader finally suggests – protectionism. In order to avoid the effects of bourgeois industry (for which he makes England responsible) this true Yankee comes up with the idea of artificially accelerating this development in America itself. Besides, his opposition to England involves him in a Sismondesque praise of the petty bourgeoisie in Switzerland, Germany, China, etc. This is the same fellow that once used to mock France for her similarity to China. The only positive interest in the book is the comparison of negro slavery in the United States with the earlier English negro slavery in Jamaica etc. He shows how the main strength of the negro in Jamaica etc. always arose from freshly imported

Savages, for the negroes under English treatment could not only *not* maintain their population but even lost up to two thirds of the annual imports, while the present negro generation in America is a home-grown product, more or less yankee-ised, English speaking, etc. and thus *capable of emancipation*.

The *Tribune* naturally heralds Carey's book with a full fanfare. Besides, both have one thing in common: they represent the protectionist, that is industrial, bourgeoisie in America in the guise of Sismondesque-philanthropic-socialist anti-industrialism. And that is the secret of the *Tribune's* claim to be the 'leading journal' in the United States, despite all its 'isms' and socialistic posturing.

Your article on Switzerland[2] was naturally a direct body blow to the editorial in the *Tribune* (against centralisation etc.) and *their* Carey. I have continued this hidden war in my first article on India[3] in which I present the destruction of local industry by England as *revolutionary*. That will be very shocking for them. By the way, the entire economy of the British in India was swinish and is so to this very day.

As for the stationary character of this part of India despite all the purposeless movement on the political surface, it is explained completely by two mutually supporting circumstances: 1. the public works concern of the central government; 2. along with that, the entire empire – apart from a couple of larger cities – was broken up into villages which had completely independent organisations and which formed small worlds in themselves. These villages are depicted as follows in a parliamentary report:[4]

> A village, geographically considered, is a tract of country comprising some 100 or 1,000 acres of arable and waste lands; politically viewed, it resembles a corporation or township. Every village is, and appears always to have been, in fact, a separate community or republic. Officials: 1. The *Potail*, Goud, Mundil, etc., as he is termed in different languages, is the head inhabitant, who has generally the superintendance of the affairs of the village, settles the disputes of the inhabitants, attends to the police, and performs the duty of collecting the revenue within the village . . . 2. The *Curnum*, Shanboag, or Putwaree, is the register. 3. The *Taliary* or *Sthulwar* and 4. the *Totie*, are severally the watchmen of the village and of the crops. 5. The *Neerguntee* distributes the water of the streams or reservoirs in just proportion to the several fields. 6. The *Joshee*, or astrologer, announces the seedtimes and harvests, and the lucky or unlucky days or hours for all the operations of farming. 7. The *smith* and 8. the *carpenter* frame the rude

instruments of husbandry, and the ruder dwelling of the farmer. 9. The *potter* fabricates the only utensils of the village. 10. The *washerman* keeps clean the few garments. . . 11. The *barber*. 12. The *silversmith*, who is also often the *poet* and *schoolmaster* of the village in one person. Then the *Brahmin* for worship. Under this simple form of municipal government, the inhabitants of the country have lived from time immemorial. The boundaries of the villages have been but seldom altered; and although the villages themselves have been sometimes injured, and even desolated, by war, famine and disease, the same name, the same limits, the same interests, and even the same families have continued for ages. The inhabitants give themselves no trouble about the breaking up and division of kingdoms; while the village remains entire, they care not to what power it is transferred, or to what sovereign it devolves; its internal economy remains unchanged.

The Potail is usually a hereditary office. In some of these communities, the lands of the village are cultivated in common, in most, each occupant tills his own field. Inside each there is slavery and a caste system. The waste lands are for common pasture. Weaving and spinning are done at home by wives and daughters. These idyllic republics, which merely guard the *borders of the village* jealously against the neighbouring village, still exist fairly untouched in the north-western parts of India which have just fallen to the English. I do not think that anyone can imagine more solid conditions for Asiatic despotism in stagnation. And however much England has Ireland-ised the country, the break-up of these stereotyped original forms was the sine qua non for Europisation. The tax collector alone was not able to achieve it. The destruction of all the ancient industries was involved and this robbed these villages of their self-supporting character.

In Bali, the island off the east coast of Java, Hindu religion and a Hindu organisation (whose traces and those of the Hindu influence are to be found, incidentally, throughout Java) is still untouched. As for the *question of property*, this is a great *controversy* among English writers on India. In the mountainous area south of Krishna, property appears at all events to have existed on the basis of land and soil. In Java, however, Sir Stamford Raffles, one time *English* governor of Java, in his *History of Java*,[5] notes that, over the entire area of Java, 'where rent to any considerable amount was attainable, the sovereign is absolute landlord'. In any case, throughout Asia, the Mohammedans seem to have decided in principle on 'property-lessness on the land'.

I must also note that the aforementioned villages already figured in Menu and that the whole organisation is depicted by him as: 10 people under a higher tax collector, then 100, then 1,000.

Write soon.

[1] H.C. Carey, *The Slave Trade, Domestic and Foreign: Why it Exists and How it May be Extinguished*, London 1853.
[2] Engels, 'The Political Situation in the Swiss Republic' (*New York Daily Tribune*, May 17, 1853).
[3] Marx, 'British Rule in India' (*New York Daily Tribune*, June 25, 1853).
[4] This extract is taken from a British parliamentary report on India, and was given here in the original English.
[5] T.S. Raffles, *The History of Java*, 2 vols, London 1817.

18. Marx to Cluss   *September 15, 1853*

. . . I think that the 'commercial decline' will begin in Spring, as in 1847 . . . I still hope to get so far as to retire to solitude for a couple of months so as to write my *Economy*. It seems that I will not achieve even that. This continual scribbling for newspapers bores me. It takes up too much of my time, separates things, and means nothing. However independent one would wish to be, one is still tied to the papers and their public, especially when you need money like me. Pure scientific work is something utterly different, and the honour of appearing beside some APC,[1] some 'Lady Correspondent' or some 'Metropolitanus' is certainly not a matter of envy.

[1] Franz Pulszki.

1857

. . . Proudhon is now publishing an 'economic Bible' in Paris.[1] Destruam et aedificabo.[2] He has, as he says, presented the first part in his *Philosophie de la Misère*. He will now 'reveal' the second part. The prattle is now translated into German by Louis Simon, the well-groomed clerk of Königswärter (or suchlike, the well-known banker of the National Bank) in Paris. I have a more recent work by one of Proudhon's pupils here: *De la Réforme des Banques, par Alfred Darimon*, 1856.[3] Inspired by the old man. The démonetisation de l'or et de l'argent or the transformation of toutes les marchandises into instruments d'échange au même titre que l'or et l'argent.[4] The work is introduced by Emile Girardin and written in admiration of Isaac Pereire. So we are left to imagine what kind of socialist coups d'état Bonaparte will seek refuge in at the last moment . . .

[1] P.J. Proudhon, *Manual of the Stock Exchange Speculator* (5th edition), Paris 1857.
[2] Latin: 'I will destroy and I will build again.'
[3] *On the Reform of the Banks*. See also *Grundrisse* Penguin, pp.113-237 (esp. pp. 115-125).
[4] French: 'the demonetisation of gold and silver or the transformation of all merchandise into means of exchange on a par with gold and silver'.

20. Marx to Engels *April 23, 1857*

. . . I have still not yet succeeded in investigating the relationship between the rate of exchange and bullion fully, but I must do it sometime. The role played by money as such in determining the rate of interest and the money market is something striking and quite antagonistic to all the laws of political economy. The two recently-published volumes of Tooke's *History of Prices*[1] are important. It is a pity that the old man gives a quite one-sided direction to all his investigations, occasioned by direct opposition to the currency principle fellows[2] ...

[1] T. Tooke and W. Newmarch, *A History of Prices and of the State of Circulation from 1793 to 1856*, Vols. V-VI, London 1857.

[2] A reference to the theory of the currency principle put forward by Lord Overstone et al, who maintained Ricardo's theory of quantity, according to which an expansion in the amount of money with the same quantity of goods would lead to inflation in the price of goods. Overstone therefore considered it necessary to have *all* bank notes backed by metal currency. In 1844, Overstone and Co. proposed 'Peel's Bill' which empowered the Bank of England to print bank notes *without* metal currency backing *only* to the value of the national debt. In the crisis of 1847, Peel's Bill was repealed in order to help the Bank out of the crisis.

For a further discussion on this, see *Capital* Vol. III, chapter 43 in Section 5.

21. Engels to Marx
December 7, 1857

The crisis, the eternal vacillation in prices and the increasing supplies made me scribble a lot last week; so I could only send your copies of the *Guardian* and no letter.

In your last letter there is a slight mistake. You write that 'corn, sugar, etc. are now held at a price because their owners pay out the same bill of exchange as they drew, instead of selling their commodities'. They, as *drawees*, cannot pay out the bill of exchange; they have nothing to do with exchange, except for accepting it and paying out in the event of a loss. The holders of commodities can only save themselves from forced sales by taking loans on the commodity. This will be difficult under the circumstances, and in any case the yield of these loans will be reduced in the colossal fall in prices of commodities (35% in the case of sugar!), and in the certainty that as soon as a few forced sales have to be made, the commodities must fall even further. So whereas the shareholders once received ⅔ or ¾ of the *higher* value in loans, they now receive at most ½ of the *reduced* value, i.e. circa half of the previously attainable loan. This must soon cause an explosion. But it is also possible that the Mincing

Lane and Mark Lane trade will remain somewhat longer in decline and only then bring about a few large bankruptcies. That this, and bankruptcies in Liverpool and other places, will occur, is certain. There will be enormous losses in sugar, coffee, cotton, wool, leather, printed cloth, silk, etc. The cotton harvest of 1857 – around 3 million bales (probably 3 ¼ million) is now worth £15,000,000 less than in September. One firm here has 35,000 sacks of coffee on offer, and each will lose £1. The loss in East Indian cotton is just as great – 33%. The bankruptcies will come whenever the bill of exchange for these commodities falls due.

The large American firm which recently received a loan of one million from the Bank of England, after two days of negotiations, and was thus saved, was owned by Mr Peabody, the 4th-of-July-Anniversary Dinner Man. Of late, the unshakeable firm of Suse & Sibeth, the only firm apart from Frühling & Göschen whose bills of exchange in East India after 1847 were negotiable without a loading certificate of the commodity being demanded as guarantee, *is said* to have had to beg the Bank for salvation. S & S are the greatest skinflints and are so afraid that they would rather do no business if they could thereby not risk anything.

So everything looks the same as before. Eight to ten days ago, the Indian and Far Eastern traders suddenly arrived in the market, helped themselves at the lowest prices and thus assisted several manufacturers out of a terrible spot, weighed down with supplies of cotton, yarn and cloth. Since Tuesday (4th November?)[1] everything has been quiet again. Costs continue to rise for the manufacturers. Coal, oil, etc. remain quite the same on full and short-time working: only wages have been reduced by a third to a half. So nothing gets sold, and floating capital is very scarce among most of our spinners and manufacturers, and many are utterly worthless. Eight or nine small businesses have already collapsed in this period, but that is only the first sign that the crisis is affecting this class. I hear today that the Cookes, owners of the vast factory in Oxford Road (the Oxford Road Twist Co.) have sold their hunters, foxhounds, greyhounds, etc., that one of them has sacked his messenger and moved out of his palace – 'To Be Let'. They are not finished yet, but will soon be. Another fortnight and the whole show will have begun.

Norway will be badly affected by the bankruptcy of Sewell & Neck; it was not affected until now.

It looks wonderful in Hamburg. Ullberg and Cramer (of Sweden, gone bankrupt owing 12,000,000 marks – of which 7 million are bills of exchange!) *possessed a capital of not more than 300,000 marks!!!* So a whole series of people have ended up not being able to raise the cash for a single bill that has fallen due, and have perhaps a hundred times their value in really worthless bills in their desks. No panic has ever been so complete and classic as the one in Hamburg now. *Everything is worthless*, absolutely without value, except silver and gold. Christian Matth. Schröder, a very old and rich firm, also went bust last week. J.H. Schröder & Co. of London (his brother) telegraphed to say that if two million marks were enough, he could send the silver for it. Answer: three million or nothing. He could not afford the three million, and Christian Matthias was out. We have debtors in Hamburg and we don't even know if they exist or are bust. The whole Hamburg affair arises from the most amazing bill-jobbing you ever saw. This has been at its most ludicrous between Hamburg, London, Copenhagen and Stockholm. The American crash and the fall in commodities then brought the whole thing out into the open, and Hamburg is commercially ruined for the moment. German industrialists, especially in Berlin, Saxony and Silesia, are badly hit by it once more.

Cotton is now at 6⁹⁄₁₆d for the middling sort and will probably fall to 6d. But the factories here can only have full-time working again if the prices are not immediately driven *over* 6d by their consequently increased production. But that will be the immediate result.

The crisis affects the philistines here mostly in their drinking habits. No one can bear being at home with the family and their trouble, the clubs are packed out and the consumption of liquor increases daily. The deeper you are in a hole, the more you try to cheer up. And then, the next morning, you present the most striking example of moral and physical blues.

I will set to work on the encyclopaedia again this week and get as far through the articles under 'C' as possible. I cannot work much or for any length now, but I will do what I can . . .

[1] A note pencilled in by Marx.

22. Engels to Marx

December 9, 1857

A few hasty details on the crisis. In Hamburg, where the old and famed Giro Bank has played down the crisis to the point of madness with its pedantry, the following has occurred: Schunck, Souchay & Co. here had drawn a bill of exchange in Hamburg. In order to proceed with the utmost caution, they send the drawee some Bank of England 'seven day bills', although the bills were for commodities etc. These were returned with a protest, as so much waste paper, and the Exchange rightly protests. Nothing is worth anything any more except silver! Exchanges with Schunck, S & Co. – Endossement and two other equally good firms have not fallen under 12½% for two whole months until last week.

N.B. If I name the firms concerned, then you realise that this is amongst ourselves. I could roast alive if such an abuse of confidential information ever came to light.

The commodity firms in Liverpool and London will soon tumble. It looks grim in Liverpool; the fellows are quite pale and have scarcely enough energy to file for bankruptcy. The faces in the Exchange there, so I was told by someone who was there last Monday, are three times as long as they are here. By the way, the storm clouds are getting bigger and blacker. The spinners and manufacturers are paying out as wages and for coal the money they received for products, and when that is used up, they are done for. The market yesterday was more depressed and more sultry than ever before.

Someone told me that he knew of five or six Indian firms which *have* to go bust in the next few days.

The fellows are only noticing now that the money swindle was the worst thing about the crisis, and the more they see that, the worse they look.

My health is good. Probably better tomorrow or the day after. Herewith a stack of *Guardians*. Have a look through the small local news items – there are some very interesting facts there.

23. Engels to Marx   *December 11, 1857*

Still very busy with bad debts and falling prices.

Over-production, in this crisis, has been more general than ever before, and is even apparent in imported food produce and in corn. That is the tremendous thing and it must have colossal consequences. As long as over-production is only confined to industry then it is only half a story; but as soon as agriculture, both in the tropics and in the temperate zones, is involved, then the thing is gigantic.

The form in which over-production is contained is always more or less that of expansion of credit, but more particularly now, bill-jobbing.

The habit of making money by drafting on a banker or a firm dealing with 'exchange business', and of covering – or not – this against depreciation, according to the arrangements, is a *rule* on the Continent and in the continental firms in England. All the commission houses here do it. This habit is practised most colossally in Hamburg, where over 100 million marks are in circulation in bills. But even elsewhere bill-jobbing is frightening, and Sieveking & Mann, Josilin & Co., Draper Pietroni & Co. – and other London firms went broke because of it. They were mainly the *drawees* in this line. The matter is so arranged here in English manufacturing and in domestic trade that people, instead of paying cash within a month, let themselves be drawn for a bill after a lapse of 3 months and are paid the interest on it. In the silk industry this grew in proportion to the growth in silk prices. In short, everyone has worked more than he is capable and is over-traded. Over-trading, however, is not synonymous with over-production, although the result is identical. A mercantile community which owns £20 million in capital thus owns a specific part of its production , trade and consumption capacity. If they then, through bill-jobbing, use this capital for production on a contract which needs £30 million in capital, then they increase production by 50%; consumption also increases through prosperity but not at all to the same extent – say 25%. At the end of a set period there is an accumulation of goods of 25% over the bona fide, that is, over the average demand *even in prosperity*. This by itself should cause a crisis, even if the money market, the sure indicator of trade, did not give a warning of it. So if the crash comes then, apart from this 25%, at least another 25% of the stocks of all necessities becomes a pig in a poke. This over-production arising from credit expansion and over-trading can be studied in all its details in the present crisis. There is nothing new in the situation itself, but only in the remarkably clear form which the development has taken: in 1847 and 1837–1842 it was not at all as clear.

That is the pretty situation of Manchester and the cotton industry: prices are low enough to permit what the philistine calls a sound business. But as soon as the slightest expansion of production starts, cotton shoots up, since there is none in Liverpool. So one has to continue working short-time, even if there are orders. And there are indeed plenty of orders, but *from places which have not yet felt the intensity of the crisis*, and the commission agents know that and so do not buy; they would otherwise have no end of problems and end up with bad debts.

The market today has fallen again. Yarn, which was worth 14 to

14½d is now offered at 11¼d and anyone offering 10½d gets it. The Indians are out of the market. The Greeks are sitting tight with corn, almost all of them, since that is their main return cargo (from Galacia and Odessa). The Germans cannot sell, for the same reasons. America is out of the question. Italy is struggling under the fall in all her raw products. Another four weeks and the whole show will turn very sour. Small spinners and manufacturers are going down every day.

Mercks of Hamburg only saved themselves with a 15 million loan from the government, and in *one* day their firm here managed at least to pay off the spinners, whose accounts were overdue. The boss at Mercks in Hamburg is the ex-Reich minister, Dr Ernst Merck, lawyer, but also shareholder . . .

24. Engels to Marx *December 17, 1857*

The crisis makes me hellishly breathless. Every day there is a fall in prices. In addition, they are getting us by the roots of our hair. My old man was in a fix today and we had to lend him some money. But I don't think it is serious; but it is all quite immaterial now.

Manchester is being drawn further into it all. The continuous pressure on the market is having enormous repercussions. No one can sell anything. Every day one hears of lower offers, and anyone with any decency does not offer for sale any more. It looks grim among the spinners and manufacturers. No yarn agent sells any yarn for weaving to the manufacturers except against cash or security. Some small ones have already gone, but that is small fry yet.

Mercks are in a jam, both here and in Hamburg, in spite of two large subventions. They are expected to go to the wall shortly. Only extra-ordinary circumstances could save them now. The Hamburg firm is said to have around 4 or 5 million marks capital in the bank for 22 million in liabilities (13 marks = £1). Other aspects indicate that the crisis has already reduced the capital to 600,000 marks.

We still have four distinct crises to come: 1. in imported produce; 2. in corn; 3. among spinners and manufacturers; 4. in home trade – next spring at the earliest. It has already begun – very merrily – in the wool districts.

Do not forget to make a note of the balance sheets of the bankrupts – Bennoch, Twentyman, Reed in Derby, Mendes da Costa, Hoare, Buxton & Co. All are very educational.

Your judgment on France has since been almost literally confirmed in the newspapers. The crash there is certain and only then will the Central and North German swindlers be brought in.

I hope you have made a note of the negotiations concerning Mac-Donald, Monteith, Stevens (London and Exchange Bank)? The affair of the London and Exchange Bank with their borrowed notes as security is the most wonderful thing I have ever read.

Apart from Hamburg, North Germany has still not been drawn into the crisis. But that is now starting. Heimedahl (silk-lining makers and sellers) of Elberfeld and Linde & Trappenberg (small ware man-ufacturers) of Barmen are bankrupt. Both were respectable firms. The North Germans have mostly had only losses until now; with them, as here, the temporary explosion of the money market has not had such a terrible effect as to make goods unsellable for any length of time.

Vienna is also becoming involved.

Lupus is now eating humble pie; we were right.

Misery among the proletariat is also beginning. At present there is not much in the way of revolution to be seen: the long period of pros-perity has demoralised them frightfully. In the streets the unemployed are still wandering around and begging. Garotte robberies are increas-ing, but not badly.

Nowadays I have a lot to do with people, in order to follow up the crisis, so that I have damned little time left to work for Dana. That must be settled in the meantime. What is he writing? And what is the situation about payment for it? . . .

The Manchester market reports are still appearing in the Saturday and Wednesday editions of the *Guardian*. Today I have sent you a whole packet of them. Today there are also some statistics on workers in it.

Congratulations on prophesying the Bank Act.

25. Marx to Engels   *December 18, 1857*

. . . I am working quite stupendously, mostly until 4a.m. You see, it is two pieces of work: 1. writing the fundamentals of the *Economy*[1] (that is quite necessary in order to let the public get to the bottom of the thing and to help me as an individual get rid of this nightmare).

2. The *present crisis*. Apart from articles for the *Tribune*, I am merely making notes, which still takes up valuable time. I think we should put

out a pamphlet *together* in spring, as a *re-announcement* to the German public that we are still here, always the same. I have plans for three large books – on England, Germany, France. All the material for a history of America is available in the *Tribune*. It can be put together later. By the way, I should be glad if you could possibly send me the *Guardian* daily. It doubles my work and interrupts me if I have to catch up on a whole week or so . . .

[1] *A Contribution to the Critique of Political Economy.*

26. Marx to Lassalle   *December 21, 1857*

. . . The present crisis in trade has spurred me on to working on the fundamentals of the *Economy*, and also to prepare something on the present crisis. I am forced to spend the day . . . working for my daily bread. So only the night remains for *real* work and then I am often disturbed by feeling unwell . . .

1858

27. Marx to Engels

. . . I am exceedingly pleased to hear that your health is improving. I myself have been taking medicine for three weeks and only stopped the dosage today. I had done too much work at night – with the assistance of only lemonade on the one hand, but an immense deal of tobacco on the other. By the way, I have made some nice developments. For example, I have thrown overboard the whole doctrine of profit up till now. By mere accident – Freiligrath found me some volumes of Hegel originally belonging to Bakunin, and he sent me them as a present – I leafed through Hegel's *Logic* again and found much to assist me in the *method* of analysis. If I ever have time for that kind of work again, I would find great pleasure in writing two or three pages on the *rationale* which Hegel discovered – but also mystified – to make it accessible for the common man.

The dregs of fadaise[1] among all modern economists are at their most concentrated in Monsieur Bastiat's *Harmonies économiques*.[2] Only a crapaud[3] would be capable of cobbling together that kind of harmonistic mishmash . . .

---

[1] French: 'absurdity'.
[2] F. Bastiat, *Economic Harmonies*, Paris 1851.
[3] French: 'frog, toad' (also term for Frenchman)

28.   Marx to Engels

January 29, 1858

. . . I have now reached a point in my work on economics where I need some practical advice from you, since I cannot find anything relevant in the theoretical writings. It concerns the *circulation* of capital – its various forms in the various businesses: its effect on profit and prices. If you could give me some information on this, then it will be very welcome . . .

29.   Marx to Lassalle

February 22, 1858

. . . I would like to tell you how things stand with my work on economics. I have in fact had the final draft to hand for several months. But the process is very slow, because things on which one has concentrated one's study for many years always produce something new when you think you have finished with it, and that demands new consideration. In addition, I am not a master of my own time, but rather a servant. Only the night remains free and very frequent attacks and recurrences of a liver complaint again disturb work at night. With all this, it would be easier for me if I could publish the whole work in unstitched booklets. This would perhaps have the additional advantage that a bookseller might be found more quickly since there is less capital tied up in the whole business. Of course, you will make an undertaking to see if you can find a publisher in Berlin. By 'booklets' I mean the kind of thing that Vischer's *Ästhetik*[1] appeared in serially.

The work we are discussing is a *Critique of Economic Categories* or, if you like, the system of bourgeois economy in a critical description. It is both a description of the system and, in describing it, a critique of the same. I am not at all sure how many pages the whole thing will involve. If I had time, peace and the means to write it out in full before handing it over to the public, I would greatly condense it, since I have always loved the method of condensing. But if – and perhaps this is easier for the public to understand, but certainly harmful for the form – if it is printed serially, then the whole thing would be greatly expanded. NB. As soon as you are sure that the thing can be done in Berlin – *or that it cannot* – please be so good as to write so that, if it is not possible, I can try in Hamburg. Another point is that I must be *paid* by the bookseller who undertakes the job – a stipulation which might ruin my chances in Berlin.

The presentation – by which I mean the style – is quite scientific, and so not liable to police prosecution in the normal sense. The whole thing is divided into 6 books. 1. On Capital (contains several introductory chapters). 2. On the Ownership of Land. 3. On Wage Labour. 4. On the State. 5. International Trade. 6. The World Market. I obviously cannot avoid polemicising against Ricardo, just as he, as bourgeois, is forced to commit blunders, *even* from a strictly economic *viewpoint*. But in general the critique and the history of political economy and of socialism should form the subject of another book. Finally, the short *historical sketch* of the development of economic categories or relationships should be yet another book. After all, I have a feeling that now, after fifteen years of study, when I can at last analyse the thing, storms from outside will probably interfere. Never mind. If I finish too late to call the attention of the world to these matters, then the failure is obviously my own . . .

[1] F.T Vischer, *Aesthetics, or the Science of Beauty*, 3 vols, Leipzig 1846–1857.

30. Marx to Engels   *March 2, 1858*

. . . Can you tell me how often you renew the machinery, in your factory for example? Babbage maintains that in Manchester the bulk of machinery is renovated every 5 years on average. This seems somewhat startling to me and not quite trustworthy. The average time for renewing machinery is *one* important moment in the explanation of the cycle of several years which industrial movement has followed since large-scale industry was consolidated . . .

31. Engels to Marx   *March 4, 1858*

. . . It is difficult to say anything definite on the question of machinery; but in any case Babbage is wrong. The safest criterion is the percentage which every manufacturer puts aside for the depreciation of his machinery, so that in a certain period his machines will have fulfilled their service. This percentage is usually 7½%, so that the use of machinery is covered by annual savings for 13⅓ years, so that it can be renewed with no loss. For example, if I have £10,000 worth of machinery. After one year, when I balance my books, I deduct

from	£10,000.00
7½% depreciation	750.00
	9,250.00
Outlay for repairs	100.00
The machinery costs me	9,350.00
At the end of the second year I deduct from	
7½% of £10,000, 7½% of £100	757.10
	8,593.10
Pay for repairs	306.10
The whole machinery now costs	£ 8,900.00

etc. Now 13⅓ years is certainly a long time, and bankruptcies and changes can occur, and one can open new branches, sell old machinery, introduce new improvements; but if this calculation were not entirely correct, then practice would have changed it long ago. Old and sold machinery does not immediately become scrap iron, since there are still buyers among small spinners etc., who can use it. We still have machinery in use which is at least twenty years old; and if one could sometimes have a look inside rattly old concerns then one would see old world junk at least 30 years old. Since, with most machines, only a few parts become so worn that they must be replaced after five or six years, or even after fifteen years, if the working principle of the machine has not been superseded by new inventions, the wastage can be replaced quite easily. (I refer especially to spinning and pre-spinning machinery), so that it is difficult to set a positive limit to the life span of such machines. Now, the improvements of the last twenty years in spinning machines are not such that they cannot almost all be incorporated into the existing *framework* of the machinery, for they consist mostly in separate small parts. (Admittedly, in carding, the enlargement of the card-cylinder was a major improvement which replaced old machinery for *good* quality products; but for ordinary sorts, the old machinery will still be good enough for a long time.)

Babbage's assurance is so absurd that, if it were true, industrial capital in England would continually decrease and money would have to be pitched after it. A manufacturer who turns over his capital five times in four years, i.e. 6¼ times in five years, would have to earn another 20% on around three quarters of his capital (the machinery), on top of an average profit of 10% annually, in order to replace his old machinery without loss — that is, make a profit of 25%. And then the cost of all articles would be increased enormously, almost more than by wages; and what would be the advantage of having machinery then? The annual wages bill amounts to perhaps one third of the price of machinery — certainly less in simple spinning and weaving mills, and depreciation is supposed to amount to a fifth! — it is ridiculous. There is certainly not a single establishment in England, in the usual line of big industry, that replaces its machinery every five years. Anyone so stupid would inevitably go bust at the first change; the old machinery, even if it were much worse, would then have an advantage over the new, and could produce much more cheaply, since the market is not geared to those who add 15% for depreciation on every pound of twist, but to those who only add on 6% (four-fifths approx. of the annual depreciation of 7½%) and so sell more cheaply.

Ten or twelve years is enough to give the bulk of machinery new character and so to replace it more or less. The period of 13⅓ years is naturally so affected by bankruptcies, the breakdown of essential parts which make repairs too costly, and similar events, that one can make it somewhat shorter. But not less than ten years . . .

32. Marx to Engels   *March 5, 1858*

. . . My best thanks for your enlightening remarks on machinery. The period of thirteen years corresponds, as far as is necessary, to my theory, since it assumes one *unit* for one epoch of industrial reproduction which more or less coincides with the period in which great crises repeat themselves, crises whose course is naturally determined by quite different moments, according to their period of reproduction. The important thing for me is to find *one* moment in the direct material conditions of big industry which decides the cycles. With the reproduction of machinery, in contrast to that of circulating capital, one is forced to think of the Moleschotts, who pay too little attention to the time of reproduction of the skeleton, and rather, like the economists, content themselves with the total reproduction-time of the human body. Another question which I need only as an approximate illustration is how – for example, in your factory or manufacturing business – the floating capital is divided into raw material, wages, and how much is left with your banker? Further, how do you *calculate* the turnover in your book-keeping? The theoretical laws for this are very simple and self-evident. But it is good to have an idea of how it works in practice. The method of accounting among merchants is naturally based on even greater illusions, partly, than those of the economists; but on the other hand they justify the practical illusions with theoretical ones. You talk of 10 p.c. profit. I suppose that you do not take into account the interest, and this probably is accounted beside profit. In the 'First Report of the Factory Commissioners' I find the following statement as an average illustration:

Capital sunk in building and machinery.................................£10,000

Floating capital.. 7,000

£   500 interest on 10,000 fixed capital

£   350 ditto on floating capital

£   150 Rents, taxes, rates

£   650 Sinking fund of 6½% for wear and tear of the fixed capital
_____

£ 1,650

£ 1,100 Contingencies (?), carriage, coal, oil
_____

£ 2,750

£ 2,600 Wages and salaries
_____

£ 5,350

£10,000 For about 400,000 lbs of raw cotton at 6d.
_____

£15,350

£16,000 for 363,000 lbs twist spun. Value £16,000. *Profit* £650, or about 4.2%. The wages of the operative here are thus about one sixth.

Here the total profit in any case is only about 10%, including interest. But Mr Senior, who wrote in the cause of the manufacturers, talks of an average profit in Manchester of 15% (including interest). It is very regrettable that the *number* of workers is not given in the above statement; and also that the proportion between the given *salaries* and the actual *wages* is not given.

In any case, as even the best economists, such as Ricardo him very self, resort to quite infantile chatter when they enter the bourgeois treadmill, I stumbled across this particular passage in Ricardo when reading him yesterday. You remember that A. Smith, who is still very old-fashioned, maintained that foreign trade, compared with domestic trade, accounted for only one half of the encouragement to the productive labour of a country etc. Ricardo then answers with the following illustration:

> Smith's argument seems false to me: for although two sets of capital, one Portuguese and one English, are used, as Smith assumes, only *one* capital is employed in foreign trade and it is double the capital used at home. Given that Scotland uses a capital of £1,000 in the production of linen, which is then used for a similar capital invested in the English silk-manufacture. £2,000 and a proportional quantity of labour is used in the two countries. If England then discovers that it can get more linen from Germany for the silk which it previously exported to Scotland, and if Scotland discovers that it can get more silk from France in return for its linen then it did from England, then England and Scotland will immediately cease trading with one another, and domestic trade will be replaced by foreign trade. But although two additional sets of capital are involved in this trade, one from Germany and one from France, will the same contribution from Scotland's and England's capital not continue and will not the same amount on industry be set in motion as was the case with domestic trade?

The supposition that in this situation Germany would buy its silk in England instead of in France and that France would buy its linen in Scotland instead of in Germany is a bit too much for a fellow like Ricardo.

Friend Thomas Tooke has died, and with him the last English economist of any value . . .

33. Marx to Lassalle   *March 11, 1858*

. . . The first instalment[1] must in any case be relatively self-contained, and since the basis for the whole argument is contained in it, it would be difficult to keep it under 5-6 sheets. But I will consider that in the final draft. It contains 1. Value 2. Money 3. Capital in general (the production process of capital, the circulation process of capital, the unity of both or capital and profit, interest). This forms a separate brochure. You will yourself have discovered in your studies on economics that Ricardo contradicts his own (correct) definition of value when discussing the development of profit, which has led, in his school, to a complete abandonment of the fundamentals or to the most sickening eclecticism. I think that I have clarified the matter. (In any case, the economists will find on closer inspection that it is a dirty business altogether) . . .

As for the total number of sheets, I am indeed most unclear, since the material for the book only exists in the form of monographs in my notebooks, which often go into much detail which would disappear in the compilation. And it is by no means my intention to work for the same length of time on each of the six books which make up the whole; instead, I will only write out the fundamental concepts in the last three, and in the first three – which contain the truly economic argument, I cannot avoid explanations everywhere. I do not think that all that can be done in less than 30–40 sheets . . .

---

[1] It was Marx's intention to add a chapter on capital to the first part of his *Contribution to the Critique of Political Economy*. Later he decided to publish this chapter separately in a second part – the reasons for this are given in letter 34 below. This second part then became the preparatory work for *Capital*.

34. Marx to Engels

April 2, 1858

. . . The following is a short outline of the first part. The whole crap will divide into six books. 1. On capital 2. Land Ownership 3. Wage Labour 4. The State 5. International Trade 6. World Market.

1. *Capital* falls into four sections. a) Capital in general. (*This is the material for the first booklet*). b) *Competition* or the action of many capitals against each other. c) *Credit*, whereby the capital appears as a general element in relation to the separate capitals. d) *Share capital* as the most highly developed form (going over into communism) together with all its contradictions. The transition of capital to land ownership is at once historical, since the modern form of land ownership is a product of the effect of capital on feudal and other land ownership. Similarly the transition of land ownership to wage labour is not only dialectical but

also historical, since the final product of modern land ownership is the general introduction of wage labour, which in turn appears as the basis of the whole crap. Well (it is difficult for me to write today) we are now come to the 'corpus delicti'.[1]

I. *Capital. First Section. Capital in General.* (Throughout this section we assume that the wage is always set at its minimum. The movements of wages themselves and the rise and fall of the minimum belong to the consideration of wage labour. In addition land ownership is set = 0, that is, we are not yet concerned with land ownership as a particular economic relationship. Only in this way is it possible to avoid dealing with everything in every relationship.)

1. *Value.* This is reduced entirely to the quantity of labour; time as a measure of labour. Use-value – whether subjective, as usefulness of labour, or objective as the utility of the product – appears here only as the material pre-condition for value, and is meanwhile produced by the determined economic form. Value as such has no other 'material' than labour itself. This definition of value, first worked out sketchily by Petty, and clearly by Ricardo, is only the most abstract form of bourgeois wealth. It already presupposes 1. the destruction of natural communism (in India etc.); 2. the destruction of all undeveloped, pre-bourgeois modes of production which are not governed in their totality by exchange. Although it is an abstraction, it is an historical abstraction which can only be assumed on the basis of a particular economic development of society. All objections to this definition of value are either deduced from less developed relations of production, or based on a confusion which validates more concrete economic conditions, from which value is abstracted and which is therefore seen as a further development of it, against this definition of the abstract and undeveloped form of value. These objections were more or less justified by the lack of clarity among Messrs Economists themselves on the question of how this abstraction related to later, more concrete forms of bourgeois wealth.

The category of money arises from the contradiction of the general characteristics of value in its material existence in a particular commodity etc. – these general characteristics are the same ones that later appear in money.

2. *Money.*

A few things about precious metals as carriers of money relationships.

a) *Money as a measure.* A few notes on the *ideal* measure in Steuart,

Attwood, Urquhart; in a more comprehensible form in the priests of labour-money (Gray, Bray etc. Several opportune blows against the Proudhonists). The value of a commodity translated into money is its *price*, which meanwhile only appears in this *purely formal* distinction from value. According to the general law of value a particular quantity of money then only expresses a particular quantity of realised labour. In so far as money is a measure, the variability of its own value is irrelevant.

b) *Money as a means of exchange or simple circulation.*

Here we only need to consider the simple form of this circulation itself. All the conditions which determine its further course are separate from it and so will be considered later. (We assume more developed relations.) If we call commodity C and money M, then simple circulation follows two cycles or syllogisms: C–M–M–C and M–C–C–M (the latter is the transition to section (c)), but the points of departure and return are not necessarily identical or merely accidental. The most that could be deduced from the so-called laws of the Economists is that money does not circulate within its own terms but is included under and determined by higher movements. All this is to be treated separately. (It belongs partly to the theory of credit; but partly it must also be dealt with at points where money comes up again, but more fully defined.) Thus money is considered here as a means of circulation (*coin*). But at the same time also as the *realisation* (and not merely an ephemeral realisation) of price. From the simple definition that the money posited as *price* is already nominally exchanged for money before it is actually exchanged, follows automatically the important economic law that *the amount of the circulating medium is determined by the prices and not vice versa.* (In this connection some historical observations on the controversy relating to this point.) It follows further that velocity can replace quantity, but that a *definite quantity* of money is necessary for the simultaneous acts of exchange, in so far as these are not related to each other as plus and minus; this balancing and allowance only behave in anticipation of each other at this point. I will not go into the further development of this section. Just note that the opposition of C–M and M–C is the most abstract and superficial form of the possibility of crisis. From the development of the law for determining the circulating amount by prices we have pre-requisites which by no means exist for all business situations; the absurdity of this is that, for example, the flow of money from Asia to Rome and its effect on the prices there is simply attributed to modern commercial relationships. The most abstract conditions, when observed more closely, always indicate a further concrete, historically determined basis. (Of course, they are abstracted from that in this definition.)

c) *Money as Money*. This is a development of the form M–C–C–M. Money as an independent manifestation of value in opposition to circulation; as a material existence of abstract wealth. Even in circulation, it shows how much it is not only a means of circulation but also a realisation of price. The property (c), where (a) and (b) are only functions of it, is that money is the general commodity of contracts (here the variability of its value, through the determination of value by labour time, is important), is the object of hoarding. (This function still appears to be important in Asia and generally in the Ancient World and Middle Ages. It now only exists in subordinate form in the banking system. In times of crisis, the importance of money reappears in this form. Money in this form is considered along with the world-historical delusion concerning it etc. Destructive properties etc.) As a realisation of all higher forms in which all relations of value are outwardly settled. But money ceases to be an economic relation when fixed in this form, and is effaced in its material carriers, gold and silver. On the other hand, in so far as it enters circulation and is then again exchanged against C, the closing process (the consumption of the commodity) withdraws it from the economic relation. Simple money circulation does not contain the principle of self-reproduction and so it points beyond itself. With money – as the exposition of its functions shows – we suppose *capital*, given that value enters circulation and contains itself. This transition is also historical. The antediluvian form of capital is merchant capital, which always produces money. At the same time, there was a development of real capital from money or merchant capital, which gained control of production.

d) If we consider this simple circulation by itself – and it is the surface of bourgeois society in which the deeper operations from which it arises are obscured – we find no difference between the objects of exchange, except formal and transient differences. This is *the realm of liberty, equality and property based on 'labour'*. Accumulation, as it appears here in the form of hoarding, is then only increased thriftiness etc. We then have some absurdity from the advocates of economic harmony on the one side, and the modern free traders (Bastiat, Carey, etc.), concerning the more developed relations of production and their antagonisms, when they try to turn it into their *truth* in the most superficial and abstract manner. We have absurdity from the Proudhonists and suchlike socialists, who oppose this exchange of equivalents (or what is supposed to be such) and its corresponding ideas of equality etc. to the inequalities etc. which this exchange produces and from which it results. In this sphere, the law of appropriation in the form of appropriation through labour appears as the exchange of equivalents, so that the exchange only gives the same value in another material form. In short, everything here is 'lovely', but also comes to a terrible end because of the law of equivalence. For we now come to

3. *Capital*.

This is actually the important part of this first section, and I must have your opinion in particular. But today I cannot write any more. My bilious attack is making it difficult for me to hold the pen and the lowering of my head to the paper makes me dizzy. So until next time.

[1] Latin: 'the heart of the matter'.

35. Engels to Marx   *April 9,1858*

I have been very busy studying the abstract of the first half booklet, for it is a very abstract abstract indeed, as cannot be avoided in a short space, and I often followed the dialectical transitions only with difficulty, since I have become most unused to any abstract reasoning. The arrangement of the whole thing into six books could not be improved on at all and it pleases me enormously, although I am still not entirely clear on the dialectical transition from land ownership to wage labour. The exposition on the history of money is also very fine, although I am not entirely clear about some details, since I usually have to look out the historical basis itself. But I think that, as soon as I have reached the end of the chapter in general, and when I have a better view of the drift, I will write to you more fully about it. The abstract, dialectical tone of this resumé will naturally disappear in the complete work . . .

36. Marx to Engels   *May 31, 1858*

. . . During my absence, a book by Maclaren[1] appeared in London, on the entire history of currency, and, judging by the extracts in the

Economist, it is first-rate. The book is not yet in the library, since things only appear there months after publication. But I naturally have to read it before my own presentation. So I sent my wife into the City to the publisher. But to our dismay, the book cost 9/6, which was more than our entire life's savings. So I would be very grateful if you could send me a postal order for this amount. I probably will not find anything new in the book; but judging by the review given in the *Economist* and by the extracts which I have read myself, my theoretical conscience will not allow me to proceed without knowing all about it . . .

[1] J. Maclaren, *A Sketch of the History of Currency; Comprising a Brief Review of the Opinions of the Most Eminent Writers on the Subject*, London 1858.

37. **Marx to Lassalle** *November 12, 1858*

. . . As for the delay in sending the manuscript, I was hindered firstly by my illness and later I had to catch up on some professional work. But the real reason is this, that I had the material in front of me, and just had to decide on its form. But the style of everything I had written still smacked of my liver complaint. And I had a twofold reason for not letting this text be ruined on medical grounds:

1. It is the result of fifteen years of study, the best part of my life.

2. For the first time it proposed an important and scientific view of social relations. So I owe the Party not to deform the thing with such a dull and wooden style that arises from a liver complaint.

I am not aiming at an elegant presentation, but only at writing in my usual style, which was impossible during the months of illness, at least on this theme, although I was obliged to write at least two printed volumes of English editorials de omnibus rebus et quibus aliis[1] and so wrote them . . .

[1] Latin: 'on everything and a little more'.

38. **Marx to Engels** *November 29, 1858*

. . . My wife is copying the manuscript, and it will not be finished before the end of this month. The reasons for this delay: long intervals of physical malaise which has now stopped in the cold weather. Too much domestic and financial trouble. Finally: the first section has become more wide-ranging, since the first two chapters of it – of which the *first*, the *Commodity*, was not even written into the first draft, and the *second*, *Money or Simple Circulation*, was only in a very sketchy form – have been greatly expanded, more than I originally intended . . .

1859

39. Marx to Engels

circa January 13, 1859

... The manuscript is about 12 sheets (3 folded sections) and –
don't collapse – although its title is 'Capital in General', these sections
do not yet contain *anything* about capital, but only the two chapters:
1. *Commodity* 2. *Money or Simple Circulation*. So you see that the part we
worked over in detail (in May, when I visited you) has still not appeared
yet. This is good for two reasons. If the thing is a success, then the third
chapter on capital can follow quickly. Secondly, since, in the nature of
things, the dogs cannot reduce their critique of the published part to
mere tendentious scolding, and because the whole thing looks exceedingly serious and scientific, the canaille are forced to take my views on
capital rather seriously. By the way, I think that, apart from any practical purposes, the chapter on money should be interesting for
experts ...

40. Marx to Weydemeyer

February 1, 1859

... My *Critique of Political Economy* is being published in booklets
(the first parts appear in 8–10 days from now) by Franz Duncker in
Berlin (the Bessersche bookshop). Duncker was only swayed to take this
step by some extraordinary zeal and powers of conviction by Lassalle.
But he still left one back door open. *The final contract depends on the sale of the
first parts.*

I divide the whole political economy into 6 parts.

Capital; Land Ownership; Wage Labour; the State; Foreign Trade; World Market.

Part I on capital is split into four sections.

Section I. Capital in general comes in three chapters. 1. *Commodity* 2. *Money or simple circulation* 3. *Capital*. 1. and 2. about 10 sheets form the contents of the first booklets to appear. You will understand the *political* reasons which made me decide to withhold the third chapter on 'Capital' until I have a good foothold.

The contents of the published booklets are as follows.

First Chapter: The Commodity.

A: *Historical material for the analysis of the commodity*. (William Petty (Englishman under Charles II); Boisguillebert (Louis XIV); B. Franklin (first early writings of 1719); the Physiocrats, Sir James Steuart; Adam Smith; Ricardo and Sismondi.)

Second Chapter: Money or Simple Circulation.

1. *Measure of Value.*

B. *Theories on the unit of measure of money*. (End of 17th century, Locke and Lowndes; Bishop Berkeley (1750); Sir James Steuart; Lord Castlereagh; Thomas Attwood; John Gray; the Proudhonists.)

2. *Means of Circulation.*

a) *Metamorphosis of Commodities*

b) *Circulation of Money*

c) *Coins. The symbol of value.*

3. *Money.*

a) *Hoarding*

b) *Means of Payment*

c) *World Money (money of the world)*

4. *The precious metals.*

C. *Theories on the Means of Circulation and Money* (Monetary system; Spectator, Montesquieu, David Hume; Sir James Steuart; A. Smith; J.B. Say, Bullion Committee, Ricardo, James Mill; Lord Overstone and his School; Thomas Tooke, James Wilson, John Fullarton.)

In these two chapters, the basis of Proudhonist socialism, now fashionable in France, which leaves private production alone *but organises* the exchange of private products, which wants the *commodity* but not the *money*, will be run into the ground. Communism must above all dispose of this 'false brother'. But, apart from any polemical purpose, you know that the analysis of simple money forms is the most difficult part of political economy, because it is the most abstract part.

I hope to win a scientific victory for our Party. But it must show whether it is numerous enough to buy enough copies to appease the 'scientific conscience' of the bookseller. The continuation of the undertaking depends on the sale of the first parts. If I just get a final contract, then everything will be all right.

41. Marx to Engels   *February 25, 1859*

. . . I am morally certain that Duncker, *after my letter to Lassalle*, will take the booklets. The Jew Braun has not written since my manuscript arrived, and that was over four weeks ago. For one thing he was busy with the publication of some immortal 'inflammatory' work of his own (still, the Jew's *Herakleitos*,[1] although abysmally written, is better than anything the democrats could boast of) and then he will probably have to undertake the final correction of my tiny scrap. Secondly he has had a bad bump on the head, indirectly, from my analysis of money, which may have stunned him a bit. For he made the following remark about Heraclitus, which I will give you word for word in spite of its interminable length (but you must read it):

> If we have already said above that Heraclitus had declared in this fragment the true economic nature and function of money (Heraclitus here says: But everything comes from fire and fire from everything, just as commodities come from gold and gold from commodities),[2] then it is superfluous to state that we do not thereby turn him into an economist, and we are just as far from stating that he could have drawn any of the conclusions from this fragment. But although this science did not even exist at this time, nor could it have existed, and so was not the object of Heraclitus' thought, it is still correct to say that in this fragment Heraclitus – precisely because he never used analysis by reflection but only speculative concepts – recognised the essence of money in its true profundity and did so more correctly than many a modern economist, and it would perhaps be interesting, and not irrelevant to the present discussion, to see whether *modern discoveries in this field result*[3] from the consequences of this thought. (N.B. L[assalle] does not know a thing about these discoveries.)
> If Heraclitus made money the means of exchange *in opposition* to all real products involved in exchange and then allows it to have its *real existence* (I emphasise where Lassalle emphasises) then money as such is

not only one and the same product with an independent and material value, it is not a *commodity* beside other commodities, as the school of Say (nice Continental delusion this, that there is a 'school of Say') still stubbornly insist concerning metal money, but it is only the ideal *symbol* of real circulating products, it is the *symbol of value* of them and only *indicates* them. And that is partly only a conclusion to be drawn from this fragment, and partly only the existing thought of Heraclitus.

But if *all* money is only the ideal unit or the expressed value of all real circulating commodities, and only *has its real existence in those* which form its opposite, then, from the mere consequence of this thought it follows (lovely style! It follows from the 'mere consequence') that the amount of values or wealth of a country can only be increased through the increase of real commodities, but never through the increase in money, since money, instead of forming any particular moment in wealth and value (now we've got wealth *and* value; before, we had amount of values *or* wealth) by itself, only now expresses the value contained in commodities (another fine remark) and only expresses the *real value* in it as an abstract unit. (This is worthy of Ruge.) It also follows: that *all* money is equal in value to all the circulating commodities, since it only expresses the value of these as an ideal unit, and so only expresses *their* value; that, through the increase or decrease of the existing amount of money, the value of this total amount of money never changes and always stays equivalent to all circulating commodities; that, strictly speaking, one cannot talk of a *value* of all money compared with the *value* of all circulating commodities, because such a comparison would present the value of money and the value of the commodities as *two* independent values, when there is only *one* value in existence, realised concretely in the tangible products and expressed as an abstract unit of value in the money, or rather, the *value* itself is nothing but a unit abstracted from the real things in which it does not exist as such and which is given a particular expression by money; so it is not the case that the value of all money merely *equals* the value of all products, but rather that, correctly speaking, all money IS only the *value* of all circulating products. (The twofold emphasis belongs to the author.) So it follows that with an increase in the number of coins, since the value of the amount remains the same, only the value of each individual coin will fall, and with a decrease, the value of each will rise. – It also follows that, since money is only the unreal abstract thought of value and the *opposite* of *real products* and materials, money as such can have no *reality* in itself; that is, that its form needs no real valuable material, but can equally well be paper money and then it will correspond most closely to its concept. All these and many other results, which have been gained since *Ricardo's* investigation by quite different roads and which are not yet generally accepted, arise already from the simple conclusion of Heraclitus's speculative concept.

Naturally I have not paid the slightest attention to the Talmudic wisdom, but have given Ricardo a good dressing-down for his theory of money, which, incidentally, originated in Hume and Montesquieu and not with him. Thus Lassalle may feel personally offended. I did not have that intention, for I took exception to Ricardo's theory in my writings against Proudhon.[4] But the Jew Braun had written me a most ridiculous letter, in which he said he was 'interested in the rapid publication of my work, *although* he himself was involved in a great economic work' and had 'set two years aside for it'. But if I 'presented too many new things, he would abandon the project'. Well! I answered that he should fear no rivalry, for there was room for both of us in this 'new' science, and even room for a dozen more. He must now see, from my presentation of money, either that I know nothing at all about it, or that he is an ass who thinks he can judge empirical things with a few abstract phrases, like 'abstract unit' and others, and that these things must be studied – and for a long time into the bargain – in order to be able to discuss them . . .

[1] A reference to F. Lassalle's *The Philosophy of Heraclitus of Ephesus* Berlin 1858. 'Braun' was a pseudonym for Lassalle.

[2] This sentence in Greek in original.

[3] Marx's emphasis.

[4] Reference to Marx's *The Poverty of Philosophy*.

42. Marx to Lassalle *March 28, 1859*

. . . You will observe that the first section of the main chapter, which is the third on *Capital*, is not contained in the publication. I withheld this for *political* reasons, for the real battle begins in chapter 3, and I thought it advisable not to frighten anyone off from the very beginning . . .

43. Marx to Engels *July 22, 1859*

. . . You have forgotten to tell me whether you want to write a review of my book. There is much rejoicing among the fellows here. They think that it has failed *because* they do not know that Duncker has not even announced it yet. In case you do write something, you should not forget 1. that Proudhonism has been extracted by its roots, 2. that in its simplest form – in the form of *commodity* – the *specific* social (and in one way *absolute*) character of bourgeois production has been analysed. Herr Liebknecht explained to Biskamp that 'no book had ever *disappointed* him so much', and Biskamp himself told me he could not see 'what it was for' . . .

44. Marx to Lassalle   *November 6, 1859*

. . . Thank you for your efforts with Duncker. By the way, you are wrong if you think I expected much praise from the German press or even that I care a jot about it. I expected attacks or criticisms, but not a total silence, which must spoil the sales significantly. If people have been roundly cursing my communism at every opportunity, then one would expect them to let loose their wisdom now on the theoretical basis of the same. For there are economic journals in Germany as well.

The first part was extensively discussed by the German press in America, from New York to New Orleans. I only fear that it was judged to be too theoretical for the workers there . . .

1860

45. Engels to Marx
January 31, 1860

. . . To come out directly polemically and politically in Germany on behalf of our Party is quite impossible. So, what is left? Either to keep your mouth shut or to make efforts which would only be known to émigrés or American Germans but not to anyone in Germany, or even to continue in the way you began in your first booklet and I in my *Po und Rhein*.[1] I consider this way to be the best for just now, and if we can do that, then just let Vogt squeal, for we will soon have enough of a foothold again that we can publish the necessary personal statements (whenever required) in the German press. The forthcoming publication of your second booklet is of course by far the most important thing, and I hope that you will not let yourself be diverted from it by this Vogt affair.[2] Just be somewhat less conscientious about your own articles; they are still much too good for the lousy public. The *main* thing is that the thing gets written and is published; the weaknesses which you think of will never be discovered by those donkeys; and if an unsettled period sets in what will you be left with if the whole thing is interrupted before you get *Capital* finished as a whole? I know very well that other things interrupt you; but I also know that the main delays are caused by your own scruples. In the end, it is better that the thing gets published than that it never appears out of some consideration . . .

---

[1] Engels's pamphlet *Po and Rhine*, Berlin 1859.
[2] Reference to the controversy between Karl Vogt, a police spy in the democratic movement, and the German émigrés. See Marx's book *Herr Vogt*. [English translation *Herr Vogt*, New Park Publications 1982.]

46.   Marx to Lassalle   *September 15, 1860*

. . . I was delighted by your praise of my book, since it comes from a competent judge. I think I can get the second part published by Easter. The form will be somewhat different, more popular to some extent – not because of any inner need on my part, but for one thing this second part has a directly revolutionary purpose, and then the relations which I present are more concrete.

My book has attracted much attention in Russia, and a professor in Moscow has given a lecture on it. And I have just received many sympathetic letters from Russians on it. Ditto from French people who read German . . .

1862

47. Marx to Engels

... Could you write to me about all kinds of workers (without exception, except the warehouse) who are employed in your factory, for example, and tell me the proportions of one group to another? You see, I need an example for my book in order to show that, in the mechanised workshop, the *division of labour*, since it forms the basis of manufacturing and is described by A. Smith, does not exist. The phrase itself is taken from Ure. Any example will do ...

48. Marx to Lassalle

... Your warning about Rodbertus and Roscher reminds me that I still have to make notes from both and on both. As regards Rodbertus, I did not honour him justly enough in my first letter to you. There is really much good material in there. Only his attempt at a new theory of rent is almost childish, comical. According to him, you see, no raw material goes into the book-keeping of agriculture, because – the German peasant, Rodbertus assures us, does not himself count seed, feed, etc. as an expense, and does not include these as production costs, and so has *false* accounts. In England, where the farmer has been doing his accounts correctly for more than 150 years, *no* land rent can exist. So the conclusion is not the one drawn by Rodbertus, that the tenant pays a rent because his rate of profit is higher than in industry, but that, because of false accounts, he is content with a lower rate of profit. By the way, this one example shows me how the partially undeveloped state of German economic relations necessarily confuses people. Ricardo's land rent theory in its present state is unconditionally false; but everything which is adduced against it is either a misunderstanding or, at best, shows that certain phenomena do not match Ricardo's theory prima facie.[1] So the latter does not deny a theory at all. The positive counter-theories against Ricardo, however, are a thousand times more false. However childish the positive solution of Mr Rodbertus, there is still a correct tendency in it; but we cannot describe it here, for it is too broad.

As regards Roscher, I can only put the book in front of me in a few weeks and make some notes. I have reserved a footnote for myself on this fellow. Such professorial students do not fit into the main text. Roscher has a great deal of knowledge – often some quite useful literary knowledge, although I myself can see straight through this graduate of Göttingen University when he grubs constrainedly through the treasury of literature and only recognises 'official literature'; respectable. But that aside. What use is a fellow to me who knows the entire literature of mathematics and does not understand mathematics? He is a real self-satisfied, boastful, moderate, smart, eclectic scoundrel! If a professorial student like that, who, by his very nature, can never get past the learning and teaching of the learned, who never reaches self-education, if a Wagner like that was at least honest and had a conscience, then he could be useful to his students. If only he did not leave false escape routes and just said openly: 'This is a contradiction. Some say this, some say that. I, by nature, have no opinion. Now just see if you can work it out for yourself.' In this form, his pupils would, on the one hand, have some real material, and, on the other, be encouraged to research for themselves. But in any case, I am putting forward a demand which is anathema to the nature of a professor. It is an essential part of him that he does not even understand the *questions* and, from his eclecticism, really only sniffs around the harvest of existing *answers*; but even that is not honest, because he is always looking with an eye to the prejudices and the interests of his paymasters! A stone breaker is respectable in comparison to canaille like that . . .

[1] Latin: 'at first sight'.

49. Marx to Engels   *June 18, 1862*

... Otherwise I am working strongly at it, and, oddly, my brain-box is in better shape with all the poverty around than it has been for years. I am expanding this volume since the German dogs always value a book according to cubic centimetres. Apart from that, I am also finished with the crap on land rent (which, however, I do *not* even want to *mention* in this part). For a long time I have had misgivings about the complete rightness of Ricardo's theory and have at last discovered the swindle. And, since we last met, I have also discovered a few nice and surprising things for the material in this volume.

Darwin, at whom I have had another look, amuses me by saying that he applies the 'Malthusian' theory *also* to plants and animals: the whole point about Mathus was that it was to be applied *not* to plants and animals, but only to men – in geometric progression – in contradistinction to plants and animals. It is notable that Darwin recognises among the beasts and plants his own English society with its division of labour, competition, opening of new markets, 'inventions' and Malthusian 'struggle for existence'. This is Hobbes's bellum omnium contra omnes[1] and it reminds one of Hegel in his *Phenomenology*, where bourgeois society appears as a 'spiritual animal kingdom', while the animal kingdom appears to Darwin as a bourgeois society ...

By the way! If it can be done quickly, without taking up your time, I would like a prime example (and an explanation) of Italian book-keeping. It would come in useful for illuminating the *Tableau Economique* of Dr Quesnay[2] ...

[1] Latin: 'the war of all against all'.
[2] Quesnay's 'economic table' — see letter 56 below.

50. Marx to Engels   *August 2, 1862*

... It is a real miracle that I can still proceed with theoretical work, as I am now doing. But I now intend, precisely in this volume, to introduce a new chapter on the theory of rent, i.e. as an 'illustration' of an earlier statement. I will give you the story in a few words, although *it is long and complicated in the book*, so that you can give me **your opinion.**

You know that I divide capital into two parts, *constant capital* (raw material, instrumental material, machinery, etc.), whose value only *reappears* in the value of the product, and secondly *variable capital*, that is capital expended in wages, which contains less realised labour than the worker puts in. For example, if the daily wage = 10 hours and the worker works 12 hours, then he increases the variable capital by + ⅕ of itself (2 hours). I call this last surplus *surplus value* . . .

If we suppose that the *rate of surplus value* (thus, the length of the working day and the surplus of surplus labour over the necessary labour which the worker does for the reproduction of his salary) is set at, say, = 50%. In this case the worker works for himself for 8 hours of a 12 hour day, and 4 hours (½) for the employer. And this is increasing in every trade, so that any differences in the average working time are only compensation for an increased or decreased hardship of labour etc.

In these conditions, with a *similar* exploitation of the worker in *different* trades, different capitals in different spheres of production *of the same size* return very *different* amounts of surplus value and thus very *different rates of profit*, since profit is nothing but the proportion of the surplus value to the total capital advanced. This will depend on the *organic composition* of the capital, that is, on its division into constant and variable capital.

Suppose, as above, that the surplus labour = 50%. Now, if, for example, £1 = working day (even if you think of a day as a week etc.), the working day = 12 hours, the necessary labour (that producing the salary) = 8 hours, then the wages of 30 workers (or if the working day= £20 and the value of their work = £30, then the variable capital for one worker) daily or weekly = £⅔ and the value created = £1. The amount of surplus value which is produced by a capital of £100 in different trades will be very varying according to the proportion in which the capital of 100 is divided into constant and variable capital. Call the constant capital C, the variable capital V. If, for example, in the cotton industry, the proportion was C80, V20, then the value of the product would be 110 (with a 50% surplus value or surplus labour). The amount of the surplus value = 10 and the rate of profit = 10%, since the profit = the ratio of 10 (surplus value):100 (the total value of the capital expended). Imagine that in a large clothes factory, the proportion was C50, V50, so that the product = 125, and surplus value (at the rate of 50% as above) = 25 and the rate of profit = 25%. Take another industry where the ratio is C70, V30, so that the product = 115, rate of profit = 15%. And finally an industry where the proportion is C90, V10, so that product = 105, and rate of profit = 5%.

We now have, at an *equal exploitation* of labour, very different amounts of surplus value, and hence very different rates of profit, for sets of capital of the same size in different trades.

But if we take the above 4 capitals together, then we have:

			Value of the Product		
1.	C80	V20	110	Rate of profit = 10%	
2.	C50	V50	125	Rate of profit = 25%	Rate of surplus value
3.	C70	V30	115	Rate of profit = 15%	in all cases = 50%
4.	C90	V10	105	Rate of profit = 5%	

| | Capital | 400 | | Profit = 55% | |

This gives a rate of profit of $13\frac{3}{4}$% on 100.

With the *total capital* (400) of the *class*, the rate of profit would = $13\frac{3}{4}$%. And all capitalists are brothers. Competition (transfer of capital or withdrawal of capital from one trade to the other) brings capitals of the *same* amount in *different* trades, despite their different organic composition, to yield the *same average* rate of profit. In other words, the *average* profit which is made by a capital of £100, for instance, in a certain trade, does not do so as this particular invested capital – that is, not in proportion to how it produces surplus value itself – but as a *corresponding part* of the total capital of the capitalist class. It is a share, whose dividend is paid proportional to its size in the total amount of surplus value (or unpaid labour) which is produced by the total variable (paid in wages) capital of the class.

So that, in the above illustration, 1, 2, 3, and 4 can make the same *average profit*, they (each group) must sell their goods at £$113\frac{1}{3}$. 1 and 4 sell *over* their value, 2 and 3 *under* their value.

This *price*, regulated so that it = the expenses of capital + the average profit, for instance 10%, is what Smith calls the *natural price*, *cost price* etc. This *average price* is the one to which the competition between the different trades (through the transfer or withdrawal of capital) levels the prices in different trades. So competition does *not* level commodities to their *value*, but to the *cost price* which is *over*, *under* or = to its *values* according to the organic composition of the capitals.

Ricardo confuses *values* and *cost prices*. So he thinks that if an *absolute rent* exists (i.e. a rent which is *independent* of the varying fertility of soils), then agricultural produce etc., because it is *over* the cost price (the capital advanced + the average profit) is continually sold *over* its *value*. This would overturn the basic law. So he denies the absolute rent, and only accepts the differential rent.

But his identification of *values* of commodities and *cost prices of commodities* is fundamentally false, and is accepted as a tradition by A. Smith.

The fact is this:

Suppose that the *average* composition of all *non*-agricultural capital is C80, V20, then the product (at 50% rate of surplus value) = 110 and the rate of profit = 10%.

Suppose further that the average composition of *agricultural capital* = C60, V40 (this figure is fairly correct for English statistics; the rent on cattle farming etc. is irrelevant to this question, since it is determined not by itself but by the corn rent). So the product at the same exploitation of labour as above = 120 and rate of profit = 20%. If the farmer sells the agricultural produce at *its* value, then he sells it at 120 and not at *110, its cost price*. But *land-ownership* hinders the farmer (= his brother capitalists) from adapting the *value* of the product to its *cost price*. The competition between capitalists can not allow this. The landowner intervenes and fishes out the *difference between value and cost price*. A low ratio of constant capital to variable capital is an expression of a low (or relatively low) development of the productive forces of labour in a particular sphere of production. So if the average composition of agricultural capital is, for example, C60, V40, while that of non-agricultural capital is C80, V20, then that shows that agriculture has not yet reached the same stage of development as industry. (Which is easily explained since, apart from anything else, the pre-requisite of industry is the older science of mechanics and the pre-requisite of agriculture is the brand new sciences of chemistry, geology and physiology.) If the ratio in agriculture = C80, V20 (in the above conditions), then absolute rent disappears. Only the *differential rent* remains, which I have so presented that Ricardo's supposition of a continual deterioration of agriculture appears most ridiculous and arbitrary.

With the above definition of *cost price* as distinct from value, we should also note that, apart from the difference between constant and variable capital which arises from the *direct productive process* of capital, there is also the difference between *fixed and circulating capital* which arises from the *circulation process* of capital. However, the formula would be too complicated to insert it into the above.

So here you have – roughly, for the matter is fairly complex – the critique of the Ricardo theory. You will admit that by referring to the *organic composition of capital*, a whole mass of previously apparent contradictions and problems disappears . . .

You will see that in my conception of 'absolute rent', *land ownership* indeed (under certain historical circumstance) *increases* the prices of basic products. This, for communists, is a handy piece of knowledge.

Assuming the correctness of the above point of view, it is *not at all necessary* to count *absolute rent* in all situations or for *every type of soil* (assuming further the given composition of agricultural capital). It is not counted if *land ownership* – factual or legal – does *not* exist. In this case, agriculture would offer no peculiar resistance to the application of capital. It would move as freely in this element as it does in the other. The agricultural product then, like a whole series of industrial products, would be sold *under* its value at the *cost price*. *Land ownership* would then disappear de facto, even if capitalist and landowner were one person etc.

But it is superfluous to go into these details now.

The *simple differential rent* — which does not result from investing capital on land instead of any other sphere of employment — presents no problem theoretically. It is only surplus profit, which also exists in every industrial sphere of production for every capital which operates under better-than-average conditions. Only, it is tied to agriculture, because it is based on a much more solid and (relatively) more firm basis, like the different degrees of natural fertility of different kinds of soil.

51. Marx to Engels   *August 9, 1862*

. . . As for the *theory of rent*, I must naturally wait for your letter to arrive. But, for the simplification of the 'debate', as Heinrich Bürgers would say, the following:

I. The only thing which I must prove in theory is the possibility of absolute rent, without doing damage to the law of value. This is the point around which the theoretical struggle has revolved since the time of the Physiocrats. Ricardo denies this possibility; I maintain it. I also maintain that his denial is based on a theoretically false dogma inherited from Adam Smith – the supposed identity of *cost prices* and *values of commodities*.

Further, where Ricardo illustrates the thing with examples, he always assumes conditions in which either no capitalist production exists or (factually or legally) *no land ownership*. But we are concerned precisely with investigating the law when these things do exist.

II. As for the *existence* of absolute land rent, this would be a question to be resolved statistically in each country. The importance of the merely theoretical solution, however, results from the fact that, for 35 years, the statisticians and practicians have all maintained the existence of absolute land rent, while the (Ricardo-ist) theoreticians have tried to explain it away by very violent and theoretically weak abstractions. I have always found until now that the theoreticians are wrong in all such quarrels.

III. I prove that, even assuming the existence of absolute land rent, it does not follow at all that, under all circumstances, the worst cultivated land or the worst mine will return a rent; but that it is quite possible that the products will have to be sold at the market price, but *under* their *individual* value. Ricardo, attempting to prove the opposite, always supposes – theoretically falsely – that under all conditions of the market, the commodity produced under the most *unfavourable* conditions will determine the market value. You have already countered this with the correct solution in the *Deutsch-Französische Jahrbücher*.

So much as a postcript on rent.

As for Brockhaus, Lassalle promises to do his utmost, and I believe him, since he festively declared that *his* magnum opus on political economy will only be published, or be undertaken – these are in fact identical expressions with him – after my work appears ...

52. Marx to Engels
August 20, 1862

... Could you not come down here for a few days? I have over-turned so many old things in my critique that I must consult you on a few points. Writing about it all is tedious for you and me.

One point which you must know about as a practician is this. Suppose that the machinery which is installed in a new business = £12,000. On average, it might depreciate in 12 years. If then £1,000 in value is added to the commodities each year, then the price of the machinery is paid off in 12 years. Thus for A. Smith and all his followers. But in fact this is only an average calculation. With machinery which has a life of 12 years, it is the same as with a horse that has a life of 10 years or working years. Although it must be replaced by a new horse after 10 years, it would really be wrong to say that it dies by $\frac{1}{10}$ every year. Mr Nasmyth notes in a letter to the factory inspectors that machinery (at least certain machinery) runs better in the second year than in the first. At all events, during the 12 years, must the machinery be replaced annually by $\frac{1}{12}$? So what would then happen to the depreciation which is to replace $\frac{1}{12}$ of the machinery annually? Does a depreciation fund not exist for the expansion of reproduction, apart from all conversion of rent into capital? Does the existence of this fund not *partly* explain the *very different* rate at which capital accumulates in nations where capitalist production is developing and so where a good deal of fixed capital exists, compared with nations where this is not the case? . . .

53. Engels to Marx   *September 9, 1862*

. . . I have found the theory of rent really too abstract for me in the present hunt for cotton, so I must reflect on the question when I get some more peace. Similarly with the question of depreciation, although here I almost think that you are on the wrong track. The period of depreciation is, you see, not the same for all machines. But more on that when I return to the question . . .

54. Marx to Kugelmann   *December 28, 1862*

. . . I was very pleased to see from your letter that you and your friends are taking such a warm interest in my *Critique of Political Economy*. The second part is now ready at last, that is, apart from the fair copy and polishing it for printing. It will be approximately 30 sheets. It is the continuation of Part I, but appears separately under the title *Capital*, and *Critique of Political Economy* is only a sub-title. In fact it only deals with the subject of what should be the third chapter of the first part, that is 'Capital in general'. So it does not include the competition of capitals and the system of credit. What the English call 'the principles of political economy' is contained in this volume. It is the quintessence (together with the first part), and the presentation of what follows (with the possible exception of the relation between the various forms of State to the various economic structures of society) would be easily completed by others on the basis of my exposition . . .

As for the publisher, under no circumstances will I give Volume II[1] to Herr Duncker. He received the manuscript of Part I in December 1858 and it only appeared in July or August 1859. I have some hope – but not exactly a strong one – that Brockhaus will print the thing. The conspiracy of silence with which the German literary mob greeted me as soon as it noticed that the thing could not be disposed of with insults, is not very advantageous for my dealings with booksellers, leaving aside the politics of my works. As soon as the manuscript is copied out (I will begin this in January 1863), I will take it to Germany myself, since it is easier to deal with the booksellers personally.

I have *every hope* that, as soon as the German edition comes out, I can get a French edition done in Paris. I have absolutely no time myself to translate it into French, particularly since I wish either to write the continuation, that is the conclusion and the presentation of capital, competition and credit, in German, or to collect the first two parts in a text for the *English* public. I do not think that I can count on any great effect in Germany before I receive a certificate from abroad. In any case the stylistic presentation of the first booklet was very unpopular. This lay partly with the abstract nature of the subject, and partly with the limited space permitted me, and partly with the intention of the work. This part which is coming is more easily understood because it deals with more concrete situations. But scientific essays revolutionising a science can never be really popular. But once the scientific basis is set out, the popularisation is easy. If times become more stormy then one can again select the colours and inks which would make up a popular presentation of these subjects. However, I never expected the German academic experts to ignore my work so completely, even if only for decency's sake. Apart from this, I have also had the not very friendly experience of having party sympathisers in Germany, who had long busied themselves with this science and who had written overdone paeons of praise to me privately concerning Part I, not making the slightest effort to write a critique or even a summary of contents in magazines which they can use. If this is party criticism, then I confess that the secret of it is quite mysterious to me . . .

[1] The continuation of *A Contribution to the Critique of Political Economy*.

1863

55. Marx to Engels

. . . I have grave doubts about the section on machinery in my book. I have never been clear how the self-actors[1] altered spinning, or rather, since steam-power had already been introduced, how the spinner was to intervene with his motive power despite steam?

I would be pleased if you could explain this . . .

[1] Automatic spinning machine.

56. Marx to Engels

. . . In my last letter I asked you about self-actors. The question is this: how did the so-called spinner intervene *before* the invention of the self-actor? I understand the self-actor, but not the conditions preceding it.

I have added something to the section on machinery. There are a few curious questions which I ignored in the first draft. In order to get some clarity on the question, I have re-read my notebooks (extracts) on technology, and am attending a practical (only experimental) course for workers on the same by Professor Willis (in Jermyn Street, the Institute for Geology, where Huxley also gave his lectures). I can deal with mechanics as I can with languages. I can understand mathematical laws but I find the simplest technical reality involving some perception more difficult than the hardest knots.

You know, or do not know, for it is all the same, that there is a deal of argument on how a *machine* differs from an *instrument*. The English (mathematical) engineers, in their crude way, call a tool a simple machine and a machine a complicated tool. But English technologists (and, in their wake, many or most of the English economists), who pay somewhat more attention to the economy, differentiate between them, saying that, in one, the motive power originates in men, and, in others, that it comes from a natural force. So the German asses, who are mighty in such small matters, have decided that a *plough* for example is a machine and that the most complicated Jenny etc., because it is moved by hand, is not. But here there is absolutely no question that if we take a look at the machine in its *elementary* form, the industrial revolution does not proceed from *motive power*, but rather from that part of the machinery which the English call the 'working machine', that is, for example, not by the replacement of the foot which moves the machine by water or steam, but by the transformation of the direct process of spinning itself and the superseding of the human element in work, which was not merely exertion of power (as in driving the wheel by the foot), but was the process which had a direct effect on the material to be transformed. On the other hand, as soon as we are no longer talking about the *historical* development of machinery, but are talking about machinery on the basis of the present mode of production, there is just as little doubt that the *working machine* (for example, in the sewing machine) is the determining factor, as soon as this process reverts to machinery, everyone knows that it can be powered by hand, water or steam engine, according to its dimensions.

These questions are irrelevant for the mere mathematician, but they will become very important when we have to show the connection of human social relations to the development of these material modes of production.

While re-reading the technological-historical excerpts, I came to the conclusion that, apart from the inventions of gun-powder, the compass and printing – these necessary pre-requisites for bourgeois development – from the 16th to the mid-18th centuries, i.e. the period of the development of manufacture from craftsmanship until really large-scale industry, the two material foundations on which were based the preparations for mechanised industry within manufacturing were the *clock* and the mill (firstly the corn-mill and particularly the water-mill), both handed down from antiquity. (The water-mill was brought to Rome from Asia Minor at the time of Julius Caesar.) The clock was the first piece of automation applied for practical purposes; the whole theory of *production at an even rate* was developed from it. By its very nature, it was based in turn on the collaboration of semi-skilled craft and direct theory. Cardanus, for example, wrote (and gave practical formulae) on the building of clocks. Clock making was called a 'scholarly (non-guild) trade' in 16th century writings, and the development of the clock proved how different the relationship between learnedness and practice in craft production was from that for example in large-scale industry. And there is no doubt that, in the 18th century, the clock supplied the first idea of using machinery (which was, indeed, powered by springs) in production. *Vaucanson's* experiments in this field had an extraordinary and historically demonstrable effect on the imagination of English inventors.

In the case of the mill, on the other hand, the essential differences, as soon as the water-mill was developed, lay in the organisation of the machine. The mechanical driving force. Firstly the motor which it requires. Then the transmission mechanism. And finally the working machine which works the material. All of them with an independent existence from each other. The doctrine of *friction* and with it the research into the mathematical forms of wheels, cogs, etc. which the mill involved; ditto here the measuring of degree of driving force, of the best method of use etc. Almost all the great mathematicians since the middle of the 17th century proceeded from the simple water-driven corn-mill, in so far as they went into practical mechanics and theoretised on it. In fact, even the names 'Mühle'[1] and 'mill', which arose during the period of manufacture, were applied to any mechanical driving-power intended for practical use.

But with the mill, just as with pressing-machines, hammers, ploughs, etc., the real work – hitting, squashing, milling, crushing, etc. – was done *without* human labour from the very beginning, whether the motive power was human or animal. So this kind of machinery, at least in its beginnings, applied very ancient and really mechanical power which existed beforehand. And so it is almost the only machinery which existed in the manufacturing period. The *industrial revolution* begins as soon as machines are used in that process where, traditionally, the final result demanded human labour, and so where, as with those older instruments, the material to be processed *never* had anything to do with the human hand, as it had from time immemorial, and where man did not have the attribute of mere *power* from the start, by the very nature of things. If, like the German donkeys, we wish to call the application of animal (and so just as *voluntary* as human) powers 'machinery', then the application of this kind of locomotion is much older than the simplest tool . . .

¹ German: 'mill'.

57. Marx to Engels   *May 29, 1863*

. . . In the meantime I have not been idle, but I could not work. What I did achieve was partly to fill in the gaps in my knowledge (diplomatic and historical) of Russian-Prussian-Polish history, partly to read and take notes on all kinds of literary history relating to that part of the *Political Economy* which I have completed. This I did in the British Museum. Now that I am relatively capable of work again, I will cast off some of this burden and do a fair copy of the *Political Economy* for the printer (and correct it). If I could now retire to solitude, then I could finish it very quickly. At all events, I will take the thing¹ to Germany myself . . .

¹ i.e. The manuscript of *Capital*.

58. Marx to Engels   *June 12, 1863*

. . . Itzig has sent me (and perhaps you as well) his courtroom speech on *indirect taxes*. There are some good things in it, but the whole thing is firstly unbearably clumsy, garrulous and *written* in the most ridiculous learned, vainglorious style. Apart from that, it is essentially the creation of a *'pupil'* who wishes to announce himself with all haste as a 'polymath' and independent scholar. So there are masses of historical and theoretical blunders. One example suffices (in case you have not read the thing yourself). He is trying – in order to impress both court and public – to provide a kind of retrospective history of the polemic against indirect taxation, and so quotes higgledy-piggledy from the past, moving from Boisguillebert and Vauban to Bodinus etc. And now the arch-pupil appears. He leaves out the *Physiocrats*, and apparently does not know that everything which A. Smith etc. said on the subject was copied down from those who were the real heroes on this question. It is just as scholarly to call 'indirect taxation' a 'bourgeois tax' – which it was 'in the Middle Ages' but not today (at least not in those countries where the bourgeoisie is developing), as he could have discovered from Messrs R. Gladstone & Co. of Liverpool. The ass does not seem to know that the polemic against 'indirect' taxes is a catchword of the English and American friends of 'Schulze-Delitsch' et Cons., and is therefore not a catchword against them – I mean the free traders. And his *application* of one of Ricardo's statements to the Prussian land tax is very *scholarly*. (That is, totally false.) It is touching to read where he imparts *'his'* discoveries to the court, discoveries which he had made in the most profound 'science and truth' and terrible 'small hours', which are as follows:

that 'land ownership' held sway in the Middle Ages,

'capital' in modern times, and now

the *'principle* of the proletarian *layer'*, *'work'*

or the *'moral principle of work'*; and on the same day that he imparted this solution to those boors, the Senior Government Councillor Engel (with no knowledge of Itzig) imparted the same wisdom to a more cultivated audience in the music academy. He and Engel mutually congratulated themselves 'by letter' on their 'simultaneous' scientific results.

The *'proletarian layer'* and the *'moral principle'* are indeed victories for Itzig and the Senior Government Councillor.

Since the beginning of this year, I have not found the urge to write to this fellow.

If I were to criticise his rubbish, I would be wasting my time; in any case, he appropriates to himself every word as a 'discovery'. It would be derisible to rub his nose in his plagiarisms, since I will not accept any of our thoughts from him in the form in which he has corrupted them. And I cannot give recognition to these borrowings and acts of *tactlessness*. The fellow would only make use of it immediately.

So there is nothing left except to wait until he vents his anger. Then I take very strong exception to his perennial remark (as with Senior Government Councillor Engel) that 'it is not *communism'*. For then I can answer that his continual protestations — had I paid any attention to them — would have forced me to

1. show the public how and where he copied us;

2. how and where we differ from his ideas.

So, in order not to relinquish anything of 'communism' and so as not to injure him, I would have ignored him totally . . .

59. Marx to Engels

July 6, 1863

... If this hot weather permits, could you take a careful look at the enclosed 'Tableau Economique', with which I have replaced Quesnay's 'tableau',[1] and then give me your impressions. It takes in the entire process of reproduction.

You know that *A. Smith* composes the *natural* or *necessary price* from salary, profit (interest), rent – that is, reduces it to the *income*. Ricardo adopted this nonsense, although he excluded rent from the catalogue as something purely accidental. Almost *all* the economists have accepted Smith, and those who oppose him tumble into some other stupidity.

Smith himself had an inkling of the nonsense of reducing the *total* product of society to *mere income* (which can be consumed annually), when, in *every single* branch of production, he reduces the price to *capital* (raw material, machinery etc.) and *income* (wages, profit, rent). According to this, society would have to begin each year anew *without any capital*.

As for my table, which appears as a *compilation* in one of the last chapters of my work, the following is required for understanding it:

1. All figures are in millions.

2. Under 'food' we include *all* that which is involved in the annual *consumption* (or which, without any *accumulation*, which is excluded from the table, could be involved in consumption).

In Class I (Food) the *whole product* (700) consists of *foods*, which thus by their very nature are not included in *constant capital* (raw material and machinery, building work, etc.). And in Class II, the *whole product* consists of commodities which form the *constant capital*, that is, which enter the reproduction process again as raw material and machinery.

3. When the lines are *dotted*, they are *ascending*, and *continuous* when *descending*.

4. *Constant capital* is that part of the capital which consists of raw material and machinery. *Variable capital* is that part which can be exchanged for labour.

5. In agriculture, for example, one part of the same product (for example wheat) forms a food, while another part (wheat, for example) re-enters the reproduction process in its natural form (as seed, for example) as a raw material. But this does not alter the essence of it, since such branches of production figure in Class II with one property, and in Class I with another.

6. The point of the whole discussion is this:

Category I. Food. Working material and machinery (which is the part of the *same thing* which is included in the annual product as a *loss*; the unconsumed part of machinery etc. does *not* figure at all in this table) = £400 for example. Labour exchanged against variable capital = 100, and reproduces itself as 300 – when 100 replaces the wage in the product and 200 the surplus value (unpaid surplus labour). The product = 700, of which 400 represents the value of the constant capital, which has, however, been transferred totally into production and so must be replaced.

Given this ratio of variable capital and surplus value, the worker works ⅓ of the day for himself and ⅔ for his 'natural superiors'.

100 (variable capital) is thus – as indicated by the dotted line – paid out in money as wages; the worker then buys the product of this Class, that is food, for 100, with this 100 (which is indicated by the descending line). So the money flows back to the Capitalist Class I.

The Surplus Value of 200 in its general form = Profit, which later, however, is divided into *industrial profit* (including *commercial*) and into *interest*, which the industrial capitalist pays in cash, and into rent, which is also paid in cash. This cash disbursed for industrial profit, interest and rent then returns (as the descending lines indicate), since the product of Class I is purchased by it. So all the money in Class I disbursed by the capitalist flows back to him, while 300 of the 700 product is consumed by the workers, entrepreneurs, monied men and landlords. So in Class I there remains a *surplus* of 400 product (in food) and a deficit of 400 in the constant capital.

Category II. Machinery and Raw Material.

Since the *whole product of this category*, not only that part of the product which replaces the constant capital, but also that part which represents the equivalent of the wages and the surplus value, consists of *raw materials* and *machinery*, then the rent of this category cannot be realised in its own product, but only in the product of Category I. But leaving aside accumulation, as we do here, Category I can only buy as much from Category II as it requires for the replacement of its constant capital, while Category II only advances to the product of Category I that part of its product which is represented by wages and surplus value. So the workers of Category II spend their money = 133⅓ on the product of Category II. The same thing happens with the surplus value of Category II, which is divided into industrial profit, interest and rent, as in I. So 400 in cash flows to the industrial capitalist of Category I from the capitalist of Category II; and in exchange the product of the former = 400 is handed over to the latter.

Class I then buys with this 400 cash the necessary amount for replacing its constant capital = 400 from Category II, which in this way retrieves the money disbursed on wages and consumption (of the industrial capitalists themselves, of the monied men and the landlords). So Category II is left with 533⅓ of its total product, which replaces its own working constant capital.

This motion, sometimes in Category I, sometimes between Categories I and II also shows how the money returns to the respective industrial capitalists of both categories, so that they can again pay wages, interest and land rent.

Category III represents the total reproduction.

The total product of Category II here appears as the constant capital of the whole society, and the total product of Category I appears as that part of the product which replaces the variable capital (the wages fund) and the incomes of the classes which share the surplus value.

I have drawn Quesnay's 'Tableau' underneath, and will explain it in a few words in the next letter.[1]

[1] Reference to F. de Quesnay's 'Analysis of an Economic Table', in M.E. Daire *The Physiocrats*, Vol I, Paris 1846.

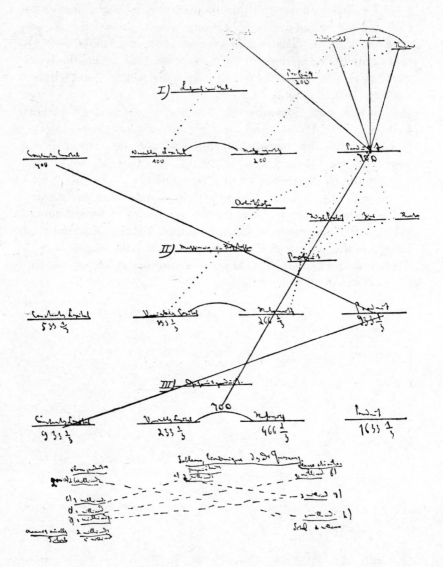

90

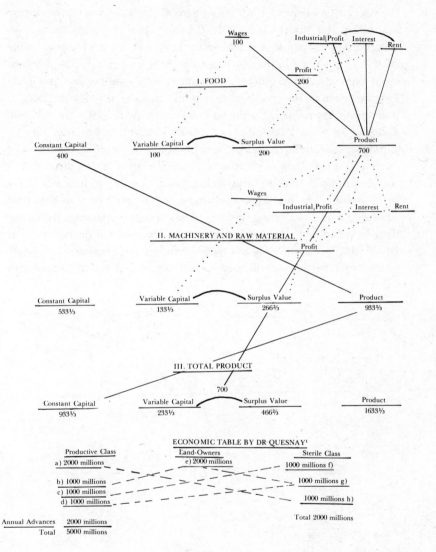

I. FOOD

Wages
100

Profit
200

Industrial|Profit   Interest   Rent

Constant Capital
400

Variable Capital
100

Surplus Value
200

Product
700

Wages

Industrial,Profit   Interest   Rent

II. MACHINERY AND RAW MATERIAL

Profit

Constant Capital
533⅓

Variable Capital
133⅓

Surplus Value
266⅔

Product
933⅓

III. TOTAL PRODUCT

700

Constant Capital
933⅓

Variable Capital
233⅓

Surplus Value
466⅔

Product
1633⅓

ECONOMIC TABLE BY DR QUESNAY[1]

Productive Class	Land-Owners	Sterile Class
a) 2000 millions	e) 2000 millions	1000 millions f)
b) 1000 millions		1000 millions g)
c) 1000 millions		
d) 1000 millions		1000 millions h)
		Total 2000 millions

Annual Advances   2000 millions
Total   5000 millions

[1] See also *Theories of Surplus Value*, Part I, chapter VI (Digression) and Addenda 8(a).

91

60.   Marx to Engels

. . . In one respect I am making good progess with my work (the manuscript for the publisher). In the final draft, it seems to me that things are taking a tolerably *popular* form, apart from a few unavoidable M–C and C–M's. On the other hand, although I write all day, I do not seem to move along as quickly as my impatience would wish – and it has long ago been at the end of its tether. In any case, it is 100% easier to understand than No.1. By the way, when I now consider the creation and see how much I have had to chop about and how I had to make up the *historical* section partly from totally unknown material, then I really have to laugh at Itzig, who now has 'his' *Economy* in hand, but who has revealed himself, in everything he has peddled so far, to be a schoolboy proclaiming – as his latest discoveries — to the world in the most sickening, most sweeping, gossipy declarations the things which we distributed to our partisans twenty years ago, and ten times better, as small coin. This same Itzig also collects all the party excrement of twenty years ago in his manure-factory in order to fertilise world history with it . . .

1864

61. Marx to Klings

October 4, 1864

. . . I have been ill for the whole of this last year (carbuncles and furuncles) – Without that, my work, *Capital*, on political economy would have been published already. Now I hope to finish it in a couple of months and to deal a theoretical blow to the bourgeoisie from which they will never recover.

Farewell and rely on it that the working class will always find a loyal champion in me.

1865

62. Marx to Engels   *May 20, 1865*

. . . I am working like a mule just now, since I must now use all the time available for work and the carbuncles are still there, although without disturbing me except in places – but not in my brain box.

In the hours when I cannot write, I do differential calculus $\frac{dx}{dy}$. I have no patience for reading anything else. Any other reading matter always drives me back to the writing desk.

This evening there is an extraordinary meeting of the International. A good old scoundrel, an old Owenist, *Weston* (a carpenter) has proposed the two theories which he always defends in the *Beehive*:

1. That a general rise in the rate of wages would not improve the lot of workers;

2. That, because of this, the Trade Unions have a *deleterious* effect.

If both of these theories – which *he* alone believes in in our group – were to be true, then we would be in a real mess, both because of the local Trade Unions and because of the rash of strikes on the Continent.

On this occasion, since this meeting is also open to non-members, he will be supported by a native Englishman who has written a pamphlet in the same style. So I am expected to refute them. So I should really be working on my reply for this evening, but I thought it more important to continue writing my book, and must therefore rely on improvisation.[1]

Naturally, I know in advance what the two main points are:

1. That wages determine the value of a commodity;

2. that, if the capitalists were to pay 5 shillings instead of 4 today, they would sell their commodities tomorrow for 5s. instead of 4 (due to the increased demand).

However lack-lustre this seems, and however much it clings to the upmost surface of appearances, it is certainly not easy to argue all the economic questions with ignoramuses who are in competition. You cannot compress a course of political economy into 1 hour. But we shall do our best . . .

[1] In late June 1865, Marx gave a lecture against Weston's views, which became the pamphlet *Wages, Price and Profit* (published in 1898). See letter 63 below.

63. Marx to Engels
June 24, 1865

. . . I read a paper to the Central Council (and it could probably be published in two sheets) concerning the questions raised by Mr Weston, on how a general rise of wages would work etc. The first part of it was an answer to Weston's inanities; the second a theoretical dispute, as far as the occasion demanded.

Now they want to print it. On the one hand, that would be very useful for me, since it connects with J. St. Mill, Professor Beesly, Harrison, etc. On the other hand, I have second thoughts.

1. since Mr Weston is not exactly flattering as an opponent;

2. since the thing contains many new things in its second part – in particularly condensed, but relatively popular form – which anticipates my book,[1] while it still passes over all kinds of things, by necessity. I wonder whether it is advisable to anticipate these things in this way? I think you can make a better decision on this than I, because you can view the matter in peace and quiet . . .

[1] Volume I of *Capital*, which Marx was preparing at that time.

64. Marx to Engels
July 31, 1865

. . . As for my work, I'll tell you the plain truth. There are still three chapters to write in order to finish the theoretical section (the first three books). Then the 4th book, the historico-literary one,[1] has still to be written, which is relatively the easiest for me, since all the questions have already been resolved in the first three books, and so this last one is more a repetition in historical form. But I cannot make up my mind to send anything off before I have the whole thing lying in front of me. Whatever shortcomings they may have, the advantage of my works is that they form an artistic whole, and I can only achieve that by my practice of never having them printed before I have them *complete* in front of me. The Jakob Grimm method is impossible for this and only works better for books which are not formed dialectically[2]. . .

[1] This planned fourth volume of *Capital* was not published until Kautsky's edition of *Theories of Surplus Value* (1905-1910), which was viewed as a separate work.

[2] Marx means that Grimm's (Editor of the great German dictionary of the 19th century and collector of folk-tales) method was not suitable for a dialectical study where all parts are seen as a unity of opposites, not disparate.

65. Marx to Engels   *November 20, 1865*

. . . Do not forget to get me the necessary data from Knowles (and *as soon as possible*). *Average weekly wages,* whether those of a mule spinner or those of a throstle spinnerwoman; *how much* yarn of *cotton* (that is *including* the wastage lost in the spinning process) on the average of the average number (or of any number, as far as I am concerned) which is spun by an individual in *one week*; and then naturally any *price* (corresponding to the wages) of cotton and the *price of yarn*. I cannot write the second chapter[1] until I have these details . . .

[1] In the first edition of *Capital*, Book I was divided by Marx into 6 chapters; in the 2nd edition, he had 7 parts and 25 chapters in Book I. So Marx here really refers to chapter 3 of the 1st edition (Part 3 of the 2nd edition).

1866

66. Marx to Engels *February 10, 1866*

. . . The most sickening thing for me was the interruption to my work, which was proceeding famously after 1st January, when my liver complaint vanished. Of course there was no question of *sitting* down. I am still troubled by that even just now. But I have been able to lie down, even if only for a short interval during the day. I could not make any progress with the really theoretical part. My brain was too weak for that. So I have expanded the section on the *Working Day* with historical material, which was not part of my original plan. The appended matter forms the sequel (*sketchily*) to your book,[1] up to the year 1865 (as I have also said in a footnote) and forms also the complete justification of the difference between your estimation of the future and its reality. As soon as my book appears, therefore, a second edition of your book will be both necessary and simple. I will supply the necessary theory. As for further historical additions which you will have to give in the appendix of your book, *all material* is pure trash and cannot be used scientifically, except for the Factory Reports, the Children's Employment Commission Reports and the Board of Health Reports. You, with your capacity for work and lack of carbuncles, should be able to master this material . . .

---

[1] Engels, *The Condition of the Working Class in England* (1st ed. 1845).

67. Marx to Engels   *February 13, 1866*

Tell, or write, Gumpert that he should send me the prescription with dosage. Since I have confidence in him, he owes it to the *Political Economy* to overlook professional etiquette and to treat me from his practice in Manchester.

I was lying fallow again yesterday, since a really vicious swine of a carbuncle has broken out on my left thigh. If I had enough money – i.e. more than $>$ – 0 for my family – and if my book was ready, then I would not care at all if I were to be consigned to the knacker's yard, alias snuffed it, today or tomorrow. But in the abovementioned conditions, I cannot have it like that.

As for this 'damned' book, as follows: it was *finished* at the end of December. The treatment of land rent alone, the penultimate chapter, almost forms a complete book in its present form. By day I went to the museum, and I wrote by night. I must plough through the new agricultural chemistry in Germany, particularly that of Liebig and Schönbein, which is more important to this subject than all the economists put together, as well as the enormous amount of material which the French have provided since my last discussion of this point. I finished my theoretical investigations on land rent two years ago. And in the meantime, of course, much has appeared – incidentally confirming my theory completely. The opening-up of Japan (I never read travelogues otherwise as a rule, unless they are professionally necessary) has been important. Hence the shift system, as the English manufacturing swine have applied it to the *same* people between 1848 and 1850, has been applied to my own person by myself.

Although it is finished, the manuscript (huge in its present form) is not accessible by anyone except myself, even you.

I began the fair copy and *style revision* on the dot on the 1st January; and I was cruising along, since it naturally gave me much pleasure to lick the child clean after so many labour-pains. But then the carbuncle intervened, so that until now I could not continue, but could only fill out all that was ready according to the plan.

By the way, I agree with you and will take the first volume to Meissner, as soon as it is ready. But I must be able to *sit* at least for the completion . . .

Do not forget to write to Watts to tell him that I have now reached the chapter on machinery . . .

68. Marx to Kugelmann   *August 23, 1866*

. . . Although I am devoting a great deal of time to preparing for the
Congress at Geneva,[1] I cannot and do not wish to go there, because no
lengthy interruption of my work is possible. I consider what I am doing
here to be much more important for the working class than anything I
could do personally at any Congress . . .

[1] The Geneva Congress of the International Working Men's Association was held from
September 3 to 8, 1866.

69. Marx to Kugelmann   *October 13, 1866*

. . . My situation (physical and bourgeois interruptions without
end) demands that Volume I must appear first, not the two at once as I
had originally intended. And it will now probably become three volumes.

The whole work breaks down into the following parts:
Book I The Process of Production of Capital.
Book II The Process of Circulation of Capital.
Book III Forms of the Entire Process.
Book IV The Theoretical History.
Volume I contains the first two books.

Book III, I think, will take up the second volume, the third will
contain Book IV.

I thought it necessary to begin at the beginning in Book I, i.e. to
provide a resume of the book I published with Duncker,[1] in *one* chapter
on commodity and money. I considered this necessary, not only for the
sake of completeness, but also because even intelligent people would not
get the right end of the stick, and so there would be something lacking in
the first presentation, particularly in the *analysis of the commodity*. Lassalle,
for example, in his *Kapital und Arbeit*,[2] where he claims to provide the
spiritual 'quintessence' of my argument, makes some enormous blunders (which incidentally continually occurs when he quite unashamedly
appropriates my research). It is comical to see how he attributes me with
literary-historical 'mistakes' when I sometimes quote from memory
without checking on things. I am still not clear myself whether I should

insert a few remarks on Lassalle's plagiarism in my introduction. Certainly, the shameless solidarisation of his worshippers against me would justify it . . .

[1] *A Contribution to the Critique of Political Economy.*
[2] F. Lassalle, *Herr Bastiat-Schulze von Delitsch, the Economic Julian, or: Capital and Labour*, Berlin 1864.

1867

70. Marx to Becker

I travelled from London last Wednesday, by steamer, and reached Hamburg on Friday afternoon in a raging storm; I was there in order to deliver the manuscript of Volume I to Herr Meissner. Printing began at the beginning of this week, so that the first volume will appear at the end of May. The whole work in three volumes. The title is: *Capital. A Critique of Political Economy*.

Volume I contains the 1st Book: 'The Process of Production of Capital'. It is assuredly the most frightening missile which has ever been launched at the heads of the bourgeoisie (including landowners). So it is important that you announce its imminent appearance in the press, the newspapers which stand open to you . . .

71. Marx to S. Meyer

April 30, 1867

. . . So why have I not answered you? Because I was continually hovering between life and death. So I had to use *every* moment available for work in order that I could finish the work for which I have sacrificed health, happiness and family. I hope that this explanation is sufficient. The so-called 'practical' men and their wisdom make me laugh. If one wished to be an ox, then one could naturally turn one's back on the horrors of humanity and only look after one's own interests. But I would have considered myself really *unpractical* if I snuffed it without completing my book, at least in manuscript.

Volume I of the work will be published by *Otto Meissner* of Hamburg in a few weeks. The title of the work is *Capital. A Critique of Political Economy*. I travelled to Germany in order to deliver the manuscript and stayed a few days with a friend in Hanover on my return journey to London.

Volume I contains the 'Process of Production of Capital'. Apart from the general and scientific exposition, I show – in great detail, and from heretofore unused *official* sources – the condition of the English (agricultural and industrial) proletariat *during the last twenty years*, ditto of the *Irish*. You will understand that all this only serves me as an argumentum ad hominem.[1]

I hope that the whole work will have appeared within a year. *Volume II* is the sequel and conclusion of the theories,[2] *Volume III* gives the history of political economy since the middle of the 17th century . . .

[1] Latin: 'proof before men'.
[2] Marx intended to combine in Vol II all the material later given in both volumes II and III.

72. Marx to Büchner *May 1, 1867*

If I permit myself, as a total stranger, to write personally to you – and in a personal, if also scientific matter – then you will excuse me because of the trust which I place in you as a man of science and a supporter of the Party.

I have come to Germany in order to deliver the first volume of my work *Capital. A Critique of Political Economy* to my publisher, Herr Otto Meissner of Hamburg. I must stay a few days here in order to see whether a rapid printing, which Herr Meissner intends, is possible, that is, whether the proof readers are capable of working in this way.

The reason I address myself to you personally is this: after publication in Germany, I would like to have the thing published in French in Paris. I myself cannot go there, at least not without danger, since I was expelled from France firstly by Louis Philippe and secondly by (President) Louis Bonaparte, and lastly continually attacked Monsieur Louis during my exile in London. So I cannot visit my translator personally. I know that your book on *Matter and Energy*[1] appeared in French and so I imagine that you could commission a suitable person for me, either directly or indirectly. Since I must get the second volume ready during the summer and the last volume during the winter, I do not have the time to undertake the French translation of the book myself.

I consider it to be very important to emancipate the French from the false beliefs in which Proudhon and his idealised petty bourgeoisie has buried them. At the recent congress in Geneva, and also in the contacts which I, as a member of the General Council of the International Working Men's Association, maintain with the Paris branch, the most terrible consequences of Proudhonism were evident.

Since I do not know how long I will stay here, could you give me an undertaking as soon as possible. If I, for my part, can ever be of service to you in London, then I will be most pleased.

[1] L. Büchner, *Energy and Matter*, Leipzig 1862.

73. Engels to Marx
June 16, 1867

For a week I have been distracted by all kinds of squabbles with Monsieur Gottfried [Ermen] and similar stories and troubles, so that I have only rarely had any peace for studying the form of value. Otherwise I would have returned the sheets[1] to you long ago. Sheet 2 seems to contain a somewhat noticeable hint of carbuncles; but that cannot be changed now, and I do not think that you should do anything about it in the addenda, for the philistines are in any case not used to this form of abstract thought, and will certainly not allow the form of value to torment them. At most, the knowledge gained dialectically here could be supported by more historical examples, to make the test of history on it, so to speak, although you have already said the necessary; but you have so much material on this that you could certainly write a good appendix to give the philistines proof, by historical means, of the necessity of the formation of money and the complementary processes.

You have made the great error of not making your train of thought in this more abstract development more accessible, by means of more small sub-sections and separate headings. You should have dealt with this section in the style of Hegel's Encyclopaedia, with short paragraphs, emphasising every dialectical transformation with a special heading and, where possible, having all digressions and mere illustrations in different script. The thing would then have looked somewhat pedantic, but a very broad class of reader would have found it easier to understand. The populus, even the most learned, is no longer used to thinking in this way, and one has to offer them every possible simplification.

Compared with the earlier presentation (Duncker), progress in the acuteness of dialectical development is very considerable, although there is much that pleases me more in the first form. It is a shame that precisely the important second sheet suffers from the effect of the carbuncles. But that cannot be altered now, and anyone capable of dialectical thought must understand it. The other sheets are very good and have given me much pleasure . . .

Five sheets sent back today.

¹ i.e. the clean proofs of Volume I.

74. **Marx to Engels**   *June 22, 1867*

Herewith four more sheets which I received yesterday . . .

I hope you will be satisfied with the four sheets. Your satisfaction up till now is more important than anything the rest of the world may say of it. In any case, I hope that the bourgeoisie will think of my carbuncles for the rest of its life. What swine they are: here is more evidence! You know that the Children's Employment Commission has been functioning for five years. After their first report, in 1863, the branches of industry which they denounced were immediately 'reprimanded'. The Tory ministry, at the beginning of this session, through Walpole, the weeping willow, introduced a Bill by which all the suggestions of the Commission, even the latest ones, were accepted. The fellows to be reprimanded, including the large metal-manufacturers, and in particular that vampire 'domestic service' keep bloody quiet. Now they present a petition to Parliament and demand – *a new investigation!* the old one (they say) was not impartial!

They calculate that the Reform Bill has absorbed all of public attention, so that the matter can be smuggled through quite nicely and privately, while, at the same time, an ill wind blows against the Trade Unions. The worst things in these 'Reports' are *the actual statements of those fellows.* So they know that a new investigation can only mean one thing – precisely 'what we bourgeois wish' – a new lease of exploitation for five years! Fortunately, my position in the 'International' allows me to draw a line across the nice calculations of these swine. It is a matter of the utmost importance. It is a question of the *abolition of torture* for 1½ million people, not including adult male working men!

As for the exposition of the *form of value*, I have followed your advice and also *not* followed it in order to behave dialectically here as well. That is: I have 1. written an appendix in which I present the *same question* as simply as possible and as pedantically as possible, and 2. divided every statement of the argument into §§ etc., *with separate headings*, as you suggested. Then in the *introduction* I tell the 'non-dialectical' reader that he should skip over pages x–y and read the appendix instead. We are not concerned only with philistines here, but with youth etc. thirsty for knowledge. Besides, the question is too decisive in the context of the whole book. Messrs Economists have until now overlooked the simplest thing of all, namely, that the equation *20 ells of linen = 1 skirt* is only the undeveloped basis of *20 ells of linen = £2 Sterling*, so that the simplest form of commodity, in which its value is still not expressed as a relation to all other commodities, but rather as something *different* to its own natural form, contains the *whole secret of the form of money* and thus, in nuce,[1] of *all bourgeois forms of product of labour*. The difficulty of exposition was avoided in the first representation (Duncker) by first giving the real analysis of the *expression of value* as soon as it developed, as an expression in money.

You are quite right about Hofmann. Incidentally, you will observe from the conclusion of my chapter III,[2] where the transformation of the master-craftsman into capitalist – as a result of mere *quantitative* changes – is indicated, that I quote *in the text* Hegel's discovery about *the law of the transformation of the mere quantitative change into a qualitative one* as something evident in history and other natural sciences. In the *footnote* to the text (at that time I was listening to Hofmann) I mention the *molecular theory*, but not Hofmann – who discovered *nothing* in this question except the final form – but Laurent, Gerhardt and Wurtz, of whom the latter is *our man*. As a result of your letter, I vaguely remembered the matter and so had a look in my manuscript . . .

[1] Latin: 'essentially, in essence'.
[2] The 3rd chapters of the 1st German edition of *Capital*, Vol. I is equivalent to chapters 7-11 of the later English editions .

75. Engels to Marx *June 24, 1867*

I received sheets up to and including 12, but have not yet read past No.8. The chapter on the transformation into capital and the origins of surplus value, in terms of presentation and content, is the high point so far. I translated it aloud to Moore yesterday, and he understood it correctly and was quite amazed at this simple method of getting results . . .

How many sheets are now set up: I can no longer tell, but it must be half the book by now? I will be delighted with the embarrassment of Messrs Economists when they reach the two abovementioned passages. The exposition of the form of value, besides, is the 'Being-in-Itself' (An-Sich) of the whole bourgeois rubbish, but the revolutionary consequence is not so obvious there, and people could slip by this abstract matter more easily and make their own phrases. But here it all ends, for the subject is as clear as day and I cannot see what they can say about it . . .

. . . Some more on the creation of surplus value: the manufacturer, and with him the Vulgar Economist, will immediately raise objections: if the capitalist only pays the worker the price of 6 hours for his 12 hours labour time, then no value can arise, for every hour of labour by the factory worker only $= \frac{1}{2}$ hour of labour $- =$ that for which they are paid $-$ so that only the value of this enters the value of the product of labour. So the usual calculation follows: so much for raw products, so much for depreciation, so much for wages (*really paid* for real hour-product) etc. However horribly shallow this argument is and however much it identifies exchange-value and price, value of labour and wages, and however absurd its supposition that 1 hour of labour only accounts for $\frac{1}{2}$ hour in the value, if only $\frac{1}{2}$ hour is paid, I still wonder that you have not already taken this into consideration, for it will *most certainly* be an objection raised against you, and it is better pre-empted. Perhaps you will return to it in the next sheet . . .

77. Marx to Engels

. . . If I get the 13th and 14th sheets of proof-copy now, you will get them on Sunday. I would like you to look at the dressing-down of Senior and the introduction to the discussion *of the working day*, before you leave. Apart from that, the paragraph on the 'working day' takes up 5 sheets, in which the real material naturally predominates. I will give you here the divisions, paragraphs, titles etc. of this appendix,[1] so that you can see how exactly I have followed your advice on the presentation of the appendix:

Appendix to Chapter I, 1

The Form of Value.

I. Simple Form of Value.

§1. *The two poles of the expression of value: relative form of value and the equivalent form.*

a) *Interdependence of the two forms.*

b) *Polarity of the two forms.*

c) *Relative Value and Equivalent, both only forms of value.*

§2. *The Relative form of value.*

a) *The equivalent relation.*

b) *Relation of value.*

c) *Qualitative content of the relative form of value contained in the relation of value.*

d) *Quantitative precision of the relative form of value contained in the relation of value.*

e) *The total relative value.*

§3. *The Equivalent Form.*

a) *The Form of Direct Exchange.*

b) *Quantitative precision not contained in the equivalent form.*

c) *The properties of the equivalent form.*

α) *First property: use-value becomes a manifestation of its opposite, of value.*

β) *Second property: concrete labour becomes a manifestation of its opposite, of abstract human labour.*

γ) *Third property: private labour becomes a form of its opposite, becomes labour in a direct social form.*

δ) *Fourth property: the fetishism of the commodity is more striking in the equivalent form than in the relative form of value.*

§4. *The form of value or the independent manifestation of value = exchange-value.*

§5. *The simple form of value = the simple manifestation of the opposites of use-value and value contained in it.*

§6. *The simple form of value of the commodity = the simple form of commodity of a thing.*

§7. *Relation of form of commodity and money form.*

§8. *The simple relative form of value and single equivalent form.*

§9. *Transition from the simple to the developed form of value.*

II. *The Total or Developed Form of Value.*

§1. *The endless series of relative expressions of value.*

§2. *The further determination contained in the developed form of relative value.*

§3. *Drawbacks of the developed relative form of value.*

§4. *The developed relative form of value and particular equivalent form.*

§5. *The transition to the general form of value.*

III. *The General Form of Value.*

§1. *The transformed form of the relative form of value.*

§2. *The transformed form of the equivalent form.*

§3. *The equal relation of development between relative form of value and equivalent form.*

§4. *Development of the polarity between relative form of value and the equivalent form.*

§5. *Transition from the general form of value to money form.*

IV. *Money Form*

(This section on Money Form is only for continuity – perhaps only half a page)

§1. *Difference between the transition from general form of value to money form and the earlier transitional developments.*

§2. *Transition from relative form of value to price form.*

§3. *The simple form of commodity is the secret of money form.*

Let us keep it at that! . . .

---

[1] Marx, 'The Form of Value'.

78. Marx to Engels

. . . I have just received sheet 20. The whole thing will probably be 40 to 42 sheets. I have received *no* other *proof copies* after the ones sent on to you. Send the ones you have back to me on your departure.

As regards the inevitable objections of the philistines and the Vulgar Economists which you mentioned (they naturally forget that, if they consider *paid labour* under the title *wages*, then they must consider *unpaid* under the title *profit* etc.), then it comes down to this question, scientifically:

How is the *value* of a commodity *transformed* into its price of production, in which:

1. the *whole labour appears as paid* in the form of *wages*;

2. while surplus labour, or surplus value takes on the form of a *price increase* in the form of interest, profit, etc., *on top of the cost price* (= price of the constant part of capital + wages).

The answer to this question presupposes:

I. that the *transformation* of, for example, *the daily value of labour power* is represented by *wages or price of daily labour*. This is demonstrated in chapter V of this volume.

II. That the transformation of surplus value is represented by *profit*, and that of *profit* by *average profit* etc. This supposes a previous presentation of the *process of circulation of capital*, since the turnover of capital etc. plays a role here. This question can thus only be presented in Book III (*Vol.2* contains Books II and III).[1] Here it will be shown whence the *mode of thought* of the philistine and the vulgar economist derives, that is, from the fact that only the immediate *form of appearance* of relations is reflected in their brains, but not in their *inner connectedness*. Incidentally, if the latter were to be true, what need for a *science* at all?

Now, if I wished to *pre-empt* all these objections, then I would ruin the whole dialectical method of argument. To put it another way. This method has the advantage that it continually *traps* these fellows and provokes them to an untimely exhibition of their donkey-headedness.

Incidentally, directly following §3 ('*The Rate of Surplus Value*') which you have just received, there comes the paragraph 'Working Day' (Struggle for the length of labour time), the treatment of which visibly demonstrates how clear Mr Bourgeois is in *practice* about the source and substance of his profit. This is also shown in the case of *Senior*, where the bourgeois swears that his entire profit and interest stems from the *last unpaid working hour*.

¹ See footnote (2) to letter 71.

79. Marx to Engels   *2a.m., August 16, 1867*

I have just finished correcting the *last sheet* (49th) of the book. The appendix – *form of value* – in *small print* takes up 1¼ sheets.

The *introduction* was also corrected and returned yesterday. So *this volume is ready*. I have only *you* to thank for making this possible! Without the sacrifices you made for me, I would have been unable to finish the monstrous labours for the 3 volumes. I embrace you, full of thanks!

Herewith 2 sheets of the proof copy . . .

80. Engels to Marx   *August 23, 1867*

I have now worked my way through circa 36 sheets and congratulate you on the complete manner in which you have clarified the most complex economic problems merely by putting things straight and placing them in their proper context, simply and almost tangibly. The same goes for the most splendid (in terms of the subject) presentation of the relation of labour to capital – in its full context and complete here for the first time. I was also quite delighted to see how you have grasped technical language, which must have given you many problems and which gave me divers misgivings. I have made pencil corrections in the margin against a few slips of the pen, and even risked a few conjectures. But how could you possibly leave the *formal* division of the book as it is! Chapter 4 is almost 200 pages long and has only four sections which are only announced by thinly-printed headings which can scarcely be found. At the same time, the train of thought is continually interrupted by illustrations and the illustrated point *never* resumes at the end of the illustration, so that one always leaps from the illustration of *one* point straight into the exposition of another point. That is dreadfully tiring and even confusing if one is not very attentive. Here a good number of sub-sections and a better emphasis of the main sections would not go amiss, and should definitely be introduced for the English edition. This aside, several points in this presentation (namely on co-operation and manufacturing) are still not clear to me, and I cannot discover which facts are related to the argument which is given only in general terms. The *outer* form of the presentation seems to indicate that this 4th chapter was the one written most hastily and least revised. But all that is not important, since the main thing is that Messrs Economists have nowhere been offered a weak spot to break in; I am indeed curious to see what the gentlemen will have to say, for you have not left them the slightest foothold. People à la Roscher will probably comfort themselves somehow, but with people here in England who do not write for three year olds, it is a different matter.

As soon as you can send me a few more sheets, I will be most pleased, for I should like to read the whole thing in context . . .

81. **Marx to Engels** *August 24, 1867*

. . . The best thing about my book is 1. (on this rests the *entire* comprehension of the facts) the *two-fold character of labour*, whether it is expressed in use-value or exchange-value, which is emphasised right in the first chapter; 2. the treatment of *surplus value independent of its special forms* of profit, interest, land rent etc. This is evident in Volume II. The treatment of the special forms in classical economy, which lumps them together with the general form, is a pot-pourri.

I would like to *write* your desiderata, arguments, queries etc. into the proof copy. This is very important for me, since I count on having a 2nd edition sooner or later. As regards chapter IV, it cost me a great deal of sweat to find the *objects themselves*, that is, in their *interconnectedness*. Then, when that was done, one Blue Book[1] after another appeared during the final *draft* and I was charmed to see my theoretical results fully confirmed by the facts. It was finally written, carbuncles and the daily knock of the creditor and all!

I must tackle you on one point – as I did many years ago – with the end of Book II (*Process of Circulation*), which I am now writing!

Fixed capital can only be replaced in kind, in, say, 10 years for example. In the meantime, its value is returned partially and gradatim[2] by the sale of commodities produced by it. This progressive return on fixed capital is only necessary for its replacement (apart from repairs and suchlike) as soon as it is dead in its material form, for example as a machine. In the *meantime*, however, the capitalist has these successive returns in his pocket.

Many years ago, I seem to remember, I wrote to you that an *accumulative fund* is formed, since the capitalist invests the returned money in the *meantime* before replacing the fixed capital with it. You came out against this theory, somewhat superficially, in a letter. I later discovered that McCulloch presents this sinking fund as an *accumulative fund*. In the conviction that McCulloch can never think properly, I abandoned the matter. His *apologetic* intention in this was already refuted by the Malthusians, but even they *admitted the fact*.

Now you, as a manufacturer, must know what you do with the returns on fixed capital *before* the moment when it has to be replaced *in kind*. And you must give me an answer on this point (without theory, *only practically*).

[1] Equivalent of a 'White Paper' – a parliamentary report.
[2] Latin: 'gradually'.

82. Engels to Marx   *August 26, 1867*

I will give a detailed answer tomorrow on the question of the replacement fund with accompanying calculations. You see, I must ask some more manufacturers whether our method is general or exceptional. It is debatable, you see, whether with £1,000 as the original cost of the machinery, where £100 would be written off in 1 year, the rule would be that, in the second year, 10% of £1,000 or 10% of £900 is to be written off etc. We do the latter, and so the thing goes on ad infinitum, at least in theory. This considerably affects accounting. But otherwise there is no doubt that the manufacturer has already *used* the replacement fund in an *average* of 4½ years, before the machinery has depreciated, or at least has it available. But this is calculated as a secure guarantee against moral depreciation, so to speak, or else the manufacturer says: the assumption that machinery has totally depreciated in 10 years is only approximately correct, that is, only on the condition that I receive the replacement fund in 10 annual amounts right from the start. In any case, you must see the calculations; the question in respect of its economic *significance* is still not quite clear to me, for I cannot see why the manufacturer should cheat the other participants in the surplus value, or the final consumers, by such a false depiction, in the long run. N.B., as a rule, the machinery depreciates by 7½%, which means a period of depreciation of around 13 years . . .

The chapter on accumulation is very fine.

83. Engels to Marx

Herewith two examples of machinery which will clarify the question for you. The rule is that an amount, usually 7½% is deducted annually from the original cost, although for simplicity I have bumped up the amount to 10%, which is indeed not excessive for many machines. Thus for example:

1860	January 1	Acquired	£1,000
1861	January 1	10% Deducted	100
			900
		New acquisitions	200
			1,100
1862	January 1	10% Deducted from £1,200 (£1,000 + £200)	120
			980
		New Acquisitions	200
			1,180
1863	January 1	10% of £1,000 + £200 + £200	140
			£1,040

etc.

In example No.1, I assume that the manufacturer invests his money in *interest* for the purpose of deductions; on the day he has to replace the old machinery, he has £1,252.11 instead of £1,000. Example No.2 assumes that he invests the money immediately, every year, in new machinery. As the last column, the value of the total acquisitions made on the last day of ten years, shows, he then has no more *value* than £1,000 in machinery (and he cannot have more, since he has of course only invested the depreciated *value* and the *total value* of the machinery cannot increase in this process), but he has expanded his factory year by year and worked with machinery which, across the eleven years, cost £1,449; thus, he has produced and earned considerably more than the original £1,000. If we assume that he is a spinner and every £ represents one spindle and a pre-spinning machine, then he has spun with an average of 1,449 spindles instead of 1,000 and, after the disappearance of the original 1,000 spindles, he entered the new period on January 1, 1866 with 1,357 spindles which were acquired in the intervening period, to which can be added another 236 for the depreciation in 1865, i.e. 1,593 spindles. Through the depreciation loan, therefore, he is able to increase the machinery by 60% over the old machinery and without investing a farthing of his *own profit* in the new equipment.

In both examples, we have omitted repairs. With a 10% depreciation, the machine ought to cover the cost of its own repairs, that is, they should be included. And they do not alter anything, since they are either included in the 10% or else they lengthen the life-span of the machine correspondingly, which comes to the same thing.

I hope that example No.2 will be clear enough for you, otherwise write, since I have kept a copy of it here.

In haste.

I. *The Manufacturer invests the Renewal Fund with an Interest of 5%.*

1856 on 1 January machinery acquired for				£1,000.00		
1857	1 January Deducted 10% for depreciation				£	100.00
1858	1 "	"	10% " "	£ 100.00		
			Interest on £ 100	£ 5.00	£	105.00
					£	205.00
1859	1 "		Interest on £ 205	£ 10.05		
			Deducted 10%	£ 100.00	£	110.05
					£	315.05
1860	1 "		Interest on £ 315.05	£ 15.15		
			Deducted 10%	£ 100.00	£	115.15
					£	431.00

1861	1 January	Interest on £ 431	£ 21.11		
		Deducted 10%		£ 100.00	£ 121.11
					£ 552.11
1862	1 "	Interest on £ 552.11	£ 27.13		
		Deducted 10%		£ 100.00	£ 127.13
					£ 680.04
1863	1 "	Interest on £ 680.04	£ 34.00		
		Deducted 10%		£ 100.00	£ 134.00
					£ 814.04
1864	1 "	Interest on £ 814.04	£ 40.14		
		Deducted 10%		£ 100.00	£ 140.14
					£ 954.18
1865	1 "	Interest on £ 954.18	£ 42.15		
		Deducted 10%		£100.00	£ 142.15
					£1,097.13
1866	1 "	Interest on £1,097.13	£ 54.18		
		Deducted 10%		£100.00	£ 154.18

Result at end of 10 years £1,252.11
or, on 1 January 1866, instead of
the depreciated £1,000.00 in machinery
£1,252.11 in cash.

II. *The Renewal Fund is invested in new machinery every year.*

	New Equipment	Depreciation Percentage	Value on 1 Jan 1866
1856 on 1 January machinery acquired	£1,000	100%	£ –
1857 1 January. Deduct. 10% of new acquis.	£ 100	90%	10
1858 1 " Deduct 10% £1,000 £100			
100 10 110		80%	22
£ 210			

1859 1	"	Deduct 10%	£1,000	£100			
			210	21	121	70%	36
					£ 331		
1860 1	"	Deduct 10%	£1,000	£100			
			331	33	133	60%	53
					£ 464		
1861 1	"	Deduct 10%	£1,000	£100			
			464	46	146	50%	73
					£ 610		
1862 1	"	Deduct 10%	£1,000	£100			
			610	61	161	40%	97
					£ 771		
1863 1	"	Deduct 10%	£1,000	£100			
			771	77	177	30%	124
					£ 948		
1864 1	"	Deduct 10%	£1,000	£100			
			948	95	195	20%	156
					£1,143		
1865 1	"	Deduct 10%	£1,000	£100			
			1,143	1,114	214	10%	193
					£1,357		
1866 1	"	Deduct 10%	£1,000	£100			
			1357	136	236	0%	236

Nominal value of new machinery   £1,593

Real value of new machinery   £1,000

@ £1 per spindle, it has produced:

1856 with	1,000 spindles		(carried)	9,486 spindles
1857 "	1,100 "		1863 with	1,948 "
1858 "	1,210 "		1864 "	2,143 "
1859 "	1,331 "		1865 "	2,357 "
1860 "	1,464 "		In 11 years	15,934 spindles
1861 "	1,610 "		Average	1,449 spindles
1862 "	1,771 "			

Carry 9,486 spindles

and begins 1866 with 1,357

236

1,593 spindles.

84. Engels to Marx
September 1, 1867

. . . The eight sheets received with thanks. The theoretical part is quite splendid, and also the exposition of the history of expropriation. But the switch to Ireland is made in the most terrible hurry and the material is processed far too little. On the first reading it is often positively unreadable. I will write more as soon as I have looked at the topic more closely. The resumé of the expropriation of the expropriators is quite brilliant, it will stand out.

It is fortunate that the book, so to speak, 'takes place' almost exclusively in England, otherwise §100 of the Russian Criminal Law would come into effect: 'Whosoever . . . incites the citizens of the state to hatred or to contempt of one another' etc. – and would lead to confiscation. Bismarck already seems to have found it necessary to launch a little mock campaign against the workers. In Erfurt or thereabouts, some Lassalle-poet, printer and publisher have been accused of high treason, and in Elberfeld even some rag of the noble Schweitzer has been confiscated. So a ban on the book in Prussia is always possible, but that would in any case have no effect in the present circumstances.

85. Engels to Marx

. . . Meissner's people in Leipzig seem to be taking a long time to get the book out. Still no announcements anywhere. Do you think that I should attack the book from a bourgeois standpoint, just to get things moving? Meissner or Siebel could easily get that into some journal. As for a ban, I cannot imagine it myself, but one can never account for the professional zeal of some lawyer or other, and once the process has started, you can rely on your old friend Lippe.

86. Marx to Engels

. . . Your plan of attacking the book from *a bourgeois standpoint* is the *best tactic of war*. But I think that – as soon as the story comes out – it would be better to let Siebel or Rittershaus have it, rather than Meissner. One must not look too closely at the activities of even the best bookseller. On the other hand, you must write a few instructions to *Kugelmann*, who has returned, on the practical aspects to be stressed. Otherwise he will write nonsense, since enthusiasm alone does not suffice. I myself, of course, cannot do that as unashamedly as you . . .

87. Marx to Kugelmann

. . . The completion of my second volume largely depends on the success of the first. Success is a prerequisite for finding a bookseller in England, and *without the latter* my material situation will remain so difficult and disturbing that I shall be unable to find either the time or the peace to get it finished quickly. These are, of course, things which I do not wish Herr Meissner to know. So it now depends on the skill and activity of my comrades in Germany, whether volume II will take a long or a short time to appear. Some sound criticism – be it from friend or foe – can only be expected by and by, since such a universal and partly difficult work needs time to be read and digested. But the next success is not determined by sound criticism but, to put it bluntly, by beating drums which will also force the foe to speak. It is not so important just *what* is said, but rather that *something is* said, *Above all, we must not lose time!* . . .

88. Engels to S. Meyer   *October 18, 1867*

. . . I hope you are able to draw the attention of the American-German press and workers to Marx's book. With the 8-hour agitation now in progress, this book with its chapter on the *working day* comes just at the right moment there and is also suitable for bringing some clarity in many aspects. You will do a great service for the future of the Party in America with every step you take to achieve this . . .

89. Engels to Kugelmann   *November 8[-20], 1867*

. . . The German press still remains silent on *Capital*, and yet it is of the utmost importance that something should happen. I found one of the articles I sent you in *Zukunft*; I regret that I did not know that it would end up in this journal, for here I would have been bolder. However, there is no harm done. The main thing is that the book gets discussed again and again. And since Marx cannot operate freely in this affair and is also embarrassed as a virgin, then the rest of us must do it. So please be so good as to tell me what success you have met with so far in the matter and which journals you think can still be used. Here we must be (as our old friend Jesus Christ said) as innocent as the doves and as cunning as the snakes. The good vulgar economists are always bright enough to protect themselves from this book and to speak of it under no circumstances, unless they have to. And so we must *force* them to. If the book is discussed simultaneously in 15–20 newspapers – and it does not matter whether favourably or unfavourably, whether in articles, letters or in footnotes to articles – just as an important publication which deserves attention, then the whole gang will howl about it all and the Fauchers, Michaelis, Roschers and Max Wirths will then *have* to discuss it. It is our damned responsibility to get these articles into journals (and *simultaneously as far as possible*), particularly in the European ones and even the reactionary ones. In the latter one could point out that Messrs Vulgar Economists shoot their mouths off in parliaments and economic meetings, but that here, where the *consequences* of their own science make an appearance, they should keep their mouths shut. And so forth. If you consider my assistance desirable, then let me know which journal you want something for; I am always at the service of the Party. My letter to Liebknecht was on the same subject, and so you can tie me down with an *unequivocal* request . . .

20th November. Since I wrote the above, Marx has told me of your letter to him, and I gather from it that, unfortunately, in your district, we can scarcely rely on any more press notices. Would it not be possible to write some *attacks* on the book, perhaps through a third person, either from the bourgeois or the reactionary viewpoint? This seems to be an expedient to me, and the articles could readily be written. Also: what is the situation in the completely or partially literary journals? . . .

90. Marx to Kugelmann   *November 30, 1867*

There is one point on which you can write to Liebknecht better than Engels or myself. And that is that, in fact, it is his duty to draw the attention of *workers' meetings* to my book. If he does not do this, then the Lassalleans will adopt the thing, which would be wrong.

Contzen (private tutor in Leipzig, pupil and supporter of Roscher) has demanded, through Liebknecht, a copy of the book from me and promised in return an extensive review of the same from his point of view. So the book was sent to him by Meissner. This would be a good start . . .

Could you tell your wife that she should first read the sections on the 'Working Day', 'Co-operation, Division of Labour and Machinery', and then that on 'Original Accumulation'. You must help her with incomprehensible terminology. I am available if there are any other problems.

There is the best chance of an exhaustive discussion of the book in France (Paris) – in the *Courrier Français*, which is unfortunately Proudhonist! – and even for a translation.

As soon as my health is better, I will write more. All the same, I hope you will write more often. Your letters always spur me on.

91. Marx to Schily   *November 30, 1867*

I wrote to Meissner immediately after receiving your letter, and told him to send you a copy of the book for Reclus. Reclus seems to me to be the right man for translating it into French, with German co-operation.

With a translation I would provide certain alterations of individual parts and also reserve the final revision for myself.

What must happen now, and as soon as possible, is that we should get things from the book into the *Courrier Français*. I do not see why Hess has to involve some third person in this. He does it best on his own. I also think that the theme of the English factory laws, which has caught his eye, is the most suitable one for an introduction. However, even that cannot be done without a few introductory words on the *theory of value*, since Proudhon has totally confused everybody on this. They think that a commodity is sold at its value if it is sold at its 'prix de revient'[1] = price of the means of production used up in it + wages (relative to the *price* of the labour added to the means of production). They do not notice that the *unpaid labour* which is contained in the commodity is an essential value-forming element equal to the paid labour and that this element of value now takes on the *form of profit* etc. They are ignorant of *what* wages are. Without an insight into the nature of value, the development of the working day etc., in short, the factory laws, have no basis. So a *few* introductory words on this are necessary . . .

[1] French: 'cost of production, cost price'.

92. Marx to Engels

December 7, 1867

. . . As regards this little Swabian journal, it would be an amusing coup if we could play a trick on Vogt's friend, Mayer the Swabian. The thing could easily be done:

First we begin by saying that, whatever one might think of the politics of the book, it pays homage to the '*German* Spirit' and so must have been written by a Prussian in exile and not in Prussia. And Prussia (we say) has long ceased to be the country in which any scientific initiative occurs or is even possible, particularly in the political or historical or social sphere. And it now represents the Russian, not the German Spirit. And as for the book itself, we must differentiate between two things, between the positive developments (the second adjective could be 'principled') which the author presents and the tendentious conclusions which he draws. And the former, since the real economic relations are treated in a materialistic way ('Mayer' loves this word because of Vogt), are a direct enrichment of science. Example: 1. the exposition of money, 2. how co-operation, division of labour, machinery and the corresponding social combinations and relations develop 'naturally'.

Now, as for the *politics* of the author, one must further differentiate. When he proves that the present society, considered economically, is pregnant with a new, higher form, then he only shows the same gradual revolutionary process in *society*, which Darwin showed in natural history. The liberal doctrine of 'progress' (this is pure Mayer) includes this and the author has done a service in showing hidden progress in which the modern economic relations are accompanied by terrifying direct consequences. By his critical conception, and perhaps malgré lui,[1] the author has put a stop to all professional socialism, that is, all utopianism.

The *subjective* politics of the author on the other hand – he was perhaps tied down by and committed to his partisanship and his past – that is to say, the manner in which he imagines or presents the final results of the present movement, the present social process, has nothing to do with its real development. If space permitted us to investigate the matter further, then we could perhaps show that his objective 'argument' negates his own 'subjective' whims.

If Herr Lassalle bawled out the capitalists and flattered the Prussian country squirearchy, then Herr Marx on the contrary shows the *historical 'necessity'* of capitalist production and lashes the merely consuming aristocratic land Junkers. Just how little he shares the ideas of his renegade pupil Lassalle on Bismarck's inner drive to institute an economic millennium, is not only shown earlier in his protests against the '*Royal Prussian Socialism*', but he also speaks out openly on pp.762, 763 when he says that the system at present existing in France and Prussia will impose the regime of the Russian knout upon the continent of Europe if it is not halted soon.

This is my idea of how we can trick the Swabian Mayer (who also printed my introduction), and however small his swinish little journal, it is still the popular oracle of all federalists in Germany and is also read abroad.

As for Liebknecht, it is indeed a disgrace that he did not immediately and spontanément[2] submit short notices to the many local journals at his disposal, which would not have necessitated any unnatural activity on his part. Herr Schweitzer and Co. understand this better, as you can see from the enclosed *Social-Demokrat* (Kugelmann sent it to me). I sent (and this is only *amongst ourselves*) a synopsis to Guido Weiss of the

Zukunft yesterday, on the one side the bowdlerised plagiarisms of von Hofstetten and on the other the original passages from my book. At the same time I wrote to him that this should *not* be published under *my name*, but as an article by *Zukunft* (or, if that was impractical, as if it came from a Berlin reader). If Weiss takes this (*and I think he will*), then not only will the Berlin worker take notice of the book because of the quotations of passages which directly interest him, but a highly useful polemic will be started and Schweitzer's plan of ignoring the book and exploiting its contents will end up in the shit. It is delightful to see how these fellows think they can develop *Lassalle's* plan. Is there anything more naive than the way in which von Hofstetten and Citizen Geib have divided up the furniture of my section on the 'Working Day' in the General Meeting of the All-German Workers Association? . . .

---

[1] French: 'in spite of himself'.
[2] French: 'spontaneously'.

1868

93. Marx to Engels

. . . I would like to know from Schorlemmer what the latest and best book (German) on agricultural chemistry is? and further, what is the situation now in the controversy between the mineral-fertilisation and the nitrogen men? (Since I last occupied myself with it, all kinds of new things have appeared in Germany.) And does he know anything about the newer Germans who have written *against* Liebig's theory on exhaustion of the soil? And does he know anything of the Munich agronomist Fraas's (professor at the University of Munich) theory of alluvion? I must be acquainted with the latest developments to some extent, for the chapter on land rent. Since Schorlemmer is the expert, he can probably give me some information . . .

94. Engels to Marx

January 7, 1868

Herewith the *Dühring*[1] and the 'Beobachter' returned. The former is very amusing. The whole article is embarrassment and funk. One sees that the good Vulgar Economist is cut to the quick and has nothing to say, except that one can only judge Volume I when Volume III has appeared, and that the fact that value is determined by labour time is unchallengeable and that there are people who express doubts on the determination of value by labour through its production costs. You see,

you have not been learned enough for this species and have not countered the great Macleod in the decisive question! And in every line there
is a fear of exposing himself to treatment à la Roscher. The fellow[2] was
well pleased to have the thing finished, but he must have gone off to the
post box with a heavy heart . . .

[1] E. Dühring's review of *Capital*, 'Marx K., *Capital, Critique of Political Economy*, Vol.I,
Hamburg 1867'.
[2] i.e. Dühring.

95. Marx to Engels
January 8, 1868

Ad vocem Dühring.[1] It is good of the man to almost positively accept
the section on 'Original Accumulation'. He is still young. A supporter of
Carey in direct opposition to the Free Traders. And also a *private tutor*, so
not unhappy that *Professor* Roscher, who bars the way to all of them, has
got a few kicks up the backside. One aspect of his description caught my
attention. Namely, that as long as the definition of value is not determined by the labour time, as with Ricardo, it does not make people
shaky. But as it is connected with the working day and its variations, a
quite unpleasant new light is shed upon them. I think that Dühring only
discovered the book out of malice against Roscher. His fear of being
Roscher-ed in his turn is, however, very noticeable. It is extraordinary
that the fellow does not sense from the three brand new elements of the
book, 1. that, in contrast to *all* previous economy, which took the particular fragments of surplus value with their fixed forms (rent, profit,
interest) for granted *from the very start*, I discussed the general form of
surplus value, in which all things as yet unseparated are so to speak
resolved, from the start.

2. That the economists, without exception, evaded the simple fact
that, if the commodity has a double character – the use-value and the
exchange-value – then labour contained in the commodity must also be
of double character, while mere analysis of labour as such, as with Smith,
Ricardo, etc., must everywhere come up against the inexplicable. This is
indeed the whole secret of the critical conception.

3. That, for the first time, wages are presented as an irrational
manifestation of a concealed relationship, and this is presented precisely
as the two forms of wages: hourly wages and piece work. (I was aided by
the fact that such formulae often appear in higher mathematics.)

As regards Herr Dühring's modest objections to the definition of value, he will be amazed in Volume II when he finds how little the definition of value is considered to be 'direct' in bourgeois society. The fact of the matter is that *no form* of society can prevent the available labour time of the society from regulating production in one way or another. But, as long as this regulation is not carried out under direct, conscious control of society over its labour time – which is only possible with common property – but is rather determined by the movement of prices of commodities, then it remains at what you have already said so exactly in the *Deutsch-Französische Jahrbücher*.[2]

---

[1] Latin: 'as regards Dühring'.

[2] See footnote 2 of letter 6 above.

96. Marx to Kugelmann   *March 6, 1868*

. . . The extraordinarily embarrassed tone of Herr Dühring in his critique has now become clear to me. You see, he is just a very forward, insolent scoundrel who presents himself as a revolutionary in political economy. He has done two things. Firstly (following Carey), published a *Kritische Grundlegung der Nationalökonomie*[1] (about 500 pages), and a new *Natürliche Dialektik*[2] (as opposed to the Hegelian). My book has disposed of him on both counts. He has advertised it because of his hatred of Roscher etc. By the way, half intentionally and half from lack of insight, he has perpetrated some frauds. He knows very well that my method of argument is *not* Hegelian, since I am a materialist, Hegel an idealist. Hegel's dialectic is the basis of all dialectic, but only *after* the disposal of its mystical form, and precisely this differentiates my method. As for Ricardo, Herr Dühring has been sore afflicted that, in my exposition, the weak points, which Carey and a hundred others before him indicated, do *not* exist. So, with bad intentions, he tries to accuse me of Ricardo's narrow-mindedness. But never mind, I must be grateful to the man, since he is the first expert even to make a pronouncement.

In the second volume (which will probably never appear unless my situation changes) there is also an analysis, amongst others, of land ownership, and of competition only in so far as the treatment of the remaining themes demands.

During my illness (which I hope will soon cease) I have not been able to write, but have been able to master enormous masses of 'material', statistical and otherwise, which alone would have sickened those who are not used to stomach this kind of fodder and to rapid digestion of the same . . .

[1] E. Dühring, *Critical Basis for an Economic Doctrine*, Berlin 1866. (The title in German is actually *Kritische Grundlegung der Volkswirtschaftslehre*).
[2] E. Dühring, *Natural Dialectic*, Berlin 1865.

97. Marx to Engels   *March 14, 1868*

. . . At the Museum – by the by – I had a look at, amongst others, the latest writings of old Maurer (the old Bavarian Privy Councillor, who earlier played a role as one of the regents of Greece and first denounced the Russians, long before Urquhart), on the *German 'Mark-', Village- etc. Constitution*. He shows in detail that private ownership of land only appeared later etc. The stupid Westphalian Junker viewpoint (Möser etc.), to the effect that the Germans settled down each to his own patch and only then formed villages, districts etc., is completely killed. It is interesting, especially now, that the *Russian* manner of re-allocation of the land in set periods (in Germany only annually) persisted partly until the 18th or even 19th century. My view that the Asian or Indian forms of property were the original ones everywhere in Europe here receives new confirmation (although Maurer knows nothing of it). But the last trace of a claim to originality by the Russians, even in this line, vanishes. What remains for them is to be stuck fast in forms, even today, which their neighbours abandoned long ago. The books of old Maurer (of 1854 and 1856 etc.) are written in the true German learned style, but also in the more homely and readable way which distinguishes the south Germans from the north Germans (Maurer is from Heidelberg, but the case is even more true for the Bavarians and Tiroleans, like Fallmerayer, Fraas etc.). He even borrows heavily from old Grimm (relics of law etc.), that is, in content not in words. Apart from that I have had a look at the things by Fraas etc, on agronomy.

By the by, you must send me back the piece by Dühring as well as the proof-sheets of my book. You will have seen from Dühring what Carey's great discovery was, namely that humanity crosses from worse to continually better soil in agriculture. Partly because the cultivation of the hills etc., which are free of water, always descends into the damper valley. But especially because Mr Carey regards *marshes* and the like as the most fertile land, and considers that these must first be *transformed* utterly. And finally, because the English colonisation of America began with lousy New England, particularly Massachusetts, Carey's ideal country.

Thanks for your efforts with the damned book . . .[1]

I noticed from Maurer that the change in views of history and the development of 'Germanic' property etc., originated with the Danes, who, it seems, busy themselves particularly with archaeology in all corners of the globe. But although they provoke changes, there is always a hitch with them somewhere or other. For the correct initial instinct is missing, and above all a comparative measure. I noticed especially that Maurer, who often talks of Africa, Mexico etc., knows nothing at all about the Celts and so attributes the development of communal property in France solely to the Germanic conquerors. 'As if', as Herr Bruno would say, 'as if' we did not already possess a quite communistic Celtic (Wales) law book of the 11th century and 'as if' the French, precisely in recent years, had not partly excavated original communities of Celtic forms! As if! But the matter is quite simple. Old Maurer has only studied oriental (Greek-Turkish) relations, apart from the German and Ancient Roman ones.

[1] i.e. Engels's published critiques of Volume I of *Capital* (see letter 89).

98. Marx to Kugelmann

March 17, 1868

. . . I was very glad to receive M[eyer]'s letter. However, he has partly misunderstood my argument. Otherwise he would have seen that I present *big industry* not only as the mother of antagonism, but also as the child-bearer of material and spiritual conditions which will resolve these antagonisms, which can naturally not be done in a *comfortable way*.

As for the factory law – as the first condition for the working class to gain some elbow-room for development and movement – I demand it *because of the State*, as a *coercive law*, not only against the factory owners but also against the workers themselves. (Page 542, note 52,[1] I indicate the resistance of female workers to any limitation of labour time.) And if Herr Meyer has the same energy as Owen, then he can break this resistance. The *individual manufacturer* (except insofar as he tries to influence legislation) cannot do much about it, as I say ditto p.243:[2] 'By and large, this does not depend on the good or bad will of the individual capitalist etc.' and ibid. note 114.[3] Such capitalists as Fielden, Owen etc. have amply shown that, in spite of all that, the individual can be active. Their main activity must naturally be of a public nature. As for the Dollfus family of Alsace, they are humbugs who have been able to create a comfortable and very profitable *feudal relationship* with their workers through the conditions of contract. They have justly been exposed in the Paris newspapers, and precisely because of that, one of these Dollfus has lately proposed one of the most infamous §§ on press law and carried it, namely, that the 'vie privée doit être murée' . . .[4]

[1] Marx's references are to the first German edition of *Capital* Vol.I. (German ed. 1953 p.581.)
[2] ibid (1953 ed. pp.281-2).
[3] ibid.
[4] French: 'private life must be protected'.

99. Marx to Engels *March 25, 1868*

. . . *Ad vocem Maurer:*[1] his books are extraordinarily important. Not only pre-history, but the whole later development of the free Imperial towns, of the immunity of propertied landowners, of public authorities, of the struggle between the free peasantry and vassalage, assumes a completely new form.

As in Palaeontology, so in the history of Man. Things which stare us in the face are in principle – through a certain judicial blindness – not observed by the cleverest brains. Later when the time is ripe, one is amazed that everywhere there are manifestations of the thing not previously observed. The first reaction against the French Revolution and the Enlightenment connected with it, was natural, and everything became medieval and was seen Romantically, and even people like Grimm were not free of this. The second reaction is – and this corresponds to the socialist tendency, although those academics have no inkling that the two go hand in hand – is to look past the Middle Ages to the pre-history of every nation. Then they are surprised to find the most modern things in the most ancient and even egalitarian to a degree that would make Proudhon shudder.

How much we are all caught up in this judicial blindness: the Old

Germanic system survived until *quite* recently in *my* region, in the Hunsrücken. I now recall that my father spoke to me about it as an *advocate*! More proof: just as the geologists explain certain facts quite upsidedown, like Cuvier, so the philologists of the stature of Grimm translated the simplest Latin sentences wrongly, because they were influenced by Möser etc. (who, I remember, was charmed that 'Freedom' never existed among the Germans, but that 'the air is your own'). For example, the well-known passage in Tacitus: *'Arva per annos* mutant et *superest ager'* which means: They change (by lots, thus 'sortes'[2] in all the 'leges Barbarum'[3] later) the fields (arva) and common land ('ager' in opposition to 'arva' as 'ager publicus'[4]) remains, which Grimm etc. translate as: 'They cultivate new fields every year, and there is always (uncultivated) land left over'!

Similarly, the passage: 'Colunt *discreti ac diversi'*[5] is supposed to show that the Germans farmed their own farms from the very beginning, like Westphalian squires. But in the *same* place we read further: *'Vicos locant* non in nostrum morem *connexis* et *cohaerentibus aedificiis*: suum quisque locum *spatio circumdat'*[6] and these Germanic prehistoric villages still exist here and there in the form described, in Denmark. Scandinavia must naturally be as important for German jurisprudence and economy as for German mythology. And only proceeding from there, could we then decipher our past. Incidentally, Grimm etc. even find in Caesar that the Germans always formed settlements in tribal communities, not as individuals: 'gentibus cognationibusque, qui uno coiereant'.[7]

But what would old Hegel say if he learned, on the one hand that the word 'Allgemeine'[8] in German and Nordic means only 'common land',[9] and that the word 'Sundre, Besondre'[10] only meant the particular owner[11] who had split away from the common land? Then, dammit, all the logical categories would proceed from 'our intercourse'.[12]

Fraas's *Klima und Pflanzenwelt in der Zeit, eine Geschichte beider*[13] (1847) is very interesting, particularly in his proof that climate and flora alter in *historical* time. He was a Darwinist before Darwin and allows the various *genera* to develop in historical time. But he is also an agronomist. He maintains that with cultivation – and corresponding to its degree – the 'dampness' so beloved of peasants vanishes (and so plants migrate from south to north) and finally steppes are formed. The first effects of cultivation are useful, and finally destructive, through deforestation, etc. This man is just as much a well-educated philologist (he has written books in *Greek*) as a chemist, agronomist, etc. The upshot is that cultivation, if it proceeds naturally and is not *consciously controlled* (he naturally cannot allow that as a good law-abiding citizen), leaves behind deserts, Persia, Mesopotamia, etc., Greece. So another unconscious socialist tendency is revealed! . . .

[1] Latin: 'concerning Maurer'.
[2] Latin: 'lots, lottery'.
[3] Latin: 'laws of the Barbarians' (= usually Germanic tribes).
[4] Latin: 'common land'.
[5] Latin: 'they farm individually and separately'.
[6] Latin: 'they do not form villages as we do, with related and connected buildings: each one surrounds his place with a free, uncultivated space'.
[7] Latin: 'in families and tribes which settled down together'.
[8] German: 'the General'.
[9] 'Gemeinland'.
[10] German: 'The Particular'.
[11] 'Sondereigen'.
[12] See footnote 3 to letter 4 above.
[13] *Climate and Plant World in History: a History of Both*.

100. Marx to Engels   *April 22, 1868*

I have begun to work again, and am making good progress. Only, I have to limit my working time, for after about three hours my head begins to hum and feel painful. Now I wish to inform you of a 'small detail' which *occurred* to me as I was just skimming through the section of my manuscript on the rate of profit. Thereby, one of the most difficult questions finds a simple answer. It is, you see, a question of how it can happen that, with a falling value of money, or of gold, the *rate of profit* rises, and with a rising value of money, it falls.

Given that the value of money falls by $\frac{1}{10}$. Then the price of commodities, all other things being equal, rises by $\frac{1}{10}$.

If, on the other hand, the value of money grows by $\frac{1}{10}$, then the price of commodities, all other things being equal, falls by $\frac{1}{10}$.

If, with a falling value of money, the price of labour does not rise by the same proportion, then it *falls*; the rate of surplus value would then rise and so, all other things being equal, does the rate of profit. The increase in the latter – as long as the descending oscillation in the value of money continues – is due to a simple lowering of wages, and the decrease is due to the situation where the change in wages only slowly accommodates the change in the value of money. (Thus at the end of the

16th and in the 17th century.) If it were the other way about, with a rising value of money, and the wages do not fall in the same conditions, then the rate of surplus value falls and so, caeteris paribus,[1] does the rate of profit.

These two movements – the rise in the rate of profit with a sinking value of money and the fall with a rising value of money – are, *in these conditions*, both only due to the fact that the price of labour is not yet balanced by the new value of money. The phenomena (and their explanation is long since known) cease after the equalisation of the price of labour and the value of money.

Here the difficulty begins. The so-called theoreticians say: as soon as the price of labour corresponds to the new value of money, for example, if it rises with the falling value of money, then both profit and wages are expressed in so much more money. *So their relation remains the same*. So there can be no change in the rate of profit. The specialists, on the other hand, occupying themselves with the history of prices, answer with facts. Their explanations are only manners of speaking. The whole difficulty rests on the confusion of *rate of surplus value* and *rate of profit*. If we imagine that the rate of surplus value remains *the same*, e.g. at 100%, then, with a fall of $\frac{1}{10}$ in the value of money, the wage of £100 (say, for 100 men) rises to 110 and the surplus value also rises to 110. The same total quantity of labour which was earlier expressed as 200, now becomes £220. So if the price of labour is balanced with the value of money, the *rate of surplus value* can neither grow nor fall through any change in the value of money. But let us suppose that the elements – or some elements – of the *constant* part of capital fall in value as a result of a growing productivity of labour, of which they are the products. If the fall in their value is greater than the fall in the value of money, then its price will sink, despite the decreased value of money. If their fall in value only corresponds to the fall in the value of money, then their price remains unchanged. We wish to presuppose this latter case.

Thus, for example, a capital of 500 in a particular branch of industry might be composed of 400c and 100v (I am considering writing 400c etc. instead of $\frac{c}{400}$ in volume II, since that would be less involved. What do you think?), then we have, with a *rate of surplus value of 100%*: $400c + 100v \parallel + 100s = \frac{100}{500} = 20\% \text{ } rate \text{ } of \text{ } profit$. If the value of money falls by $\frac{1}{10}$, then the wages rise to 110, and ditto the surplus value. If the money price of the *constant* capital remains the same, because the value of its components sink by $\frac{1}{10}$ as a result of increased productivity of labour, then: $400c + 110v \parallel = 110s$ or $\frac{110}{510} = 21^{29}/_{50}\%$ rate of profit, i.e. an increase of about $1\frac{1}{2}\%$, while the rate of surplus value, $\frac{110s}{110v}$, is 100% as before.

The *increase in the rate of profit* would be greater if the value of the constant capital sank more rapidly than the value of money, and would be smaller if it was lower. But this will continue as long as any fall in value of the constant capital occurs, so that the same mass of means of production costs £440 and not £400 as before.

But the fact that, particularly in the real industries, the productivity of labour is given added propulsion by the falling value of money and the mere inflation of money prices and the general international race for the increased mass of money, is an historical fact and is particularly evident from 1850-1860.

The opposite case is to be deduced in analogous fashion.

Now how far, in one case, the rise in the rate of profit with a falling value of money, and, in the other, the fall in the rate of profit with a rising value of money, has an effect on the *general rate of profit* depends partly on the *relative extent* of the particular branch of production in which the change occurs, and partly on the *length* of the change, for the rise and fall of the rate of profit in particular branches of industry takes time to infect the others. If the oscillation only lasts a short time, then it remains localised . . .

[1] Latin: 'All other things being equal'.

101. Engels to Marx   *April 26, 1868*

The business of the rate of profit and value of money is very neat and very clear. Only, I am not clear how you can accept $\frac{s}{c+v}$ as the *rate of profit*, since s does of course not only fall into the pocket of the industrialist who produces it, but must also be divided with the trader etc.: unless you are taking the entire branch of business together, with no concern for the question of how s is divided up between manufacturer, wholesaler, dealer etc. I am very curious indeed to see how you develop this point . . .

To write 400c + 100v + 100s looks quite good, just as good as £400. 3s. 4d. . . .

102. Marx to Engels   *April 30, 1868*

For the case in question, it is irrelevant whether s (the surplus value) is *quantitatively* greater or smaller than the surplus value produced in the production value itself. For example, if $\dfrac{100s}{400c + 100v} = 20\%$, and this becomes, as a result of a fall of $\frac{1}{10}$ in the value of money = $\dfrac{110s}{400c + 110v}$ (assuming that the value of the constant capital decreases) then it is irrelevant whether the capitalist producer only appropriates a half of the surplus value produced by himself. For the rate of profit for him then = $\dfrac{55s}{400c + 110v}$, which is larger than before $\dfrac{50s}{400c + 100v}$. s is retained here in order to show *qualitatively* in the equation where the profit originates.

However, it is best that you should know the method of explaining the rate of profit. So I will give you the *most general* features of the process. In Book II, as you know, the *process of circulation* of capital is presented in the conditions set out in Book I. So the new determinants of form result from the process of circulation, such as fixed and circulating capital, transformation of capital etc. Finally in Book I we content ourselves with accepting that, if £110 arises from £100 during the valorisation process, these determinants meet with the elements in which they are again transformed, on the market. But now we investigate the conditions of this meeting, that is, the social interconnection of the different captals, parts of capital and the revenue (= s).

In Book III we then come on to the transformation of surplus value into its various forms and its separate opposing components.

I. *Profit* is firstly only *another name*, or another category, for *surplus value*. Since the whole labour appears to be paid through this form of wages, the unpaid part of the same necessarily appears as being not a result of labour, but a result of capital, and not of the variable part of the same, but of the total capital. The *surplus value* thereby receives the form of *profit,* without any *quantitative* difference between the one and the other. It is only the illusory form of appearance of the same.

Further, the part of capital consumed in the production of the commodity (the capital invested in its production, constant and variable, *minus* the part of the *fixed* capital which is applied but not consumed) now appears as the *cost price* of the commodity, since the part of the value of the commodity which costs *him* is regarded by the capitalist as *its* cost price, whereas the unpaid labour contained in it is not included in *its* cost price from his point of view. The surplus value = profit now appears as *the surplus of its sale price over its cost price.* If we thus call the value of the commodity V and its cost price C, then V = C + s, so V− s = C, so V is greater than C. The new category of the cost price is very necessary for the details of the later argument. From the very beginning we find that the capitalist can sell the commodity, at a profit, *below its value* (if still *above* its cost price) and this is the *basic law* for the understanding of the equalisation achieved by competition.

So if the profit firstly *only formally* differs from the surplus value, then, on the contrary, the *rate of profit* is immediately really different from the *rate of surplus value*, for in the one case $\frac{s}{v}$, in the other $\frac{s}{c+v}$, from which it follows from the start that, since $\frac{s}{v}$ is greater than $\frac{s}{c+v}$, the rate of profit is less than the rate of surplus value, unless c = 0.

With consideration of the results of Book II, however, it follows that we cannot calculate the rate of profit from any, for example weekly, produced commodity we like, but that $\frac{s}{c+v}$ here means the surplus value produced *during the year* in relation to the capital *invested* (as opposed to *turned over*) during the year. Thus $\frac{s}{c+v}$ here is the *annual rate of profit.*

Next we must investigate how a different *turnover* of the capital (partly dependent on the relation of circulating to fixed components of capital, partly on the number of turnovers of the circulating capital in one year etc.) modifies the *rate of profit* with the *rate of surplus value unchanged*.

But given the turnover and $\frac{s}{c+v}$ as the annual rate of profit, we consider how this can be changed, independently of changes in the rate of surplus value and even of its own mass.

Since s, the mass of surplus value = *the rate of surplus value multiplied by the variable capital*, then, if we call the rate of surplus value r and the rate of profit p', then $p' = \dfrac{r \times v}{c + v}$. Here we have 4 figures, p', r, v, c, and we can operate with any three of them, always looking for the unknown 4th quantity. This provides all possible cases of the movement of the rate of profit, and, to a certain extent, even of the mass of surplus value. This was naturally inexplicable to all previous thinkers.

These laws now discovered, which are for example very important for understanding the influence of the price of raw material on the rate of profit, remain correct, in *whatever* way the surplus value is later divided between the manufacturer etc. They also remain *directly* applicable, if $\dfrac{s}{c + v}$ is regarded as the relation of the socially produced surplus value to the social capital.

II. What were treated as *movements* in I, either of capital in a particular branch of production, or of social capital – movements by which its composition etc. is altered – are now treated as *differences between the masses of capital invested in the different branches of production*.

So now we find that, if the *rate of surplus value*, i.e. the exploitation of labour, is assumed to be equal, the production of value and hence the production of surplus value and hence the *rate of profit* is different in different branches of production. But competition forms an average or total rate of profit from these very different rates of profit. This, reduced to its absolute expression, can be none other than the (annual) surplus value produced by the capitalist class in relation to the capital invested in *society* as a whole. For example, if the social capital = 400c + 100v and the surplus value produced annually from it = 100s, then the composition of the social capital = 80c + 20v and that of the product (in percentage) = 80c + 20v ‖ + 20s = 20% rate of profit. This is the *general rate of profit*.

Competition between the masses of variously composed capitals inherent to the various spheres of production strives after one thing: *capitalist communism*, that is, that the *mass of capital belonging to each sphere of production* seizes a certain part of the total surplus value, in that proportion in which it forms a part of the total social capital.

Now this is only achieved if the annual output of commodities in each sphere of production (in the above situation where the total capital

$= 80c + 20v$ and the social rate of profit $= \dfrac{20s}{80c + 20v}$) is sold at the *cost price + 20% profit on the invested value of capital* (regardless of the amount the invested fixed capital which enters, or does not enter, the annual cost price). But the *determination* of the price of the commodities must also *diverge* from their *values*. Only in those spheres of production where the percentage composition of capital is $80c + 20v$ does the price C (*cost price*) + 20% of the *invested capital* coincide with their *value*. Where the composition is higher (e.g. $90c + 10v$) this price is *above* their value, where the composition is smaller (e.g. $70c + 30v$), *under* their value.

The price thus equalised, which distributes the social surplus value equally among the masses of capital in relation to their size, is the *production price* of the commodities, the centre around which the oscillation of the market prices moves.

The branches of production which contain a natural *monopoly*, even when their rate of profit is higher than the social one, are excluded from this process of equalisation. This will later be important for the exposition of land rent.

It is also necessary to explain in this chapter the various *causes leading to the equalisation* of different investments of capital, for they appear to the Vulgar Economist as so many *sources* of profit.

Further, the *altered form of appearance* which laws of value and surplus value – which were previously developed and are still valid – now adopt *after the transformation of the values into prices of production.*

III. *The tendency of the rate of profit to fall with progress in society.* This is already evident from what was developed in Book I on the *alteration in the composition of capitals with the development of the social productive force.* This is one of the greatest triumphs over the pons asinorum[1] of all previous economics.

IV. Until now we have only dealt with the *productive capital* of society = 500 (millions or billion, no matter). And indeed: $400c + 100v \parallel + 100s \times p\,'$, the general rate of profit, = 20%. We suppose that the trading capital = 100.

Then we calculate the 100s on 600 instead of 500. The general rate of profit is therefore reduced from 20% to 16⅔%. The *production price* (for simplification, we will accept that the whole 400c, i.e. including the fixed capital, is involved in the *cost-price* of the annually produced mass of commodities) now = 583⅓. The trader sells at 600, and if we ignore the fixed component of his capital, then his 100 realises 16⅔%, as much as the productive capitalists, or in other words, he appropriates ⅙ of the social surplus value. The commodities are – en masse and on the social scale – sold at *their value*. His £100 (leaving aside the fixed component) only serves him as circulating money capital. Whatever the trader swallows on top of that, either in simple swindling or in speculation on the oscillation of commodity prices or, with real specialists, in wages, even if only for lousy, unproductive labour, is regarded as profit.

V. Now we have reduced profit to the form in which it appears as practically given, i.e. in our supposition 16⅔%. *Now comes the distribution of this profit into entrepreneurial profit and interest. The interest-bearing capital. The credit system.*

VI. *Transformation of surplus profit into rent.*

VII. Finally we arrive at the *forms of appearance* which serve the Vulgar Economist as a *point of departure*: land rent originating from the soil, profit (interest) from capital, wages from labour. From our point of view, however, the matter now looks different. The apparent movement is explained. Further, the A. Smith-ian nonsense, which has become the *foundation stone* of all previous economics, to the effect that the price of commodities consists of those three revenues, that is, variable capital (wages) and surplus value (land-rent, profit, interest), is overturned. The total movement in this apparent form. Finally, since these three (wages, land-rent, profit (interest)) are the sources of income for the three classes of landowners, capitalists and workers – the class struggle is the consequences, in which the movement and the analysis of the whole crap is resolved . . .

¹ Latin: 'asses' bridge'.

103. Marx to Engels
May 4, 1868

This morning I received the enclosed letter and cutting from Schweitzer. Since he turns to me as a workers' representative of one of the most industrialised districts I must naturally answer.

It is my opinion that the Germans can withstand the lowering of the protective tariff on pig-iron and that the manufacturers are overdoing their lamentations in other commodities as well. I base this view on a comparison of the English and German exports to neutral markets. Enclosed as an example is a note on the exports to Belgium.

But at the same time, in my opinion, it is a question of exploiting this question in the Party interest and simultaneously of not allowing the English any new relief of any sort.

So my suggestion would be:

1. *No lowering of import duties* before a parliamentary inquiry into the state of the German iron-mining and manufacturing production. This inquiry should not, as Messrs Bourgeois would like, be limited merely to chambers of commerce and 'experts', but should be extended at the same time to include *worker relations* in the aforementioned branches, particularly since Messrs Manufacturers 'demand' protective tariffs only 'for the protection' of the workers and have also discovered that 'the value of iron' only consist of 'wages and freight'.

2. *No lowering of import duties* before a parliamentary inquiry on how the *railways* abuse their monopoly and before their freight- (and public transport) charges are regulated by law.

I would now like your opinion *immediately*, and the return of the enclosed equally immediately.

It is most splendid that your patriotic chamber of commerce bemoans the growing strength and danger of the International Working Men's Association.

104. Engels to Marx   *May 6, 1868*

... The piece on profit is very fine, but I will have to think it through again in order to grasp its meaning perfectly.

As regards Schweitzer. This scoundrel is only making use of the affair as another opportunity to make us rise to the bait. It is naturally not important that you should give him information this time, but principiis obsta!,[1] make sure that the fellow, having attacked the little finger, does not try to have a go at the whole hand. I myself have no doubt at all that the German iron industry can bear the protective tariff, all the more since the reduction of the tariff on pig-iron, from 7½ groschen to 5 groschen per hundredweight (from 15 to 10 shillings per tonne) can be borne and also the other reduction. The export of iron grows year by year, and not only to Belgium. What could be driven into the ground would be the individual ironworks which arose during the speculation boom of the fifties, and which are based on insufficient and poor mines. But these are mostly kaput and the vicinity of a railway would be more useful to them than all protective tariffs put together, if they are ever to become capable of life again. (There is a place like that in Engelskirchen, 500 yards below my brother's factory – coal has to be brought 2½ German miles[2] from Siegburg by rail – no wonder that it stands silent. *This* kind of works is crying out for protective tariffs and is presented as evidence that they are needed.)

The Elberfeld-Barmen chamber of commerce is the most horrible protective tariff institute there is, and it is *notorious* for that. But the main industry of the district relies on *exports*! But there is always a whole series of foundering businesses there and hence the moans.

Your plan is quite good, as regards the inquiry, and I like it a great deal. As for the railways, the freight charges in Germany are *cheaper* than elsewhere, and since freight traffic in Germany is the *principal* thing, this cannot be otherwise. They could still be reduced, and the governments have the power to do that, but the most urgent thing is a greater centralisation and equalisation of management and of freight charges, and this belongs, constitutionally, to the Imperial Diet. The cries of the iron fellows about high freight charges are generally unfounded . . .

[1] Latin: 'resist from the beginning.'
[2] = 9 English miles (1 German mile = 7,500 metres).

105. Marx to Engels   *May 7, 1868*

. . . I would now like to ask you for some information. But you can put it off if the work for the *Fortnightly*,[1] which is urgent, interrupts it.

I would dearly like, you see, to connect the examples in Volume II to those in Volume I.

In order to use the data given on p.186[2] about your factory – which is quite sufficient for illustrating the rate of surplus value – *for the rate of profit*, I would need:

1. The missing data on the capital invested in the *factory building* and the percentage of the sinking fund set aside. Ditto the warehouse. Giving the *rent* for both, if it is paid. Also the office costs and the costs of the personnel in the warehouse.

As regards the *steam engine*, I do not know what *percentage* is taken up in weekly depreciation, and so the capital invested in the steam engine is not apparent.

2. *This is the real question.* How do you calculate the *transformation of the circulating part of the capital* (i.e. the raw material, auxiliary materials, wages)? How large therefore is the *invested circulating* capital? I would like to get a *full* answer to this, or an illustrated one, namely the calculation of the transformation of the invested circulating capital . . .

[1] *Fortnightly Review*. Engels was preparing an article for this magazine.
[2] This is the page number in the original 1867 edition. See *Capital*, Vol.I, pp.204ff.

106. Engels to Marx

May 10, 1868

You received that information on the factory directly from Henry Ermen – G. Ermen's spinning-works do not concern me and young Ermen is expressly forbidden to say anything about it. If you want to write (*privately*) to Henry Ermen at Bridgewater Mill, Pendlebury, then he will probably give you the desired information. But you must tell him to give you the data relating *1860*, since there has been a great deal of construction since then. I can tell you roughly that a factory building capable of holding 10,000 spindles would cost £4,000–£5,000, including the cost of the land (we can probably make it slightly cheaper here, since it was only a single-storey shed, and land up here, as long as there is no coal beneath it, costs almost nothing). The rate of depreciation of buildings (£500-600 being deducted for cost of land) at 7.5% *inclusive of interest*. So with £3,600, £18 land rent (@ 3%) + (7.5% of 3,000 =) 225 = £243 rental of the building.

There is no *warehouse* for this factory, since G. Ermen only sells either to us or through an agent to other people, and pays 2% commission on the turnover. Taking this at £13,000, then £260 as replacement for the warehouse costs.

As regards the calculation of the turnover of circulating capital, I am not very sure what you mean by that. We only calculate the *total turnover*, i.e the sum of the annual sales. If I understand you aright, you wish to know the rate of turnover of the circulating part of capital per year, or in other words, how much circulating capital is in *business*. But this is different in almost all cases. A prospering spinner almost always (that is, excepting that period in which he is involved in expansion, or immediately afterwards) has some superfluous capital, which he invests somehow or other, but also uses at times to cover himself cheaply with cotton etc. Or he invests credit if he can and if it is worthwhile. One could suppose that a spinner, who invests £10,000 in machines (apart from the *building*, which he can of course rent out, and usually does), can get by with ⅕ – ¼ of the fixed capital in the circulating capital, so that, for the £10,000 fixed capital invested in machinery, £2,000–2,500 in circulating capital is sufficient. That is the *average* supposition in this area.

Here I leave the steam engines aside. H. Ermen has obviously told you some quite absurd tale which he has invented. If the weekly depreciation of the steam engine is £20, and annually £1,040! at a rate of 12.5%, the costs of the steam engine would be £8,320, ce qui est absurde.[1] The whole machine cannot have cost more than £1,500–2,000, and if G. Ermen wants to write off his whole machine in two years, then that sounds quite like him, but it is not commercially sound. You can ask him about this as well. But I fear that Monsieur Gottfried[2] has long taken these old account books into his own safe keeping, and then Henry Ermen will no longer be able to help you either . . .

. . . This week I have at last got no meetings or any such things and will be able to get down to some things for the *Fortnightly*. But I still do not know *how* to start. It is clear that I should start with the transformation of money into capital, but the *How* is not at all clear yet. What do you think?

[1] French: 'which is absurd'.

[2] i.e. G. Ermen, the main partner in the Manchester firm, Ermen & Engels; uncle of Henry Ermen.

107. Marx to Engels   *May 16, 1868*

. . . By the way, my main object is certainly to know how large is the *invested* circulating capital, i.e. in raw material etc. and wages, as opposed to the circulating capital in *turnover*. I now have enough statements, partly from manufacturers, who have made them to the Commissioners or private economists. But these only give the annual account. The devil of it is that, in political economy, the practially interesting and the theoretically necessary diverge enormously, so that one cannot even find the necessary material as one can in other sciences . . .

108. Marx to Engels

You seem to me to be on the wrong track with your unwillingness to present such simple figures as M-C-M etc. to the English review-Philistines. Quite the contrary. If you, like me, were forced to read the economic articles of Messrs Laler, Spencer Herbert, Macleod etc. in the *Westminster Review* etc., then you would see that all of them are fed up with economic trivialities – and also know that their readers are fed up with them – and that they are trying to season the swill with pseudo-philosophical or pseudo-scientific slang. The pseudo-gentleman makes the whole thing (which, in itself, = 0) no more understandable. Quite the contrary. The art consists in so mystifying the reader and causing him so many headaches that he finally discovers to his great relief that these hard words are only masquerades of *loci communes*.[1] In addition, the readers of the *Fortnightly* and of the *Westminster Review* flatter themselves on having the most capacious heads in England (and, you understand, in the whole world). Incidentally, if you had seen what Mr *James Hutchinson Stirling* dares to serve up to the public as 'the secret of Hegel', both in books and in reviews – Hegel himself would not understand it – then you would see – for Mr J.H. Stirling passes as a great thinker – that you really are too hesitant. *New things* are in demand. New in form and in content.

In my opinion, since you wish to commence with chapter II[2] (you must not forget, however, to call the reader's attention somewhere or other to the fact that he will find the value and money crap *newly* presented in chapter I), the following could be used as an introduction, naturally in the form you think fit:

Thos. Tooke stresses in his studies on currency that money in its function as capital flows back to its point of departure (reflux of money to its point of issue),[3] and does not flow back in its function as mere currency. This distinction, which was discovered by Sir James Stueart amongst others long before Tooke, has lately served as a polemic against the supposed influence which the issuing of credit money (banknotes etc.) is said by the high priests of the money principle to exercise on commodity prices. Our author, on the other hand, takes this particular form of circulation of money serving as capital ('serve in the *function of capital*', *A. Smith*)[3] as the point of departure for his investigation of the nature of capital itself and then as a solution to the question: how is money, the independent form of value, transformed into capital? ('Conversion into capital'[3] is the official expression.)

All sorts of businessmen, says Turgot, 'ont cela de commun qu'ils *achètent pour vendre . . . leurs achats* sont une *avance* qui leur *rentre'*.[4] *Buying in order to sell* is indeed the transaction in which money functions as capital and which determines the reflux to its point of issue, in opposition to *selling in order to buy*, in which it only *needs* to function as currency. The different order of the act of selling and buying imposes two different movements of circulation on the money. What lies behind this is the different behaviour of the *value* itself represented in the forms of money. In order to make this visible, the author gives the following figures for the two different movements of circulation, etc. etc.

I think you would make the problem simpler for yourself and the readers by using these figures . . .

[1] Latin: 'commonplaces'.
[2] i.e. *Capital*, Vol.I, chapters 4-6.
[3] In English in original.
[4] French: 'have this in common, that they *buy in order to sell . . .* their *purchases* are an *advance* which will *flow back* to them'.

109. Marx to Engels   *June 23, 1868*

. . . Yesterday by accident I came across a fine passage in A. Smith.[1] After he had explained that labour was the prime cost etc., and *approximately* said the correct things, although with continual contradictions, after he had explained ditto: 'The profits of stock, it may perhaps be thought, are only a different name for the wages of a particular sort of labour, the labour of inspection and direction. They are, however, altogether different, are regulated by quite different principles, and bear no proportion to the quantity, the hardship, or the ingenuity of this supposed labour of inspection and direction'; he suddenly turns round and tries to develop wages, profit and rent as the 'component parts of natural price' (he means = value). Amongst other things comes this beautiful passage:

> When the price of any commodity is neither more nor less than what is sufficient to pay the rent of the land, the wages of the labour, and the profits of the stock employed in raising, preparing and bringing it to the

market, according to their natural rates, the commodity is then sold for what be called its natural price. The commodity is then sold *precisely for what it is worth, or for what it really costs the person* who brings it to market; *for* though in common language the *prime* cost of *any commodity* does *not comprehend the profit* of the person who is to sell it again, yet, if he sells it at a price which does not allow him the *ordinary rate of profit in his neighbourhood*, he is evidently a *loser* by the trade; since, by employing his stock in some other way, he might have made that profit. [The existence of profits in the 'neighbourhood' is the very explanation of itself!] His profit, *besides, is his revenue*, the proper fund of his subsistence. As, while he is preparing and bringing the goods to market, he advances to his workmen their wages, or their subsistence; so he *advances to himself*, in the same manner, his own subsistence; which is generally suitable to the *profit* which he may reasonably expect from the sale of his goods. Unless they yield him this profit, therefore, *they do not repay him what they may very properly be said to have cost him*.

This second way of squeezing the profit into the prime cost – because it has already been gobbled up – is really beautiful.

The same man whose organs for pissing and procreating also coincide spiritually, had earlier said:

As soon as stock has accumulated in the hands of particular persons . . .*the value which* the *workmen add to* the materials . . .*resolves itself into two parts*, of which the one pays their wages, the other the *profits of their employer* upon the whole stock of materials and wages which he advanced.[2]

[1] Adam Smith, *The Wealth of Nations*.

[2] This and the preceding quotations are in English in the original.

110. Engels to Marx   *July 2, 1868*

. . . I wrote to Borkheim to ask him to get hold of a new Russian book: *Zemlya y volya* (*Land and Freedom*), in which a German-Russian landowner proves that the Russian peasant, since the abolition of peasant-serfdom, was *being ruined by communal property*, and Russian agriculture – both large and small – ditto. The book is supposed to contain much statistical evidence. Exchange-value has already penetrated these native communities so deeply that it would appear still applicable, even after the abolition of feudalism . . .

111. Marx to S. Meyer

July 4, 1868

. . . I am grateful that you send me a few newspapers from time to time. But it would be most valuable if you could rustle up a few anti-bourgeois things on the relations in landownership or agriculture in the United States. Since I am discussing *land rent* in Volume II,[1] some material, particularly against H. Carey's harmonies, would be welcome.

[1] Marx deals with land rent in section 6 of Volume III, while he originally intended to publish Volume III as a part of Volume II.

112. Marx to Engels

July 11, 1868

. . . You do not see the whole joke in this farce about that Mannekin Pis[1] Faucher when he tries to make out that I am a pupil of Bastiat. For Bastiat says in his *Harmonies*: 'If anyone explains to him, using the definition of value by labour time, the reason why the air has *no* value and a *diamond* a *high* value, then he would throw the book in the fire.' Since I have now performed this terrible act, Faucher must prove that I accept Bastiat's explanation that there is 'no measure' of value.

The way that Herr Bastiat explains the value of a diamond is in the following true travelling-salesman conversation:

'Monsieur, give me your diamond. Monsieur, I would do so gladly; give me in exchange your labour for a whole year.' Instead, the business friend now answers: 'My dear chap, if I were forced to labour, you will understand that I would have something other than diamonds to buy.' He says: 'But, monsieur, you did not sacrifice one minute for your acquisition.' 'Well, monsieur, try to find yourself a similar minute.' 'But, rightly, we should exchange *equal labour*.' 'No, rightly, you appreciate your services and I appreciate mine. I will not force you. Just give me a whole year, or find your own diamond.' 'But that would take me ten years of painful searching, to say nothing of a probable disappointment at the end of it. I think it would be wiser and more profitable to employ those ten years in another way.' 'That is precisely the reason why I think I can do you another *service* in only asking you for one year. I will spare you nine, and that is why I attach a great deal of *value* to this *service*.'[2]

Is this not the very image of the traveller in wine?

By the way – something the German Bastiat-ists do not know – this unhappy turn of phrase, that the value of commodities is determined not by the labour which it requires, but by the labour which it *spares* the purchaser (this drivel about the connection between exchange and division of labour is childish), is just as little an invention of Bastiat as any other of his travelling-salesman categories.

The old donkey Schmalz, that Prussian demagogue-catcher, says (in the German edition of 1818, French ed. 1826):[3]

> In general, the work of others never produces anything for us except an *economy of time*, and this economy of time is all that constitutes its *value* and its *price*. The carpenter, for example, makes a table for me, and the servant who posts my letters, cleans my suits or who fetches the things I need, both render me a *service* which is absolutely of the same nature: both *spare* me both the time which I would have been obliged to use myself in these occupations and the time which I would have needed to spend acquiring the skill and the talents which they require.[2]

Old Schmalz was a follower of the Physiocrats. He says this in a polemic against A. Smith's productive and unproductive labour and works from their basic assumption that only agriculture produces real value. He found this in *Garnier*. On the other hand, there is something similar in the follower of the Mercantilists, *Ganilh*. Ditto in the polemic against A. Smith's distinction. So the successor-polemic on two sides, neither of which have as yet the slightest idea of what value is – so we can write off Bastiat! And this is the latest discovery in Germany! It is a shame that there is no newspaper where we can reveal this plagiarism by Bastiat.

[1] A famous fountain figure in Brussels.
[2] This passage in French in the original.
[3] T. Schmalz, *Political Economy* (Translated from the German), 2 vols., Paris 1826.

113.   Marx to Kugelmann   *July 11, 1868*

... I heartily thank you for your letters. *Do not* write to Faucher. This Mannekin Pis would consider himself very important. All he has achieved is to get me, if there is a second edition,[1] to take a few deserving swipes at Bastiat in the appropriate passage on the *magnitude of value*. This was not done before because the third volume will contain its own extensive chapter on the gentlemen of 'Vulgar Economy'. By the way, you will find it quite natural that Faucher and his consorts deduce the 'exchange-value' from their own botched-up scribbles, not from the *mass of labour expended*, but from the *absence of this expenditure*, that is, from *labour saved*. And the worthy Bastiat did not even make this 'discovery' – which was so welcome to these gentlemen – for himself, but only 'copied it' in his own fashion from much earlier authors. His sources are, of course, unknown to Faucher and company.

As for the *Centralblatt*,[2] the man is making the biggest possible concession in admitting that, if anything can be imagined under the term 'value', then one must admit to my conclusions. The unfortunate man does not see that even if there had been no chapter at all on 'Value' in my book, then the analysis of the real relations which I provide would contain the proof and evidence of the real relation of value. All the gossip about the necessity of proving the concept of value is based only on the most complete ignorance, as much of the problem under discussion as of the scientific method. Every child knows that any nation which stopped work – I will not say for one year – but just for a couple of weeks, would die. And every child knows that the volume of products corresponding to the various needs calls for various and quantitatively determined amounts of total social labour. It is self-evident that this *necessity* of the *division* of social labour in certain proportions is not at all negated by the *specific form* of social production, but can only alter its *mode of appearance*. Natural laws can never be negated. Only the *form* in which those laws are applied can be altered in historically different situations. And the form in which this proportional division of labour asserts itself in a social situation and in which the connection of social labour asserts itself as a *private exchange* of the individual products of labour, is precisely the exchange-value of those products.

Science consists precisely in working out *how* the law of value asserts itself. So if one wishes to 'explain' all the phenomena which appear to contradict the law from the very start, then one would have to provide the science *before* the science. This is exactly Ricardo's mistake, when, in his first chapter on value, he takes *for granted* all the possible categories which should first be explained, in order to provide evidence of their agreement with the law of value.

In any case, the *history of theory* proves on the other hand, as you have correctly surmised, that the conception of the relation of value was *always the same*, more or less clear, more trimmed with illusions or more scientifically defined. Since the process of thought itself proceeds from these relations, and is itself a *natural process*, then real intelligent thinking must always be the same and can only improve gradually according to the maturity of development, including that of the organ by which thought is achieved. All else is chatter.

The vulgar economist has not the slightest idea that the real, daily relations of exchange can *not be identical* to the amounts of value. The whole point about bourgeois society consists precisely in the fact that, a priori,[3] there is no conscious social control of production. What is reasonable and naturally necessary is only achieved as a blindly produced average. And then the vulgar economist thinks he has made a great discovery when he insists, in opposition to the revelation of the inner connectedness, that things look different in appearance. In fact, he boasts that he clings to appearance and takes it as final. So why then do we need a science?

But there is also another side to the question. Once insight into the connectedness has been gained, all theoretical belief in the permanent necessity of existing conditions collapses before the practical collapse. So here there is an absolute interest of the ruling classes in eternalising the thoughtless confusion. And why else are these sycophantic gossipers paid, when they have no other scientific trump to play except to say that no one should devote a single thought to political economy.

However, satis superque.[4] In any case, it shows how rotten these priests of the bourgeoisie are, when workers and even manufacturers understand my book and have found their way into it, while these '*learned scribes*' (!) complain that I expect quite unbecoming things of their intellect . . .

[1] of *Capital*, Vol.I.
[2] Reference to a review of *Capital*, Vol.I in the *Literarisches Centralblatt* No.28, Leipzig 1868.
[3] Latin: 'from the start'.
[4] Latin: 'Enough and more than enough'.

114. Engels to Marx   *August 12, 1868*

It would be worth the trouble to get to the bottom of Mr Morley's motives,[1] even if only to ascertain that the weak, lousy clique system, which we used to suppose only existed in Germany, flourishes here as well. If Morley refuses the thing in spite of Beesly's influence, then he has a reason. At heart, they are bourgeois, and Mr Morley has all the reason in the world to prevent anything argued by you from reaching the public. This is due to no *'isms'*; that knocks him on the head, and so there is the pretended lack of space. But I am not afraid to present the book to the English public, but the simplest and easiest way has been cut, and we will have to look for a new way. In the meantime, the French articles will do their job and it would be good to let these come to the attention of the gentlemen at the *Fortnightly*: it would be splendid if we could still force Mr Morley to accept the thing . . .

[1] Morley, editor of the Liberal magazine *Fortnightly Review*, refused to publish one of Engels's review of *Capital*.
[2] In English in the original.

115. Engels to Marx

September 16, 1868

. . . Is there not an urgent need for a short, popular description of the content of your book *for workers*? If this is not done, then some Moses will come along and do it and bowdlerise it. What do you think? . . .

116. Marx to Danielson

October 7, 1868

. . . You cannot wait for Volume II,[1] whose appearance will probably be delayed a further six months. I cannot finish it until certain official inquiries, prepared in the past year (and 1866) in France, the United States and England are completed or published. By the way, Volume I is a completed entity . . .

[1] The Russian Danielson wanted to publish both volumes of *Capital* simultaneously in translation, and asked Marx to send him the sheets of Volume II as they appeared.

117. Marx to Engels

October 10, 1868

. . . When you were last here, you saw the Blue Book on the Irish land relations of 1844–1845. By accident, I found the Report and Evidence on the Irish Tenant Right, 1867 (House of Lords) in a little second-hand bookshop. This was a real find. While Messrs Economists treat it purely as a quarrel about dogma – as to whether land rent is payment for natural differences in soil or whether it is merely interest on capital invested in the soil – here we have a practical life-and-death struggle between farmer and landlord, as to *how far* the rent should include, *in addition to* the payment for soil difference, the interest on the capital invested in the soil not by the landlord, but by the tenant. Only in replacing the conflicting dogmas by the conflicting facts and real opposites can the hidden background become visible, and only then can one change political economy into a positive science.

118. Marx to Kugelmann   *October 12, 1868*

. . . If I speak of the 'good situation', then that is firstly in relation to the propaganda which my book has provided and the recognition which it has found among German workers since you wrote to me last. But secondly, in relation to the wonderful progress which the International Working Men's Association has made, particularly in England.

A few days ago, a bookseller from St Petersburg surprised me with the news that *Capital* was now being printed in a Russian translation. He asked for my photogram as a title-page vignette for it, and I could not refuse this small thing to 'my good friends', the Russians. It is one of the ironies of fate that the Russians, whom I have fought uninterruptedly for 25 years, and not only in German but also in French and English, were always my 'patrons'. In Paris in 1843–44, the local Russian aristocrats carried me on their shoulders. My book against Proudhon (1847), ditto the one printed by Duncker (1859), never found a greater demand than in Russia. And the first foreign nation to translate *Capital* is Russia . . .

119. Marx to Engels   *October 15, 1868*

. . . I had a meeting with Beesly. Morley's sub-editor (the editor of the scientific department) explained that my argument was irrefutable. But the article was too 'dry' for a magazine. Beesly asked me to popularise the thing without sacrificing the scientific points. This is rather difficult. But I will try. But above all he wants to provide a lengthier introduction, with personal details about my past and something on the influence of the book in Germany. This, of course, must be done by you. But there is plenty of time until I send you the bulk of the article. The whole crap should then appear in the *Westminster Review* . . .

120. Marx to Engels

November 7, 1868

. . . He [Borkheim] is translating the main sections from the Russian book[1] on the disintegration of agriculture, and has also given me a French book[2] by the Russian Schedo-Ferroti on the subject. The latter is very mistaken – he is quite a superficial fellow – when he says that the Russian communal system first arose as a result of the ban on peasants leaving the land. The whole thing is absolutely – *to the very last detail* – identical to the *original Germanic* communal system. What has been added in Russia (and this is also the case in *a part of the Indian communal system*, not in Punjab, but in the south) is 1. the *undemocratic*, but *patriarchal* character of the commune management and 2. the *collective responsibility* for taxes to the State etc. From point 2 it follows that, the harder a Russian works, the more he is exploited for the state, not only by taxation, but in food provision, horse delivery etc. during the continual troop manoeuvres, for State couriers etc. The whole crap is breaking up . . .

[1] P. Lilienfeld, *Land and Freedom*.
[2] Schedo-Ferroti (F.I. Firks), *Studies on the Future of Russia, No.10: Property of the People*, Berlin 1868.

121. Marx to Engels

November 14, 1868

Since Praxis is better than all theory, I ask you to describe to me with the *greatest exactitude* (with examples) the method by which you run your business quant à banquier[1] etc.

i.e. 1. the method of purchase (cotton etc.). With regard only to the monetary way of doing things; the bills; time for drawing them etc.

2. In sales. Bill-relationship to your buyers and to your London correspondent.

3. The relation and operations (current account etc.) affecting your banker in Manchester.

. . . Since Volume II is mostly too greatly theoretical, I will use the chapter on credit for an actual denunciation of swindle and of commercial morals.

[1] French: 'as it affects your banker'.

1869

122. Marx to Kugelmann

February 11, 1869

. . . The local treasurer of our General Council – Cowell Stepney, a very rich and respectable man, but completely dedicated to the workers' cause, if in a somewhat foolish way – asked a friend in Bonn about (German) literature on the workers' cause and socialism. This friend sent him en réponse[1] a (written) conspectus made up by Dr Held, the professor of political economy in Bonn. His marginalia show the enormous narrow-mindedness of this learned mandarin. He (Held) writes on Engels and myself here: 'Engels, *The Condition of the Working Class* etc., the best product of German socialist communist literature'. 'Karl Marx is closely connected to Engels. And from him comes the most scientific and learned work which has ever been produced by socialism, that is *Capital* etc. Although it only appeared recently, this book is still an echo of the pre-1848 movement. Therefore I mention it here in connection with Engels. The work is also (!) very topically interesting, because (!!) one can here see where Lassalle took his basic ideas.' That's a nice place too!

A private tutor in political economy at a German university has written to say that I have completely convinced him, but . . . but his position does not allow him 'and other colleagues' to *express* their agreement.

This cowardice among the mandarins of the science on the one hand, and the conspiracy of silence by the bourgeois and reactionary press on the other, is causing great harm. Meissner writes to say that the accounts from the Autumn Book Fair look bad. He is still over 200 thaler *below* his expenditure. He adds: if even half of what Kugelmann has done in Hanover could be achieved in a few larger places like Berlin etc., then we should already be into the second edition . . .

---

[1] French: 'in reply'.

123. Marx to Engels   *March 1, 1869*

. . . I received the Foster[1] on Saturday evening. The book was certainly important for its time. Firstly, because the Ricardo theory was completely developed in it, and indeed better than Ricardo – on money, rate of exchange etc. Secondly, because one can see how those donkeys, the Bank of England, the Committee of Inquiry and the theoreticians worked each other's fingers to the bone on the question: England as a debtor to Ireland. In spite of this, there was a continual rate of exchange to Ireland's disadvantage and money was exported from Ireland to England. Foster solves the puzzle for them: namely, in the depreciation of Irish paper money. Certainly, two years before him (1802), Blake had completely explained this difference between *nominal* and *real* rates of exchange, and Petty had already said the essential things – except that the thing was forgotten after him . . .

---

[1] J. Foster, *An Essay on the Principle of Commercial Exchanges etc.*, London 1804.

124. Marx to Ludlow[1]   *April 10, 1869*

Being aware of your services to the working class, I should before this have given myself the pleasure of sending you my last work *Das Kapital* (II and III volume not yet published), if I had known you to be a German reader.

In your article on Lassalle in the *Fortnightly* you say first that Lassalle propagated my principles in Germany and say then that I am propagating 'Lassallian principles' in England. This would indeed be what the French call 'un échange de bons procédés'.[2]

In the volume I send you, you will find Preface, p.VIII, note 1, the plain facts stated videlicet that 'Lassalle has taken from my writings almost literally *all his general theoretical developments'*, but that I 'have nothing whatever to do with *his practical applications'*.[3] His practical nostrums, government aid to co-operative societies, I call by courtesy *his*. It belongs in fact to, and was zealously preached, at the time of Louis Philippe, by Monsieur *Buchez*, ex-Saint-Simonian, author of the *Histoire Parlementaire de la Révolution Française*, glorifying Robespierre *and* the Holy Inquisition. Monsieur Buchez put forward his views, for instance, in the journal *L'Atelier*,[4] in *opposition* to the radical views of the French communism of that time.

Since you quote my reply to Proudhon: *Misère de la Philosophie*,[5] you cannot but be aware from its last chapter that in 1847, when all political economists and all the socialists concurred on one single point – the condemnation of *Trade Unions*, I demonstrated their historical necessity.

[1] In English in the original.
[2] 'an exchange of civilities'.
[3] See *Capital* Vol.I, FLPH Moscow 1961, p7 (footnote 1); Penguin ed, pp.89-90.
[4] *The Workshop*.
[5] *Poverty of Philosophy*.

125. Engels to Marx
November 19, 1869

. . . How is the French translation of your book getting on? I have not heard anything about it since I returned.

And so to *Carey*.

I do not think that the whole controversy at all affects real economics directly. Ricardo says that rent is the surplus of the return from more fruitful pieces of land above those which yield least. And Carey says exactly the same thing . . .

So, on the question of what rent is, they agree. The controversy concerns the manner and the means by which rent comes into existence. Now, Ricardo's description of the origins of rent (Carey, p.140)[1] is just as un-historical as all such patchwork histories by economists and resembles Carey's own great Robinson Crusoe tale about Adam and Eve, p.96ff. This is partly excusable with the old economists, including Ricardo, since they had no historical knowledge and were just as un-historical in their whole approach as other men of the 18th century Enlightenment whose so-called historical digressions were of course only façons de parler[2] which enabled them to envisage the creation of this or that in a rational way, and by which prehistoric men always think and act exactly as if they were men of the 18th century Enlightenment. But when Carey presents Adam and Eve to us as Yankee backwoodsmen, when he tries to develop his own historical theory, then he cannot expect to be believed, so he does not have that excuse.

The whole controversy would be pointless if Ricardo, in his naivety, had not described the more fruitful land as simply 'fertile'. The most *fertile* and *most favourably situated* land is the first to be cultivated according to Ricardo. That is just how any thinking citizen of a land which has been cultivated for centuries would envisage the thing. Now Carey latches on to the 'fertile' and accuses Ricardo of maintaining that those stretches of land which were most capable of yield *by themselves* were the first to be cultivated, and says: No, on the contrary, the most fruitful areas *by themselves* (the valley of the Amazon, the Ganges delta, Tropical Africa, Borneo and New Guinea etc.) are precisely not yet cultivated, and the first settlers always cultivate the *self-draining* stretches first – that is, those on hills and on slopes – because they cannot do otherwise, although, by nature, these are the *poorer* areas. And when Ricardo says: fertile *and the most favourably situated*, then he is saying the same thing, except that he does not notice that he is expressing himself loosely and that a contradiction can be found in these two qualifications which are connected by '*and*'. But when Carey, p.138, gives a description and maintains that Ricardo is putting his first settlers in the valley while Carey puts them on the hills (in his picture of naked rocky heights and impracticable slopes of 45 degrees), then he is simply lying about Ricardo.

Carey's historical examples, insofar as they relate to *America*, are the only valuable things in this book. As a Yankee, he went through the process of settling himself and could follow settlements from their beginnings, and so he knows his facts. Nevertheless, there are many uncritical remarks here which still have to be laid bare. But the invention and the stupidity begins when he starts discussing Europe. And the fact that Carey is not blameless even in reference to America is shown by the zeal with which he tries to prove the worthlessness, indeed the *negative* quality of the value (by which the land can be worth minus 10 dollars per acre) of uncultivated land, and by the way he praises the self-sacrifice of societies which make desert land usable for humanity at the price of their own certain ruin. It must make an odd impression when this is told in the land of colossal land swindles. By the way, *prairie land* is not mentioned anywhere here, and elsewhere it is passed over very quietly. The whole story about the negative quality of value of desert soil and all his calculations and proofs are best contradicted by America itself. If these things were true, then America would not only be the poorest country, but would become *relatively* poorer each year, because an increasing amount of labour would be wasted on those worthless areas.

As for his definition of rent: 'the amount received as rent is interest upon the value of labor expended, *minus* the difference between the productive power (the rent-paying land) and that of the newer soils which can be brought into activity by the application of the same labor that has been there given to the work'[3] –pp.165, 166 – this may be correct here and there within certain limits, especially in America. But, at best, rent is such a complicated thing which depends on so many other conditions that even this is only true, ceteris paribus,[4] of two *adjoining* pieces of land. Ricardo knew as well as he does that the interest for the value of labour expended is also contained in rent. If Carey defines land as such as worse than worthless, then rent *must* naturally be 'interest upon the value of labor expended' or else, as he tells us on p.139, must be theft. Admittedly, C[arey] does not explain the transition from theft to interest.

I think that the *origin* of rent in different countries, and even in one and the same country, is not at all the simple process that both Ric[ardo] and C[arey] imagine. With Ric[ardo], as I say, this is excusable, since it is the story of the fisher and the hunter in the realm of agriculture. This is no economic *dogma*; but C[arey] wants to create one from his theory and present it as such to the world, although quite separate historical studies should be used here than Mr Carey's. There may even have been places where rent arose à la Ricardo, and others where it arose à la Carey, and again others where quite different developments took place. And Carey should also be informed that in those places where fever – and particularly tropical fever – is a factor, the economy just stops. Unless he understands his theory of population like this: with the increase in population, the surplus population would be forced to work the most fruitful, i.e. the most unhealthy, stretches of land, and here they either succeed or they succumb, and then Carey has happily created a harmony between himself and Malthus.

In Northern Europe, rent arose neither à la Ricardo nor à la Carey, but simply out of the feudal burdens which were later raised to their rightful economic level by competition. In Italy, it was different again, vide[5] Rome. So it is impossible to calculate how much rent in countries with an old culture is really original rent and how much interest there is on the labour involved. And as soon as it is proved that rent – even without putting my work into the land – can grow, it becomes quite irrelevant. The grandfather of Sir Humphrey de Trafford in Old Trafford near Manchester was so swamped by debt that he did not know whether he was coming or going. His grandson, after paying off all the debts, had an income of £40,000 per annum. So if we now deduct circa £10,000 for building work, then we still have £30,000 annual value of the farm estate which perhaps brought in £2,000 80 years ago. If, in addition, £3,000 is calculated as interest on the work and capital invested, which is a lot, then there remains an increase of £25,000, or five times the earlier value, including the improvements. And all that is not due to the employment of labour, but because labour has been employed in something else adjoining, because the estate adjoins a town like Manchester, and milk, butter and vegetables can sell well there. The same thing happens in the larger framework. From the moment when England became a country which imported corn and cattle, and even earlier, the density of the population was a factor in the determining of rent, quite independently of the labour employed on the land in England as a whole. Ricardo, with his most favourable situated lands, also takes heed of the involvement of the *market*, while Carey ignores it. And if he then says: the land itself has only a negative value, but the *situation* has a positive value, then he thereby admits what he had denied, that land, precisely because it can be monopolised, has or *can* have a value independent of the labour employed. But C[arey] keeps as quiet as a mouse on this score.

It is also of no consequence whether or not the labour employed in the land in cultivated countries pays its own way. More than 20 years ago, I maintained that, in the present society, no instrument of production could last for 60 to 100 years, and no factory, and no building etc., has ever covered its production costs at the end of its existence. I still believe, all in all, that this is perfectly correct. And if C[arey] and I are both correct, then that proves nothing about the rate of profit and nothing about the origin of rent, but only proves that bourgeois production, even by its own definition, is idle.

You have probably had enough of these random notes on C[arey]. They are very jumbled up, since I have not made any notes. As regards his historical-materialist natural-scientific tone, then its entire value =

that of the two trees, the tree of life and that of knowledge, which he did not of course plant for his own Adam and Eve, who had to toil away in the backwoods, but rather for their descendants in his tome on Paradise. The ignorance and slovenliness here can only be equalled by the shamelessness which allows him to make his debut with this stuff.

You will not ask me to read the remaining chapters. It is the purest rubbish, and he is not very free with his jokes either. I will send you the book as soon as I am in town, because there is no post box here big enough to take it . . .

[1] H.C. Carey, *A Manual of Social Science*, Philadephia 1865.
[2] French: 'manners of speaking'.
[3] This passage in English in the original.
[4] Latin: 'all other things being equal'.
[5] Latin: 'see'.

126. Marx to Engels   *November 26, 1869*

I did not feel very well this week and the thing under my arm is still very painful. So I have not thanked you earlier for your notes on Carey, whose volume I received yesterday.

In my book against Proudhon,[1] where I still accepted *Ric[ardo]'s* theory of rent completely, I already argued against what was wrong there, wrong even from his (R[icardo]'s) point of view.

> Ricardo, after postulating bourgeois production as necessary for the determination of rent, nevertheless applies the concept of rent to the landed property of all ages and all countries. This is an error common to all economists who present bourgeois relations of production as eternal categories.

Mr Proudhon had naturally transformed R[icardo]'s theory immediately into some moral expression of equality and thus found in R[icardo]'s defined rent, 'an immense *land register*, which is produced contradictorily by landlords and farmers . . . in a higher interest, and whose ultimate result must be to equalise the possession of land etc.'.

I then remarked, among other things:

> Land assessment based upon rent can only be of practical value within the conditions of present society. Now we have shown that the farm *rent* paid

by the farmer to the landlord is a fairly accurate expression of *rent* of land only in the countries most advanced in industry and commerce. And even this rent often includes *interest* paid to the landlord on capital invested in the land. The location of the land, the vicinity of towns and many other circumstances influence the farm rent and modify rent in general . . . On the other hand, rent cannot be the *invariable* index of the *degree of fertility of a piece of land*, since the modern application of chemistry is constantly changing the nature of the soil, and geological knowledge is just now, in our days, beginning to *revolutionise all the old estimates of relative fertility* . . . fertility is not so natural a quality as might be thought; it is closely bound up with the *social relations* of the time.'[2]

With regard to the development of culture in the United States itself, Mr Carey ignores the most well-known facts. For example, the English agricultural chemist Johnston, in his notes on the United States, argues: the farming emigrants who went from New England to New York State left worse soil for better soil (not 'better' in Carey's sense, that the land has first to be cultivated, but in the chemical and also the economic sense), and the farming emigrants from New York State who settled down firstly on the other side of the Great Lakes, say in Michigan for instance, leave better land for worse etc. The settlers of Virginia exploited the most suitable land (both in terms of situation and of fertility) for growing their main crop, tobacco, so terribly that they had to move on to Ohio etc., which had a worse soil for the same crop (although not for wheat etc.). The nationality of the emigrants also had a say in the places of settlement. The people from Norway and our own Alpine forests went to the wild northern forests of Wisconsin, the Yankees kept to the prairies in the same territory etc.

Prairies, both in the United States and in Australia, are in fact a thorn in C[arey]'s flesh. According to him, a soil which is not absolutely clad in forest is by nature infertile, and so is all meadow land.

The joke is that Carey's two great conclusions (in relation to the United States) stand in direct contradiction to his own dogma. *Firstly*, under the diabolical influence of England, people, instead of cultivating the good prime land of New England in a sociable way, disseminated over the worse (!) areas of the West. Thus, a move from better to poorer soil. (By the by, C[arey]'s 'dissemination', as opposed to 'association', is all cribbed from Wakefield.) *Secondly*, the trouble in the south of the United States is that the slave-owners (whom Mr C[arey] as a man of harmony defends elsewhere in all his earlier writings) start cultivating the better soil too prematurely and pass by the poorer soil. So they begin with the better soil, which should never happen! If C[arey] was convinced by this example that the real farmers – here, the slaves – are motivated neither by economic nor by any other reasons of their own, but by *external necessity*, then he could put two and two together and see that this situation might also arise in other countries.

According to his theory, culture in Europe should have originated in the mountains of Norway and proceeded then to the Mediterranean countries, instead of marching the other way.

Carey tries, with a most absurd and fantastical theory of money, to conjure away the awkward economic circumstance that, in contrast to all other improved machinery, the machinery of the earth, which according to him is *always improving, increases* the costs of its products – at least periodically – instead of making them cheaper (this was one of the circumstances which Ricardo envisaged; and even with his nose he could see no further than the history of grain prices from about 1780 to 1815 in England).

As a harmoniser, Carey first proves that there are no antagonisms between capitalist and wage-labourer. The second step is to prove that there is a harmony between a landowner and a capitalist, and this can be done by presenting landownership as *normal*, even if it has *not yet* developed. The great and decisive difference between a colony[3] and an old civilised country is that in the latter the masses are excluded from land and soil, whether it is fruitful or not, whether cultivated or not, by *land ownership*, while in the colony the soil relatively speaking can still be owned by the labourer himself — this situation must on no account be mentioned. It must play absolutely no role in the swift development of the colonies! The awkward *'question of property'*, and here it appears in its most awkward form, would kick a leg from underneath harmony.

As for the deliberate distortion that, because the natural fertility of the soil in a country with developed forces of production is naturally an important condition for the production of surplus value (or, as Ricardo says, affects the rate of profit), it must conversely follow that the richest and most developed production must then take place in the most naturally fruitful areas; thus, for example, Mexico must be superior to New England; as for this, I have already given my answer in *Capital*, p.502ff.[4]

Carey's only positive contribution is that he maintains the progress from worse to better soil just as one-sidedly as Ric[ardo] maintains the opposite, while in reality land with unequal degrees of fertility is always cultivated at the same time and so a very careful distribution of strips of land of different kinds took place among the members of Germanic communities, and among the Slavs and the Celts, which made the later arguments about common land so difficult. But as to the progress of culture in the course of history, then we have progress simultaneously in both directions – according to the number of conditions, or again one or the other direction holds sway during a specific period.

The thing that turns the *interest* on capital invested in the land into an element of the *differential rent* is precisely the fact that the landowner receives this rent from capital which was invested in the soil, not by *himself*, but by the tenant farmer. This well-known fact relating to all of Europe should not exist, economically speaking, because the tenancy system has *not yet* developed in the *United States*. However, the thing occurs here in another form. In the end, the land jobber, and not the tenant farmer, is paid the *price* of the land for the capital expended by the latter. The history of the pioneers and of land jobbers in the United States often recalls the great horrors which occur for example in Ireland . . .

[1] i.e. *The Poverty of Philosophy*.
[2] These three quotes from the *Poverty* are in French in the original, since that book had not yet been translated from the French into either German or English.
[3] By 'colony', Marx (like Carey) means an uninhabited country which is being settled.
[4] i.e. p.502ff of the first edition of Volume I.

127. Engels to Marx   *November 29, 1869*

It is very fine that, even in the one field where one *ought* to be able to believe he has some knowledge – the history of the colonisation of the United States – Carey is shown up. After this, au fond,[1] there is not much left of the fellow . . .

Here in the Free Library and the Chatham Library[2] (which you know) I have found another mass of very valuable source material (apart from the books with second-hand information), but unfortunately no Young or Prendergast, nor the English edition on Breton[3] Law which was done for the English government. Wakefield, however, has turned up again. And various things by old Petty. Last week I ploughed through the tracts of old Sir John Davies (Attorney General for Ireland under King James); I do not know if you have read them – they are the main sources – but you will certainly have found them quoted a hundred times. It is truly a shame that one cannot get the original sources everywhere, because one can find infinitely more there than from the commentators who always confuse and complicate everything which was clear and simple. From the above it becomes clear that ownership of common land in Ireland still existed in full force Anno 1600 and was introduced in the appeals of Mr Davies (on the confiscation of forfeited lands in Ulster) as evidence that the land did not belong to the individual owners (the peasants) and so either belonged to the lord who forfeited it or to the Crown from the very start. I have never read anything more beautiful than this plea. The distribution occurred every two or three years. In another pamphlet he describes the incomes etc. of the clan chiefs quite exactly. I have *never* found these things quoted, and if you can use them, I will send you the details. And I have caught Monsieur Goldwin Smith out nicely. This man, you see, has never read Davies and so makes the most absurd statements to excuse the English. But I will catch the fellow . . .

[1] French: 'basically'.
[2] In Manchester.
[3] i.e. Ancient Irish.

128. Marx to Kugelmann   *November 29, 1869*

. . . You must excuse my long and somewhat criminal silence; I have had to catch up on a vast amount of work, not only for my scientific studies, but also quoad[1] the *International*, and also because I am learning *Russian* since I have been sent a book from Petersburg on the condition of the working class (including, of course, peasants) in Russia,[2] and finally because my health has by no means been satisfactory . . .

[1] Latin: 'in respect of'.
[2] i.e. N. Flerovsky, *The Condition of the Working Class in Russia*, St Petersburg 1869.

1870

129. Marx to De Paepe[1]

I am writing this letter primarily to ask you a personal favour. You probably know that a section of the English bourgeoisie have formed a kind of 'Land League' against the 'Land and Labour League' of the workers. Their ostensible aim is to transform land ownership in England into allotment property and to create a peasantry for the greater good of the people. Their actual aim is to attack the landed aristocracy. They wish to bring the land into free circulation in order to transfer it from the hands of the landlords into the hands of the capitalists. To this end they are publishing a series of popular pamphlets, under the title of 'The Cobden Treaties', which paint small-property ownership in a rosy hue. Their great paragon is *Belgium* (principally *Flanders*). It appears that the peasants in that country live in Paradise. They have got in touch with M. Laveleye who provides them with facts for their orations. Now, since I deal with land ownership in the 2nd volume of *Capital*, I would find it useful to go into the details of the constitution of land ownership in Belgium and of Belgian agriculture. Could you be so kind as to send me the *titles of the principal books* which I would have to consult?

---

[1] This letter written in French in original.

130. Marx to Engels
February 10, 1870

... I have read the first 150 pages of *Flerovsky's*[1] book (they cover Siberia, Northern Russia and Astrakhan). This is the first book to tell the truth about economic conditions in Russia. The man is a firm enemy of what he calls 'Russian optimism'. I have never had any rosy views on this communistic El Dorado, but Fl[erovsky] surpasses all my expectations. It is indeed wonderful, and in any case a sign of change, that such a thing can be printed in Petersburg.

'U nas prolyetariev malo, no zato massa nasheyo rabocheyo klassa sostoit iz rabotnikov, kotorikh uchast' khuzhe, chem uchast' vsyakoyo prolyetariya.'[2]

The presentation is quite original, sometimes reminds one most of Monteil. One can see that the man has travelled everywhere himself and has made his own observations. He has a burning hatred of the landlord, the capitalist and the official. No socialist doctrine, no mysticism of the land (although some on the form of land ownership), no nihilistic ecstasies. Here and there some well-meaning rubbish which is, however, suitable for the level of development of the people for whom the book is destined. In any case, this is the most important book to appear since your *Condition of the Working Class* ...

[1] See footnote to letter 128.

[2] Russian: 'There are few proletarians here, but the mass of our working class consists of workers whose condition is worse than that of any proletarian'.

131. Marx to Engels
April 14, 1870

... Lafargue has met a very learned Russian woman in Paris (a friend of his friend Jaclard, an excellent young man). She told him that *Flerovsky* – although his book passed the censor during the liberal fit – has been exiled to Siberia, if you please, for the same. The translation of my book has been confiscated before publication and has been banned.[1]

During the coming week or at the beginning of next you will receive: *Landlord and Tenant Right in Ireland. Reports by Poor Law Inspectors. 1870*, ditto *Agricultural Holdings in Ireland. Returns. 1870*.

The Reports of the Poor Law Inspectors are interesting. Amongst other things, they show, as in their *Reports on Agricultural Wages* (which you already have), that the conflict between *labourers* on the one hand, and *farmers and tenants* on the other has begun since the famine. As for the Reports on 'Wages', if we accept that the present figures for wages are correct, and these are probably based on other sources, then the *earlier wage figures* were either set too *low* or the earlier parliamentary returns on the same (which I will look out for you from my parliamentary papers) were set too *high*. On the whole, however, my view[2] in the section on Ireland has been confirmed, namely that the wage increases were more than counterbalanced by price increases in food and that, except at harvest time etc., a relative surplus of labourers has been created in spite of emigration. Also important in the *Landlord and Tenant Right Reports* is the fact that the development of machinery has transformed a mass of handloom weavers into paupers . . .

The two Reports of the Poor Law Commissioners show very plainly: 1. that since the famine the clearing of labourers' cottages from the estates has begun *as in England* (not to be confused with the suppression of the 40-shilling freeholders after 1829;[3] 2. that the Encumbered Estates proceedings have replaced the turned-out bankrupt landlords with a mass of *small profiteers* . . .

[1] This was not in fact true since the translation was still being done, completed in October 1871 and published in April 1872.
[2] See *Capital*, Vol.II, chapter 5, Section 5 (f).
[3] See letter 132 below.

132. Engels to Marx   *April 15, 1870*

. . . Your conclusions on the parliamentary reports agree with my results. But we should not forget that the process of clearing the 40-shilling freeholders is ultimately combined with that of the clearing of labourers since 1846, because, until 1829, leases for 21 or 31 years *and a life* (if not longer) were drawn up to create freeholders, so that a man could only be a freeholder if he *could not be free during his own lifetime*. These leases almost never excluded sub-division. They were partly still in effect in 1846 or else their consequences were there, which meant that the peasants were still tied to an estate. Ditto to those pieces of land which were then in the hands of middlemen (who usually had leases of 64 years and three lives or even 99 years), which often reverted only between 1846 and 1860. Thus, these processes more or less combined with each other, or else the Irish landlord was never, or rarely, able to be certain that the labourers in particular, more than any other traditional small tenants, were to be driven out. The same thing happens in England as in Ireland: the land must be worked by labourers who live in *other Poor Law Unions*, so that the landlord and his tenants remain free of the Poor Tax. Senior says the same thing, or rather his brother Edward, Poor Law Commissioner in Ireland. The great instrument which is clearing Ireland is the *Poor Law*.

The land which has been sold since the Encumbered Estate Court, according to my notes, amounts to as much as ⅕ of the whole; the buyers are indeed mostly profiteers, speculators etc., *mostly Irish Catholics*. Sometimes also graziers grown rich. Nevertheless, there are still *only* circa 8,000 to 9,000 *landowners* in Ireland . . .

133. Marx to Kugelmann   *June 27, 1870*

. . . Last year I counted on having a second edition of my book after the Easter book fair and consequently the receipts from the first edition. But you can see from the enclosed letter from Meissner, which arrived today, that all that is still a long way off. (Could you please send me the letter back.)

Messrs German professors have lately felt called upon to take notice of me here and there, if only in an absurd way; for example, A. Wagner in a booklet on land ownership, Held (of Bonn) in a booklet on agricultural credit facilities in the Rhine Province.

Herr Lange (*Über die Arbeiterfrage*, etc., 2nd edition)[1] gives me fulsome praise, but only with the aim of making himself important. Herr Lange, you see, has made a great discovery. The whole of history can be subsumed under a single natural law. This natural law is the *phrase* (the Darwinian expression in this application becomes a mere phrase) 'the struggle for life', and the content of this phrase is the Malthusian law of population, or rather of over-population. So instead of analysing the 'struggle for life', as it is expressed historically in various particular forms of society, one only needs to transform every concrete struggle into the phrase 'struggle for life' and then this phrase in turn into the Malthusian 'population fantasy'. One must admit that this is a very penetrating method . . . for pompous, pseudo-scientific, high-faluting ignorance and idle thinking.

What this same Lange has to say about the Hegelian method, and my application of it, is truly infantile. Firstly he understands rien[2] of Hegel's method, and so secondly even less of my critical way of applying it. In a way, he reminds me of Moses Mendelssohn. This archetypal windbag, you see, wrote to Lessing to ask how he could possibly consider taking 'that dead dog Spinoza' au sérieux![3] In the same way, Herr Lange is amazed that Engels, myself etc. could take that dead dog Hegel au sérieux, when Büchner, Lange, Dr Dühring, Fechner and so on have long agreed that they – poor deer[4] – have long since buried him. Lange is so naive as to say that I move in the empyreal matter 'with the rarest freedom'. He has no idea that this 'free movement in matter' is nothing but a paraphrase for the *method* with which I treat the matter – i.e. the *dialectical method* . . .

As for Meissner's pressure for volume II, not only have I been interrupted all winter by illness, I also found it necessary to swot up on my Russian, since the treatment of the land question necessitated studying Russian conditions on the land in the original sources. In addition, the English government published a series of Blue Books (soon to be completed) on the Irish Land Question. Finally – entre nous[5] – I would have liked a second edition of Volume I beforehand. If this came before the final draft of Volume II, then that would only disturb me . . .

---

[1] F. Lange, *On the Workers Question. Its Relevance to the Present and the Future*, Winterthur 1870.

[2] French: 'nothing'.

[3] French: 'seriously'.

[4] This expression in English in original might be a mistake for 'poor dear'.

[5] French: 'between ourselves'.

1871

134. Marx to S. Meyer

January 21, 1871

. . . In Petersburg there has appeared, semi-officially, an *Archive of Legal Medicine* (in Russian). One of the contributing doctors published an essay in the last quarto-volume, 'On the Hygienic Condition of the West European Proletariat', in which he quoted mainly from my book – albeit with acknowledgements. As a result of this, the following misfortune has occurred: the censor has received a mighty reprimand from the Minister of the Interior, the editor-in-chief has been sacked, and the number itself, or all the copies that could be seized – has been burned!

I do not know whether I told you that I have had to teach myself Russian since the beginning of 1870, and I can now read it fairly fluently. This arose because I was sent from Petersburg Flerovsky's very important work – *The Condition of the Working Class (especially peasants) in Russia*, and since I also wished to acquaint myself with the economic (excellent) works by Chernyshevsky (who was thankfully sent to the Siberian mines seven years ago). The rewards matched the labour which a man of my years must make to master a language which is so far removed from the classical, the Germanic and the Romance languages. The intellectual movement which is now taking place in Russia shows that something is moving in the deep. Heads always connect with the body of the people by invisible threads . . .

135.   Marx to W. Liebknecht   *April 13, 1871*

. . . Engels wants me to tell you that his essay[1] in the *D[eu]tsch-F[ranzösische] Jahrbücher* has now only historical value, and so is no longer suitable for practical propaganda. On the other hand, you can print lengthy extracts from *Capital*, for example things from the chapter on 'primitive accumulation'[2] etc. . .

[1] i.e. Engels, *Outlines for a Critique of Political Economy*, 1844.
[2] *Capital*, Vol.I, Part 8.

136.   Marx to Danielson   *June 13, 1871*

I will deal with the 'First Chapter' with pleasure,[1] although I cannot begin it for another *two weeks*. An illness of eight weeks has created a backlog of work which must be dealt with before anything else. Then I will send a catalogue of smaller corrections as well.

As for the continuation of my work, the report of our friend[2] is based on a misunderstanding. I considered a complete revision of the manuscript to be necessary. Apart from that, necessary documents have not been available until now, but they will soon arrive from the United States . . .

[1] The Russian publicist Danielson had asked Marx to send him the revised first chapter of *Capital*, Vol.I so that it could be translated into Russian.
[2] In his letter to Marx of May 23, 1871, Danielson had talked of 'our common friend' who had said that Meissner would not publish Volume II until Volume I had sold out.

137.   Marx to Danielson   *November 9, 1871*

Herewith a few alterations, partly only printing errors. The alterations ad[1] p.192, p.201, p.288, Note 205a and p.376, are of some importance, because they deal partly with the content.

It would be superfluous to *wait* for the revision of the 1st chapter since my time has been so taken up for months (and in the near future there is little hope of improvement in this) that I cannot get down to my theoretical work at all.

Certainly, I shall one fine morning put a stop to all this, but there are circumstances, where you are in duty bound to occupy yourselves with things much less attractive than theoretical study and research . . .[2]

[1] Latin: 'to'. The page numbers refer to the first edition of *Capital*, 1867.
[2] This paragraph is in English in the original.

1872

138. Marx to Lachâtre[1]   *March 18, 1872*

I applaud your idea of publishing the translation of *Capital* in serial parts. In this form, the work will be more accessible to the working class and, for me, this is more important than any other consideration.

That was the good side of your coin, but there is the other side. The method of analysis which I employed and which has never yet been applied to economics, makes the reading of the first chapters fairly difficult, and it is to be feared that the French public, always impatient for results and anxious to know the relationship of general principles to immediate questions affecting it, will be frightened away because it cannot make immediate progress.

This is a disadvantage which I can do nothing about, except to forewarn and forearm those readers who desire the truth. There is no Queen's Highway in science, and only those who do not fear exhaustion in climbing the steep paths have any chance of reaching the brilliant heights.

[1] This letter in French in original.

139. Marx to Danielson   *May 28, 1872*

This reply has been so delayed because I was always hoping to be able to enclose both the first copies of the *second German edition of 'Capital'* and of the *French translation* (Paris) with this letter. But the German and French booksellers have dragged their feet so much that I can put it off no longer.

Firstly, best thanks for the beautifully bound copy,[1] the translation is *masterly*. I would be pleased to have another, unbound, copy for the British Museum.

I regret that something *absolute* (in the strictest sense of the word) prevented me from beginning the revision of the second edition before the end of December 1871. It would have been very useful for the Russian edition.

Although the French edition (translated by Mr Roy, the translator of Feuerbach) has been prepared by a great master of both languages, the translation is often too literal. So I was obliged to rewrite whole passages in French to make them palatable for the French public. Later it will be so much easier to translate from the French into English and the Romance languages.

I am so overworked, and in fact so much interfered with in my theoretical studies that, after September, I shall *withdraw* from the *commercial concern*[2] which, at this moment, weighs principally upon my own shoulders, and which, as you know, has its ramifications all over the world. Mais,[3] est modus in rebus,[4] and I can no longer afford – for some time at least – to combine two sorts of business of so very different a character . . .[5]

[1] Of the Russian translation of *Capital*, Vol.I.
[2] i.e. The General Council of the International.
[3] French: 'but'.
[4] Latin: 'there is a measure to all things'.
[5] This paragraph is in English in the original.

140. **Marx to Sorge**   *June 21, 1872*

. . . As for my *Capital*, the first German consignment[1] will appear next week, ditto the first French[2] in Paris. You will receive some copies of both (consecutively) from me for yourself and some of your friends. 10,000 copies of the French edition have been printed (with the words 'entirely revised by the author' on the title page – and not merely as a phrase, for I had the devil's own work with it) and 8,000 have already been allocated before the first consignment.

In Russian, those books already printed must pass before the censor before they can go out to the public, and he has to make a legal complaint about them if they do not pass the test.

From Russia, I received a letter about the Russian translation of my book (which is masterly):

> Two censors in the censor's office have started on the book and their decisions on it have been laid before the committee of censure. Even before it was read, it was decided in principle that this book should not be stopped merely because of the author's name, but should be investigated thoroughly to see how much it really matched up to its title. The following is a resumé of the decision unanimously adopted by the committee and given as a report to the central administration:
>
> 'Although the author is a complete socialist in his convictions and the whole book has a completely defined socialist character, but in consideration of the fact that the presentation cannot be described as accessible for everyone and that, on the contrary, it possesses the form of strictly mathematical scientific proofs, the Committee declares the prosecution of this work before the courts to be impossible.'

And so it received a passport to the world. 3,000 copies have been printed. It was published in Russia on March 27 and by May 15, 1,000 copies were already sold . . .

[1] Of the second German edition of *Capital*, Vol.I.
[2] Of the first French edition of *Capital*, Vol.I.

141. Marx to Danielson   *December 12, 1872*

. . . I await with anticipation the critique (in manuscript)[1] along with everything else printed you can lay hands upon in this line. One of my friends, you see, wants to write about the reception of my book in Russia.

The publication of the French translation has been interrupted by unpleasant accidents, but will recommence in a few days.

An Italian translation is in preparation . . .

I would really like to have a look at Professor Sieber's (of Kiev) book on Ricardo's teachings on value and capital[2] – which also contains a discussion of my book . . .

In Volume II of *Capital* I will deal very extensively with the Russian form of land ownership in the relevant section.[3]

Another thing. I would like to publish something on Chernyshevsky's life, personality, etc., in order to stir up sympathy for him in the West. But I need some details.

[1] A reference to the article by J. Zhukovsky, 'Karl Marx and his Book on Capital', which appeared in the magazine *Vestnik Europia (European Messenger)* in 1877.

[2] N. Sieber, *Ricardo's Theory of Value and Capital*, Kiev 1871.

[3] This plan was not carried out due to Marx's illness and to lack of available material.

1873

142. Marx to Danielson

January 18, 1873

. . . As regards Ch[ernyshevsky], it depends on you whether I will deal with the purely scientific or also the other side of his activity. Naturally, he will only figure in Volume II of my work as an economist. I know a large part of his writings . . .

143. Marx to Engels

May 31, 1873

. . . I told Moore here about a problem which I have been wrestling with in private for a long time. But he thinks that the matter cannot be resolved, or at least, is not to be resolved pro tempore[1] because of the many and largely unknown factors involved. The thing is this: you know the tables which give prices, discount rate, etc. etc. in their movement during the year, in ascending and descending zigzags. I have tried several times – for the analysis of crises – to calculate these ups and downs as irregular curves, and thought (I still think that it is possible with enough tangible material) that I could determine the main laws of crises mathematically. Moore, as I say, considers the matter impracticable, and I have decided to give it up for the time being . . .

[1] Latin: 'for the moment'.

144. Engels to Marx

November 29, 1873

. . . In the perevod *Kapitala*[1] chapters 2 to 5[2] (including machinery and large industry) are done by him,[3] so that it is quite a large section. He is now translating some English things for Polyakov.[4]

Yesterday I read in French the chapter on the factory laws. With all respect for the art which has transformed the chapter into elegant French, I still feel sorry for the beautiful chapter. Strength and blood and life have gone to the devil. The possibility that the everyday writer can express himself with some sort of elegance has been paid for in the castration of the language. It is becoming more and more impossible to create any thoughts in this kind of modern 'proper' French. Even the re-arrangement of sentences, which has become necessary almost everywhere because of the pedantic and formal logic, removes anything striking and anything living from the presentation. I would regard it as a great mistake to take the French fabric as the basis for an English translation. In English, the powerful expression of the original should not be weakened; what is lost by necessity from the really dialectical passages is balanced out by the greater strength and conciseness of the English in many other parts . . .

[1] Russian: 'the translation of *Capital*'.
[2] i.e. Chapters 2-5 of the first edition of Volume I = chapters 4-20. (Sections II to VI.)
[3] i.e. Lopatin, one of the translators of *Capital* into Russian.
[4] This name given in Russian script in original. Polyakov published the translation of *Capital* in Russia.

1875

145. Marx to Lavrov[1]

February 11, 1875

Today I am sending you the German edition in one volume (I no longer have any 'Hefte'[2] available) and the first six parts of the French edition. In the latter there are many changes and additions (see for example *booklet 6, p.222* against J. St. Mill – a striking example of how bourgeois economists, even with the best of intentions, instinctively take the wrong road at the very moment when they are about to grasp the truth). The most important changes contained in the French edition, however, are in the sections that have not yet been published, that is, the chapters on accumulation.

My best thanks for the publications which you sent me. The ones which interested me particularly were the articles 'Chto dyelayetsya na rodinye'.[3] If I had the time, I would take some extracts for the *Volksstaat*. The 'Nye Nashi'[4] are excellent people. I have a slight suspicion that our friend Lopatin has a hand in this article.

I was sent a whole parcel of books and official publications from St Petersburg, but – it was stolen, probably by the Russian government. Amongst other things there were the reports *Komissii po syel'skomu khozyaistvu i syelslskoy proizvodityel'nosti v Rossii* and *Po podatnomu voprosu*,[5] absolutely necessary things for the chapter in the second volume where I shall deal with land ownership, etc. in Russia.

My health has much improved since my stay in Karlsbad, but on the one hand I am still obliged to limit my working hours severely, and on the other I have caught a *cold* since I returned to London, and it has not stopped bothering me.

I will come and see you when the weather is more pleasant.

[1] This letter in French in original.
[2] German: 'booklets', serial parts of the whole volume.
[3] Russian: 'What is Happening in Our Country'.
[4] Russian: 'Not Ours' – a Siberian sect, described by Lopatin in an article in the Russian journal *Vperyod* ('Forward') whose members denied the State, God, religion, property, the Family, law and bourgeois morality.
[5] Russian: *Commissions on Agriculture and for Agricultural Productivity in Russia, On the Tax Question.*

146. Marx to Lavrov[1]   *June 18, 1875*

. . . The commercial crisis is developing. Everything now depends on the news from the Asian markets and particularly from the markets in Western India, which have become more and more glutted for several years now. The definitive crash could be delayed in certain conditions, which are, however, not very likely.

The shortening of the periods between great crises is truly remarkable. I have always considered the periods not to be of a constant length, but of a diminishing length; it is particularly satisfying to find that it shows such manifest signs of a descending movement; that is a bad omen for the longevity of the capitalist world.

[1] This letter in French in original.

147. Engels to Lavrov   *November 12[-17], 1875*

At last, returning from a trip to Germany, I got down to your article,[1] which I have just read with great interest. Here are my observations on it, in German (which will allow me to be more concise).[2]

1. I can accept the *theory of development* in Darwin's teaching, but I regard D[arwin]'s method of proof (struggle for life, natural selection) only as a first, provisional, incomplete expression of a newly-discovered fact. Until Darwin, those very people who now see nothing but a *struggle* for existence everywhere (Vogt, Büchner, Moleschott etc.), stressed only the *co-operation* of organic nature, and the fact that the kingdom of plants

provides the kingdom of animals with oxygen and food, and how the kingdom of animals delivers carbon dioxide and fertiliser to the plants, as Liebig, for example, stressed. Both conceptions have a certain justification within set limits, but the one is as one-sided and narrow as the other. The interaction of bodies in nature – both dead and living – includes harmony as well as collision, struggle as well as co-operation. So when some self-professed naturalist takes it upon himself to reduce the whole manifold wealth of historical development to the one-sided and paltry phrase 'struggle for existence', a phrase which can only be taken cum grano salis[3] even in the realm of nature, then he is condemned out of his own mouth.

2. Of the three 'ubezhdennyie Darwinisty'[4] mentioned by you, only Hellwald deserves mention. Seidlitz is at best only small fry and Robert Byr a novelist whose novel *Dreimal* is presently being serialised in *Uber Land und Meer*.[5] And that's where his entire braggery belongs as well.

3. Without wishing to denigrate the advantages of your method of attack, which I would call psychological, I would have chosen another. All of us are influenced to some extent by the intellectual medium in which we prefer to move. In Russia, whose public you know better than I, and in a propagandistic journal which aims at the 'svyazuzhshii affekt',[6] at the moral feeling, your method is probably better. In Germany, where false sentimentality has caused so much damage, and still does, it would not be suitable, it would be misunderstood and sentimentally distorted. With us, hatred is more urgent than love – at least at the moment – and above all we need to shed the last remnants of German Idealism, we need to establish material facts in their historical rights. So I would – and in time will possibly get around to it – attack these bourgeois Darwinists something as follows:

The whole Darwinist doctrine of the struggle for existence is simply Hobbes's doctrine of bellum omnium contra omnes[7] and the bourgeois economic doctrine of competition, together with the Malthusian population theory, transferred from society into natural life. Once this trick has been performed (and I, as mentioned sub 1[8], question its unconditional justification, especially with regard to the Malthusian theory), then these same theories can be transferred back from organic nature to history, and one could then claim that their validity as eternal laws of human society has been established. The childishness of this operation is so apparent that we do not need to waste words on it. But if I wished to go further into the matter, I would do so by presenting these men firstly as bad *economists* and only secondly as bad naturalists and philosophers.

4. The basic difference between human and animal society is that the animals, at most, *collect*, while men *produce*. This single, but cardinal, difference alone makes it impossible to carry laws of animal societies over into human society with no further ado. It makes it possible, as you rightly note, 'chelovek vel borybu ne tolyko za sushchestvovanye, no za naslazhdenya i *za uvelichenye svoyich naslazhdenii* . . . gotov byl dlya vysshego naslazhdeniya otrechsya ot nizshich'.⁹ Without questioning your other conclusions from this, I would infer further, working from my premises: human production thus, at a certain stage, reaches such a height that not only necessities but also luxuries – even if at first only for a minority – can be produced. The struggle for existence – if we can allow this category for the moment – is transformed into a struggle for pleasures, no longer for mere means of *existence*, but for means of *development, socially produced* means of development, and the categories from the animal kingdom no longer apply to this stage. But if, as is now the case, production in its capitalist form creates a far greater quantity of the means of existence and development than the capitalist society can consume, because it artificially keeps the great mass of real producers away from these means of existence and development; if this society is forced by its own law of survival to increase this production continually – which is already too great for society – and so periodically, every ten years, has to destroy not only a mass of products but also the productive forces themselves – what sense is there then in chatter about 'the struggle for existence'? The struggle for existence can then only consist in the producing class taking the control of production and distribution away from the class which was previously entrusted with it but has now become incompetent, and exactly that is the socialist revolution.

It is to be noted in passing that the mere consideration of past history as a series of class struggles suffices to expose the shallowness of the conception of the same history as a slightly varying expression of the 'struggle for existence'. So I would never do these false naturalists that favour.

5. For the same reason, I would have formulated your sentence another way, although it is quite correct in content:

'shto ideya solidarnosti dlya oblegcheniya boryby mogla . . . vyrasti nakonec do togo, shtoby okhvatiti vse chelovechestvo i protivpostavitee yego, kak solidarnoye obshchestvo bratyev, ostalynomu miru mineralov, ratsenii i zhivotnykh'.¹⁰

6. On the other hand, I cannot agree with you that the 'boryba vsech protiv vsech'[11] was the first phase of human development. In my opinion, the social impulse was one of the most important levers for the development of men from the apes. The first men must have lived in groups, and, as far as we can peer into the past, we find that this was the case.

November 17. I was interrupted again and I continue these lines today in order to send you them. You will see that observations rather refer to the form and to the method of your attack than to the substance. I hope you will find them clear, I wrote them in haste, and, in re-reading them, I would have liked to have changed many words, but I fear that would make the manuscript illegible . . .[12]

[1] 'Socialism and the Struggle for Existence', appeared in the magazine *Vperyod* ('Forwards') in September 1875.

[2] This paragraph in French in original.

[3] Latin: 'with a pinch of salt'.

[4] Russian: 'convinced Darwinists'.

[5] *Over Land and Sea*.

[6] Russian: 'emotion of solidarity'.

[7] Latin: 'the war of all against all'.

[8] Latin: 'under note 1'.

[9] Russian: 'that Man not only conducted a struggle for existence, but also one for pleasure and *for an increase in pleasure* . . . he was prepared to renounce the lowest pleasure for the highest'.

[10] Russian: 'the idea of solidarity for facilitating the struggle could finally . . . grow so much that it took hold of all humanity and posited it as a united society of brothers against the rest of the world of minerals, plants and animals'.

[11] Russian: 'the war of all against all'.

[12] This paragraph in French in original.

1876

148. Marx to Sorge

... Could I get from New York (*at my own expense of course*) the American book catalogues from 1873 to the present? I would like to find out for myself (for Volume II of *Capital*) what useful things about American agriculture and land ownership have appeared, ditto about credit (panic, money, etc., and all that goes with it).

The English papers make no sense at all of the great scandals in the United States.[1] Have you kept any American papers on the subject? ...

---

[1] A reference to the swindle and corruption scandals which occurred during the founding of the large railway companies etc.

1877

149. Marx to Engels

March 5, 1877

Herewith some Dühringiana. I found it impossible to read the fellow without always beating him extensively about the head.

Now that I have found in reading him (and the section from Ricardo onwards, which I have not yet read, must contain some fine pearls) what the gift of patience is, but also what a club in the hand is good for, I can enjoy him in peace in future. Once you have worked your way into the lad so that you have his method at your fingertips, then you find him a fairly entertaining scribbler. Meanwhile he has done me a great service as a diversion during my annoying catarrh . . .

150. Engels to Marx

March 6, 1877

Many thanks for your lengthy labours on the 'Critical History'.[1] That is more than I need to discredit the fellow[2] completely in this field. In fact, Lavrov is almost right in saying that the fellow has been treated too leniently until now. When I now read over the course on economy, now that I know the fellow and his ways, and now that I no longer need to fear discovering some dodge behind the rubbish, and now that the whole pompous fadaise[3] appears in its nakedness, I find that some more antipathy would not be out of place . . .

---

[1] i.e. Chapter 10 of Section II of Engels's *Anti-Dühring*, which Marx wrote for Engels.
[2] Dühring.
[3] French: 'absurdity'.

151. Marx to Engels   *March 7, 1877*

Since I might forget this later on, I will add this contribution to my last epistle:

1. The most important point in Hume's conception of the influence of an increase in the amount of money on the stimulation of industry – a point which also shows most clearly (if there could even be any doubt at all about it) that this increase only occurs, to his mind, during a depreciation of precious metals, and one point to which Hume returns several times, as can be seen from the extract I sent you – is that *'the price of labour'* only increases at the last moment, after all other commodities. Now *Mr Dühring does not breathe a word* about this, since, however much he sings Hume's praises, he treats him just as superficially as anyone else. Apart from that, if he had noticed the problem, which is more than questionable, he could not exactly celebrate the theory in front of workers, and so he had to burke the whole.

2. My peculiar mania for treating the Physiocrats as the first methodical (and not just occasionally so, like Petty etc.) *analysts of capital* and the *capitalist method of production* was something I did not wish to abandon. Once I have said this in plain words, my point of view could be taken up by quacks and immediately garbled before I have a chance of presenting it. So I have not dealt with this in the exposé I sent you.

But for Dühring it might have been fitting to indicate the following two passages in *Capital*. I quote from the *French* edition because it is less sketchy than in the German original:

With reference to the 'Tableau Economique':[1]

> Annual reproduction is a very simple process to understand, as long as it is solely considered as the sum total of annual production: but all the elements of the latter must be brought into the market. There, the movements of capital and revenues meet, mingle and are lost in a general movement of displacement – the circulation of social wealth – which distorts the observer's view and provides very complex problems for analysis. The great merit of the Physiocrats is that they were the first to attempt to depict, in their 'tableau economique', the annual production as it emerged from circulation. Their presentation was in many respects closer to the truth than that of their successors. (pp.258, 259)[2]

With reference to the definition of 'travail productif':[3]

Classical political economy has always maintained, now instinctively, now consciously, that the characteristic of productive labour was the creation of *surplus value*. Its definitions of productive labour changed in relation to the advance in the analysis of surplus value. The Physiocrats, for example, declared that only agricultural labour was productive. And why? Because it alone gave a surplus value which, for them, only existed in the form of land rent. (p.219).[4]

Although the Physiocrats did not unravel the mystery of surplus value, they knew at least that it [is] 'une richesse indépendente et disponible qu'il (the owner of it) n'a point achetée et qu'il vend'[5] (Turgot) (p.554 *Capital*, German 2nd edition) and that it could not escape *circulation* (see *Capital*, pp.141-145) . . .

[1] French: 'economic table'.
[2] This and the following passage in French in the original. The page numbers refer to the French edition of 1872 – here see *Capital*, Vol.I, FLPH Moscow 1961, pp.590-1; Penguin ed, pp.737-8.
[3] French: 'productive labour'.
[4] See *Capital*, Vol.1, FLPH Moscow 1961, pp.509; Penguin ed, p.644.
[5] French: 'An independent and available wealth which he (the owner of it) has not bought and which he sells.'

152. Marx to Engels   *July 25, 1877*

. . . *An example of the 'great acuity' of the professorial socialists:*

Even with the great acuity at Marx's command, the problem cannot be resolved: 'Use-values' (the fool forgets that we are talking about '*commodities*'), i.e. the vehicle for *pleasures* etc., cannot be '*reduced*' to their opposite, to quantities of efforts, to sacrifice etc. (The idiot believes that I want to 'reduce' the *use-values* to *value*, by comparison of value.) That is a substitution of alien things. The *identi*fication of *different kinds* of use-values can only be explained by a reduction of the same to a common use-valuable.

(Why not rather to . . . *weight?*).[1] — Thus dixit[2] Herr *Knies*, the critical genius of professorial economy . . .

[1] The German word 'Gewicht' (weight) here has the connotation of 'balance' (German: 'Gleichgewicht'), since Marx stressed the first part of the word '*Gleich*setzung' (*iden-ti*fication) shortly before. 'Balance' was the bourgeois economic ideal.
[2] Latin: 'he said'.

153. Marx to Engels

August 1, 1877

... A propos *'value'*, Kaufmann, in the first chapter of his *Teoriya Kolyebanya Tsyen*[1] on 'value' (which is very paltry, in fact absolutely faulty, but not uninteresting), makes the following absolutely correct remark after a review of assorted epigones of sophistication among contemporaneous German, French and English scholastics:

> In our review of the doctrines on value ... we saw that the political economists have quite understood the importance of this category ... However, all those who dealt with economic science were aware of the fact that the meaning of value was enormously increased in figures of speech, but in fact then forgot this as quickly as they could, as soon as they had pontificated upon it to some extent in the introduction; it is impossible to quote *even a single example* where the remarks on value stand in any organic relation to what is said about other questions – where the statements on value in the introduction exert any influence at all on the following discussions. Here I have naturally referred only the pure category of 'value', separate from *'price'*.

This indeed is the signature of all vulgar economy. Adam Smith initiated it; his few profound and surprising applications of the theory of value are contained in passing statements which have no influence at all on his deductions ex professo.[2] Ricardo's great sin, which made him indigestible from the start, was precisely the attempt to prove the correctness of his theory of value by those economic facts which seemed to contradict it most ...

[1] In fact, chapter 2 of I.I. Kaufmann, *Theory of Price Fluctuation. An Investigation*, Charkov 1867.
[2] Latin: 'official, real'.

154. Marx to Schott

November 3, 1877

Best thanks for your letters.

Your offer to procure me some things from France, Italy, Switzerland, etc. is very welcome, although I am unwilling to make too great a demand on you. By the way, I can easily wait, without being hindered in my work in any way, because I alternate between the various parts of the work. In fact, I began *Capital* privately precisely in the opposite order (beginning with the third, historical section) to that in which the public received it, although Volume I, lately attacked, was prepared for print-immediately, while the other two remained in the raw state which all research originally possesses . . .

1878

155. Engels to Bracke   *April 30, 1878*

... I think you anticipate the future a little too much in your conception of the 'Reichseisenbahn'[1] and of the monopoly of tobacco. Apart from the enormous growth in power which Prussia would gain firstly from total financial independence of any control and secondly from direct control of the two new armies – that of the railway clerks and that of the tobacco sellers – and the power and corruption of assigning positions – apart from all that, we should not forget that any transference of industrial and commercial functions into the hands of the State today could have a double significance and a double effect, according to circumstances: one would be reactionary, a retreat to the Middle Ages, and one progressive, a step towards communism. But we in Germany have just crawled out of the Middle Ages and are only now in the process of entering modern bourgeois society with the aid of big industry and crisis. What is required for the greatest possible development is precisely the *bourgeois* economic regime which concentrates capital and forces opposites to a climax, particularly in the north-east. The economic dissolution of feudal conditions east of the Elbe is, in my opinion, the most urgent development for us. Then comes the dissolution of the small factory in industry and of the workshop in the whole of Germany and their replacement by large-scale industry. And that, in the end, is only the good side of the tobacco monopoly — with one blow, one of the most infamous cottage industries would be transformed into big industry. On the other hand, State tobacco workers would also be placed under the

Emergency Laws, be robbed of the right of coalition and of striking, which would be even worse. Imperial railways and the tobacco monopoly are not necessarily State industries for us – at least, the railways not *yet*, they are only just becoming that in England; Post and Telegraph, on the other hand, *are* necessarily so. And for all the disadvantages which would be brought by these new State monopolies, the only compensation would be that there would be an easy new phrase for agitation. For a State monopoly which was only arranged for financial and power-political purposes, and not from a pressing inner need, would not give us even one correct argument. And the foundation of the tobacco monopoly and the abolition of the tobacco cottage industry would take at least as much time as the longest possible life of Bismarckism. You can also rely on the Prussian State to debase the *quality* of the tobacco and increase the prices so much that the supporters of free enterprise will point gleefully at this indictment of State communism and the people will be forced to concede. The whole thing is one of Bismarck's ignorant fantasies, quite worthy of his 1863 plan to annex Poland and to Germanise it in three years . . .

[1] 'Imperial Railway' – a name for the nationalised railway system under the control of the central government of the German Empire, as opposed to the multitude of privately-owned railways in Germany at that time.

156.   Marx to Danielson[1]   *November 15, 1878*

. . . In regard to the second edition of the *Capital*, I beg to remark:

1. I wish that the *divisions into chapters* – and the same holds good for the *subdivisions* – be made according to the French edition;

2. that the translator compares always carefully the second German edition with the French one, since the latter contains many important changes and additions (though, it is true, I was also sometimes obliged – principally in the first chapter – to 'aplatir'[2] the matter in its French version).

3. *Some changes* I consider useful – I *shall try to get ready* for you at all events *within eight days*, so that I may dispatch them Saturday next (today is Friday).

As soon as *the II volume* of the *Capital* will go in print – but this will hardly be before the end of 1879 – you shall get the manuscript in the way demanded.

I have received some publications from Petersburg, for which my best thanks. Of the polemics of *Chicherin* and other people against me, I have seen nothing, save what you sent me in 1877 (one article of Sieber, and the other, I think, of Mikhailov[sky], both in the 'Fatherlandish Annals', in reply to that odd would-be Encyclopaedist – Mr Zhukovsky). Professor Kovalevsky, who is here, told me that there had been rather lively polemics on the *Capital*.

The English crisis, which I announced on p.354 of the French edition in a footnote, has finally broken on us during the last few weeks. Some friends – theoreticians and businessmen — begged me to suppress this footnote, because it seemed ill-informed to them. They were so convinced that the crises in North and South America and those in Germany and Austria would have to, so to speak, 'discount' the English crisis.

The first country where business will follow an *ascending* curve will be the *United States* of North America.[3] Only this improvement will there set in under conditions altogether altered – for the worse. The people will try in vain to get rid of the monopolising power and the (as far as the *immediate happiness* of the masses is concerned) baneful influence of the great companies swaying industry, commerce, property in land, railroad, finance – at an always accelerating rate since the outbreak of the Civil War. The best Yankee writers are loud in proclaiming the stubborn fact that, if the Anti-Slavery War has broken the chains of the black, it has on the other hand enslaved the white producers.

The most interesting field for the economist is now certainly to be found in the United States, and, above all, during the period of 1873 (since the crash in September) until 1878 – the period of chronic crisis. Transformations – which to be elaborated did require in England centuries – were here realised in a few years. But the observer must look not to the older States on the Atlantic, but to the newer ones (*Ohio* is a striking example) and the newest (*California* for instance). The imbeciles in Europe, who fancy that theoreticians like myself and others are at the root of the evil, might learn a wholesome lesson by reading the *official* Yankee reports.

You would much oblige me by some information which you as a banker must possess – on the present state of Russian finance.

[1] This letter is in English in the original (but see Note 3 below).
[2] French: 'to level out, to make simple or plain'.
[3] This sentence and the preceding paragraph are in French in the original.

1879

157. Marx to Danielson[1]

April 10, 1879

. . . And now, primo, I am obliged to tell you (cela est tout-à-fait confidentiel)[2] that I have been informed from Germany, my II volume *could not be published so long as* the present regime was maintained in its present severity. This news, considering the status quo, did not surprise me, and, I must confess, was far from annoying me – for these reasons:

Firstly: I should under no circumstances have published the II volume before the present English industrial crisis had reached its climax. The phenomena are this time singular, in many respects different from what they were in the past and this – quite apart from other modifying circumstances – is easily accounted for by the fact that never before the *English crisis was preceded* by tremendous and now already five years lasting crisis in the *United States, South America, Germany, Austria,* etc.

It is therefore necessary to watch the present course of things until their maturity before you can 'consume' them 'productively', I mean *'theoretically'*.

One of the singular aspects of the present state is this: There have, as you know, been crashes of banks in Scotland and in some of the English counties, principally the Western (of Cornwallis and Wales) ones. Still the real *centre of the money market* – not only of the United Kingdom, but of the world –, *London*, has till now been little affected. On the contrary, save a few exceptions, the immense joint stock bank companies, like the Bank of England, have as yet only *profited* of the general prostration. And what this prostration is, you may judge from the utter despair of the English commercial and industrial philistine of seeing ever better times again! I have not seen the like, I have never witnessed a similar moral dislocation although I was in London in 1857 and 1866!

There is no doubt, one of the circumstances favourable to the London money market is the state of the *Bank of France*, which, since the recent development of the intercourse between the two countries, has become a *succoursale*[3] to the Bank of England. The Bank of France keeps an immense amount of bullion, the convertibility of its bank notes being not yet re-established, and at the signal of any perturbation of the London stock exchange French money flows in to buy securities momentarily depreciated. If, during last autumn, the French money had been suddenly withdrawn, the Bank of England would certainly have had refuge to its last remedy *in extremis*, the *suspension of the Bank Act*, and in that case we would have had the monetary crash.

On the other hand, the quiet way in which the restauration of cash payments was effected in the United States, has removed all strain from that corner upon the resources of the Bank of England. But what till now mainly contributed to prevent an explosion within the London money market, is the apparently quiet state of the banks of *Lancashire* and the other industrial districts (saving the mining districts of the West), though it is sure and ascertained, that these banks have not only invested great part of their resources in discounting of bills of, and advances upon, unprofitable transactions of the manufacturers, but have as for instance at Oldham, sunk a great part of their capital in the foundation of new fabrics. At the same time stocks, mainly of cotton produce, are daily accumulating not only in Asia (India principally) whither they are sent on consignment, but at Manchester etc. etc. How this state of things could pass away without a general crash among the manufacturers, and, consequently, among the local banks reacting directly upon the London money market – is difficult to foresee.

Meanwhile strikes and disturbances are general.

I remark *en passant*[4] that during the past year – so bad for all other business – the *railways* have been flourishing, but this was only due to extraordinary circumstances, like the Paris exhibition etc. In truth, the railways keep up an appearance of prosperity, by accumulating debts, increasing from day to day their *capital account*.

However the course of this crisis may develop itself – although most important to observe in its details for the student of capitalistic production and the professional théoricien[5] – , it will pass over, like its predecessors, and initiate a new 'industrial cycle' with all its diversified phases of prosperity, etc.

But under the cover of this 'apparently' solid English society, there lurks another crisis – *the agricultural* one which will work great and serious changes in its social structure. I shall recur to this subject on another occasion. It would lead me too far at present.

Secondly: The bulk of materials, I have not only from *Russia*, but from the *United States* etc., make it pleasant for me to have a 'pretext' of continuing my studies, instead of winding them up finally for the public.

Thirdly: My medical adviser has warned me to shorten considerably my 'working day' if I were not desirous to relapse into the state of 1874 and the following years where I got giddy and unable to proceed after a few hours of serious application.

In regard to your most remarkable letter I shall confine myself to a few observations. The railways sprang first up as the 'couronnement de l'oeuvre'[6] in those countries where *modern industry was most developed*, England, United States, Belgium, France etc. I call them the 'couronnement de l'oeuvre' not only in the sense, that they were at last (together with steamships for oceanic intercourse and the telegraphs) the *means of communication* adequate to the modern means of production, but also in so far as they were the basis of immense joint-stock companies, forming at the same time a new starting point for all *other sorts* of joint-stock companies, to commence by banking companies. They gave in one word an impetus never before suspected to the *concentration of capital* and also to the accelerated and immensely enlarged *cosmopolitan activity of loanable* capital, thus embracing the whole world in a network of financial swindling and mutual *indebtedness*, the capitalistic form of 'international' brotherhood.

On the other hand, the appearance of the railway system in the leading states of capitalism allowed, and even forced, states where capitalism was confined to a few summits of society, to suddenly create and enlarge their capitalistic *superstructure* in dimensions altogether disproportionate to the bulk of the social body, carrying on the great work of production in the traditional modes. There is, therefore, not the least doubt that in those states the railway creation has accelerated the social and political disintegration, as in the more advanced states it hastened the final development, and therefore the final change, of capitalistic production. In all states, except England, the governments enriched and fostered the railway companies at the expense of the public exchequer. In the United States to their profit great part of the public land they received as a present, not only the land necessary for the construction of the lines, but many miles of land along both sides the lines, covered with forests etc. They became so the greatest landlords, the small immigrating farmers preferring of course lands so situated as to ensure their produce ready means of transport.

The system inaugurated in France by Louis Philippe, of handing over the railways to a small band of financial aristocrats, endowing them with long terms of possession, guaranteeing the interest out of the public pocket, etc. etc., was pushed to the utmost limit by Louis Bonaparte whose régime, in fact, was essentially based upon the traffic in railway concessions, to some of which he was so kind as to make presents of canals, etc.

But in Austria, and Italy above all the railways were a new source of unbearable state indebtedness and grinding of the masses.

Generally, the railways gave of course an immense impulse to the development of foreign commerce, but this commerce in countries which export principally *raw produce* increased the misery of the masses. Not only that the new indebtedness, contracted by the governments on account of the railways, increased the *bulk of imposts* weighing upon them, but from the moment every local production could be converted into cosmopolitan gold, many articles *formerly cheap*, because invendible to a great degree, such as fruit, wine, fish, deer, etc., became *dear* and were withdrawn from the consumption of the people, while, on the other hand, the *production itself*, I mean the special *sort of produce* was changed according to its *greater or minor suitableness for exportation*, while formerly it was principally adapted to its consumption *in loco*. Thus for instance in Schleswig-Holstein agricultural land was converted into pasture, because the export of cattle was more profitable, but, at the same time, the agricultural population was driven away. All the changes very useful indeed for the great landed proprietor, the usurer, the merchant, the railways, the bankers and so forth, but very dismal for the real producer!

It is, to conclude by this my letter (since the time for putting it to post draws nearer and nearer), impossible to find real analogies between the United States and Russia. In the former the expenses of the government diminish daily and its public debt is quickly and yearly reduced; in the latter bankruptcy is a goal more and more appearing to become unavoidable. The former has freed itself (although in a most infamous way, for the advantage of the creditors and at the expense of the menu peuple)[7] of its paper money, the latter has no more flourishing fabric than that of paper money. In the former the concentration of capital and the gradual expropriation of the masses is not only the vehicle, but also the natural offspring (though artificially accelerated by the Civil War) of an unprecedented rapid industrial development, agricultural progress etc.; the latter reminds you rather of the times of Louis XIV and Louis XV, where the financial, commercial, industrial superstructure, or rather the *façades* of the social edifice, looked (although they had a much [more] solid foundation than in Russia) like a satyre upon the stagnant state of the bulk of production (the agricultural one) and the famine of the producers. The United States have at present much overtaken England in the rapidity of economical progress, though they lag still behind in the extent of acquired wealth, but at the same time the masses are quicker, and have greater political means in their hands, to resent the form of a progress accomplished at their expense. I need not prolong the antitheses.

A propos. Which do you consider the best Russian work on credit and banking?

Mr. Kaufmann was so kind as to send me his book on 'theory and practice of banking', but I was rather astonished that my former intelligent critic in the Petersburger *Messager de l'Europe*, had converted himself into a sort of Pindar of modern stock exchange swindling. Besides, considered merely – and I expect generally nothing else of books of this kind – from Fachtstandpunkt,[8] it is far from original in its details. The best part in it is the polemics against paper money.

It is said that certain foreign bankers with whom a certain government desired to contract new loans, have asked as a guarantee – a constitution. I am far from believing this, because their modern method of doing the business was, till now at least, and would be, very indifferent as to forms of government.

[1] This letter in English in original.
[2] French: 'this is quite confidential'.
[3] French: 'a branch'.
[4] French: 'in passing'.
[5] French: 'theoretician'.
[6] French: 'crowning achievement'.
[7] French: 'little people'.
[8] German: 'the standpoint of the specialist'.

158. Marx to Cafiero[1]   *July 29, 1879*

My most sincere thanks for the two copies of your work! Some time ago I received two similar books, one written in Serbo-Croat, the other in English (published in the United States), but they both sinned in attempting to give a succinct and popular resumé of *Capital* while simultaneously keeping too pedantically to the scientific *form* of the argument. In this way, I think they more or less flew wide of the main target of the resumés, which was to impress the public. And that is the great superiority of your work!

As for the concept of the thing, I believe I am not mistaken in finding an apparent gap in your observations in the introduction, which is that there is no proof that the *material conditions* necessary for the emancipation of the proletariat are spontaneously engendered from the process of production . . .[2]

For the rest, I share your opinion – if I have understood your introduction correctly – that we should not over-burden the minds of those whom we wish to educate. Nothing is preventing you from returning to the matter at a favourable moment in order to emphasise further this materialist basis of *Capital* . . .

[1] This letter in French in original.

[2] After this, Marx had written and then deleted: 'and the class struggle which finally becomes social revolution.

'The thing that distinguishes critical and revolutionary socialism from its predecessors, in my opinion, is precisely this materialist basis. It shows that, at a certain stage of historical development, the animal has to transform itself into a man.'

1880

159. Marx to Domela-Nieuwenhuis *June 27, 1880*

. . . After reading your essays in the *Jahrbuch der Sozialwissenschaft* (Vol.I, Part II), I have not the least doubt that you are quite the most suitable man to give the Dutch a resumé of *Capital*. – I also note en passant that Herr Schramm (K.A.S. p.61),[1] *misunderstands* my *theory of value*. He could have noticed this just from a footnote in *Capital*, where I say that A. Smith and Ricardo are [wrong] when they confuse *value* and *production price* (and that is to say nothing about *market prices*), that the connection between 'value' and 'production price', i.e. between 'value' and the prices which oscillate around the 'production price', do not belong at all to the theory of value as such and even less can they be *anticipated* by general scholastic phrase-mongering.

The second part of *Capital* cannot appear in Germany in the present circumstances, which is quite fortunate for me [in] so far as certain economic phenomena have entered a new stage of development in this very period, and these demand new study.

---

[1] K.A. Schramm, *The Foundations of Economy*, Leipzig 1876. Marx refers to page 61, but this should be p.81.

1881

160. Engels to Kautsky

. . . Since you are thinking of coming here soon, an extensive *written* critique of your book,[1] which you most kindly sent me, would be a fairly superfluous task, for I shall certainly have the pleasure of discussing it with you in conversation, and so I will restrict myself to a few minor points.

1. What you say on p.66 etc. is rendered invalid by the fact that there are other, real differences between surplus value and capital profit than the percentage calculation on the variable or on the total capital. In *Anti-Dühring* p.182[2] the relevant main sections of *Capital* are presented.

2. Even the professorial socialists obstinately call upon us proletarian socialists to solve their puzzle for them – how to avoid some imminent over-population and the resulting danger of the collapse of the new order of society, then that is still no reason why I should do these people a favour. I consider it a pure waste of time to dispel all the scruples and doubts of these people – which are only a result of their own confused superwisdom – or even, for example, to refute all the enormous mass of rubbish which Schäffle alone has collated in his many weighty works. We would also end up with a fair-sized volume just to correct all the *false references* from *Capital* which these gentlemen have supposedly quoted. They should first learn to read and to copy before demanding answers to their questions.

In addition, I do not regard the question at all urgent at a moment when mass production in America – which has only just developed –

and *really* large-scale agriculture formally threatens to suffocate as under the weight of food produce; on the eve of a revolution which will of necessity have this consequence, among others, that the *earth will only begin to be populated* – as you say pp.169-170, although you pass over this point far too lightly – and which *needs*, *urgently*, a great increase in population in Europe as well.

Euler's calculations have exactly the same value as the one about the silver coin which, invested in Anno 1 of our calendar at an accumulating interest, would now be worth something like $\frac{1.2^{144}}{60}$ guilder, which is a lump of silver larger than the earth. When you say p.169 that the social situation in America is not so very different from that in Europe, then that can only apply to the big towns on the coast or even only to the outward legal forms there. The great mass of the American population certainly live in conditions which are extremely favourable for an increase in population. This is shown by the flood of immigration. And even so, 30 years will be required to double it. There is no need for scaremongering.

There is of course the abstract possibility that the human population will become so great that limits to growth must be set. But if the communist society should find itself compelled to regulate the production of people in the same way that it will already have regulated the production of things, then precisely this society and this one alone, will be in a position to do so without difficulty. I do not think that it should be so difficult for such a society to reach a planned result which has already been reached naturally and without a plan in France and Lower Austria. In any case, it will be up to those people to choose whether, when, how and which means they use. I do not feel obliged to make suggestions or to give you any advice on this. These people will doubtless be able to consider the matter as well as ourselves.

By the way, in 1844 I wrote (*Deutsch-Französische Jahrbücher*, p.109): 'Even if Malthus were entirely correct, then this transformation would have to be undertaken on the spot, since it alone, and the education of the masses which it provides, would make it possible to place a moral restriction on the urge to procreate which Malthus himself presents as the most effective and simple counter-measure to over-population.'

And now enough of this, we can discuss the other points when we meet. You are quite correct to come here. You are one of the few from the younger generation who takes the trouble to really learn something and that will stand you in good stead in escaping the atmosphere of 'un-criticism' which is rotting all the present historical and economic literature of Germany.

[1] K. Kautsky, *The Influence of Population Increases on Social Progress*, Vienna 1880.
[2] See *Anti-Dühring*, Section II, chapters 5-8.

161. Marx to Danielson[1]   *February 19, 1881*

. . . I have read with the greatest interest your article[2] which is in the best sense of the word 'original'. Hence the boycotting. If you break through the webs of routine thought, you are always sure to be 'boycotted' in the first instance; it is the only arm of defence which in their first perplexity the *routiniers*[3] know how to wield. – I have been 'boycotted' in Germany for many many years, and am still so in England, with that little variation that from time to time something so absurd and asinine is launched against me that I would blush to take any public notice of it. But try on! The next thing to do – in my opinion – is to take up the wonderfully increasing *indebtedness of the landlords*, the upper class representatives of agriculture, and show them how they are 'crystallised' in the retort under the control of the 'new pillars of society'.

I am very anxious to see your polemics with the *Slovo*. As soon as I shall sail in more quiet waters I shall enter more fully upon your *Esquisse*.[4] For the present I cannot omit one observation. The soil being exhausted and getting not the elements – by artificial and vegetable and animal manure etc. – to supply its wants, will with the changing favour of the seasons, of circumstances independent of human influence – still continue to yield harvests of very different amounts, though, summing up a period of years, as for instance from 1870 to 1880, the stagnant character of the production presents itself in the most striking character. Under such circumstances the favourable climatic conditions pave the way to a *famine year* by quickly consuming and setting free the mineral fertilisers still latest on the soil, while *vice versa* a *famine year*, and still more a series of bad years following it, allow the soil-inherent minerals to accumulate anew, and to work efficiently with returning favour of the climatic conditions. Such a process goes of course everywhere on but *elsewhere* it is checked by the modifying intervention of the agriculturist himself. It becomes *the only regulating factor* where man has ceased to be a 'power' – for want of means.

So we have *1870* an excellent harvest in your country, but that year is a *climax year*, and as such immediately followed by a very bad one; the year *1871*, the very bad harvest, must be considered as the starting point for a new little cycle, till we come to the new climax year 1874, which is immediately followed by the famine year 1875; then the upwards movement begins again, ending in the still worse famine year 1880. The summing up of the years during the whole period proves that the average annual production remained the same and that the mere natural factors have alone produced the changes comparing the single years and the smaller cycles of years.

I wrote you some time ago, that if the great industrial and commercial crisis England has passed through, went over without the culminating financial crash at London, this *exceptional* phenomenon was only due to – French money. This is now seen and acknowleged even by English routiniers. Thus the *Statist* (January 29, 1881) says: 'The money market has only been so easy as it has been during the past years *through an accident*. The *Bank of France* in the early autumn permitted its stock of gold bullion to fall from £30 millions to £22 millions . . . *Last autumn undoubtedly there was a very narrow escape.*' (!)

The *English railway system* rolls on the same inclined plane as the European *public debt system*. The ruling magnates amongst the different railway-nets directors contract not only – progressively – new loans *in order to enlarge their network*, id est the 'territory', where they rule as absolute monarchs, but they enlarge their respective networks *in order to have new pretexts for engaging in new loans* which enable them to pay the interest due to the holders of obligations, preferential shares etc., and also from time to time to throw a sop to the much ill-used common shareholders in the shape of somewhat increased dividends. This pleasant method must one day or another terminate in an ugly catastrophe.

In the *United States* the railway kings have become the butt of attack, not only, as before this, on the part of the farmers and other industrial *'entrepreneurs'* of the *West*, but also on the part of the grand representative of commerce – the *New York Chamber of Commerce*. The Octopus railway king and financial swindler *Gould* has, on his side, told the New York commercial magnates: 'You now attack the railways, because you think them most vulnerable considering their present unpopularity; but take heed: after the railways *every sort of corporation* (means in the Yankee dialect *joint stock company*) will have its turn; then, later on, *all forms of associated capital*; finally *all forms of capital*; you are thus paving the way to

– *Communism* whose tendencies are already more and more spreading among the people.' M. Gould 'a le flair bon'.[5]

In India serious complications, if not a general outbreak, is in store for the British government. What the English take from them annually in the form of rent, dividends for railways useless to the Hindus; pensions for military and civil servicemen, for Afghanistan and other wars, etc. etc. – what they take from them *without any equivalent* and *quite apart* from what they appropriate to themselves annually *within* India – , speaking only of the *value of the commodities* the Indians have *gratuitously* and annually to send over to England, it amounts to *more than the total sum of income of the 60 millions of agricultural and industrial labourers of India!* This is a bleeding process, with a vengeance! The famine years are pressing each other and *in dimensions* till now not yet suspected in Europe! There is an actual conspiracy going on wherein Hindus and Mussulmans cooperate; the British government is aware that something is 'brewing', but this shallow people (I mean the governmental men), stultified by their own parliamentary ways of talking and thinking, do not even desire to see clear, to realise the whole extent of the imminent danger! To delude others and by deluding them to delude yourself – this is: *parliamentary wisdom* in a nutshell! Tant mieux![6]

Can you tell me whether Professor Lankester's '*Chapter on Deterioration*' (I have seen it quoted in your article) is translated into Russian? He is a friend of mine.[7]

Last month we had here Russian visitors, amongst others Professor Sieber (now settled at Zürich) and Mr Kablukov (Moscow). They were all day long studying at the British Museum.

No news of our 'mutual' friend?[8]

A propos. *Janson's* last statistical work – comparing Russia with Europe – has made much sensation. I should be glad to see it . . .

---

[1] This letter in English in original.

[2] i.e. Danielson's 'Sketches on our People's Economy after the Reform', which appeared in the periodical *Slovo* ('The Word') in October 1880; later published as a book in 1893.

[3] French 'routinist, pen-pusher'.

[4] French: 'sketch'.

[5] French: 'has a good nose'.

[6] French: 'So much the better!'

[7] E.R. Lankester, *Degeneration. A Chapter in Darwinism*, London 1880.

[8] H. Lopatin – arrested in 1877 in Russia.

162.   Marx to Zasulich[1]

A nervous ailment, which has assailed me periodically for the past ten years, has prevented me from replying sooner to your letter of 16th February. I regret that I cannot give you a concise explanation suitable for publication of the question which you did me the honour of asking.[2] Several months have passed since I promised a paper on the same subject for the Committee of St Petersburg. However, I hope that a few lines will suffice to leave you in no doubt about the misunderstanding concerning my supposed theory.

In analysing the genesis of capitalist production, I said:

> Thus, the capitalist system is based on the radical separation of the producer from the means of production ... The basis of this whole evolution is the *expropriation of the peasants*. Only in England has this been accomplished in a radical manner ... But *all the other Western European countries* are undergoing the same process.[3] (*Capital*, French edition, p.315)

The 'historical inevitability' of this process is thus expressly restricted to *Western European countries*. The reason for this restriction is indicated in this passage from chapter XXXII:

> *Private property* produced by the labour of the individual ... is supplanted by *capitalist private property*, which rests on the exploitation of the labour of others, on wage labour. (*ibid*., p.340)[4]

Thus in this development in Western Europe we are dealing with the *transformation of one form of private property into another form of private property*. With the Russian peasantry, on the contrary, *their communal property will be transformed into private property*.

The analysis in *Capital*, therefore, offers reasons neither for nor against the vitality of the rural community, but the special study which I have made of it, and for which I found material in original sources, has convinced me that this community is the fulcrum for the social regeneration of Russia; but in order for it to function as such, the destructive influences which assail it on all sides must first be eliminated and then normal circumstances for a spontaneous development will be assured ...

[1] This letter in French in original.

[2] On 16th February 1881, Vera Zasulich wrote to Marx:

'You would render us a great service if you gave us your opinion on the possible future of our village communities and on the theory that all the countries of the world must inevitably pass through all the phases of capitalist production.' Marx drew up five draft replies to this letter.

[3] See *Capital*, Vol.I, FLPH Moscow 1961, pp.714-16; Penguin ed, pp.874-6. Marx quotes here from the French edition, which differed slightly from the German original – Marx described it as possessing 'a scientific value independent of the original and should be consulted even by readers familiar with German' (*Capital*, Vol.I, p.22 FLPH ed.).

[4] See *Capital*, Vol.I, FLPH Moscow 1961, p.714.

163. Engels to Bernstein

March 12, 1881

. . . Otherwise the paper[1] is generally very good, individual editions are very good indeed, and a few less doctrinaire articles, like the one on State Socialism, would not go amiss. How can one lump Turgot, one of the very first economists of the 18th century, together with that most practical man of haute finance, Necker, the ancestor of the Lafittes and Pereires, and even with the dismal Calonne, the man who lives from hand to mouth, a real aristocrat – 'Après nous le déluge'?[2] How can these men, especially Turgot and even Necker, be compared with Bismarck, who at best just wants money at any price – à la Calonne, and then how can Bismarck be compared with Stoecker, or with Schäffle and Co., who all go in such different directions? If the bourgeoisie lump them all together, then that is no reason why we should do the same thing uncritically. Exactly this is the root of doctrinairism: one *believes* the partisan and narrow-minded statements of one's opponents and then builds a system on those statements which actually stands or falls by them. With Bismarck, it is money, more money, and three times money, and so his excuses for it only change in appearance. Give him another kind of majority in parliament and he will jettison all his plans and make quite different ones. So one can never ever find a statement of bankruptcy of modern society in anything said by such a theoretically unreasonable and such a practically vacillating animal as Bismarck; and just as little in the spiritual St Vitus' Dances of a fool like Stoecker, nor in the rubbish of 'thinking men' à la Schäffle. These people never 'think' about declaring the bankruptcy of society (they find it enough to 'think'). Rather, they only live in order to patch society up again. But Schäffle, for example, is a 'thinking man': in essence, the stupid Swabian confesses that he has reflected for full ten years on one (the simplest) point in *Capital* before grasping it, and then his understanding is pure idiocy!

It is simply a partisan falsification by the Manchester bourgeoisie to call every interference of the State in free competition 'Socialism': protective tariffs, guilds, tobacco monopolies, nationalisation of certain branches of industry, the merchant navy, the royal porcelain factory. We should *criticise* this, but not *believe* it. If we do the latter and develop a theory on that basis, then the theory will collapse along with its premises, i.e. with the simple proof that this supposed socialism is nothing but feudal reaction on the one side and, on the other, an excuse to print money with the side effect of transforming as many proletarians as possible into employees and pensioners of the State, and of organising an army of workers alongside the disciplined army of war and of civil servants. Compulsory voting brought about by superiors in the State instead of by factory foremen – that's a fine kind of socialism! But that is where we end up if we believe the bourgeoisie – and they do not believe it themselves, but only claim to: that the State = Socialism.

[1] The daily socialist newspaper, *Der Sozialdemokrat* (1879-1890), central organ of the SPD during illegality. Edited by Bernstein from 1881.
[2] French: 'after us let the floods come'.

164. Marx to Sorge   *June 20, 1881*

...I had already received two other books before your copy of Henry George[1] – one from Swinton and one from Willard Brown: so I gave one to Engels, and one to Lafargue. Today I have to limit myself to formulating my opinion of the book, concisely.

Theoretically, the man is totally arrière.[2] He has understood nothing about the nature of *surplus value* and so scurries around, in the English manner, in speculations which even the English have abandoned concerning the independent parts of surplus value – the relation of profit, rent, interest etc. His basic dogma is that *everything would be all right* if the land rent were paid to the State. (You will also find this kind of payment in the *transitional measures* contained in the *Communist Manifesto*). This view originally belonged to bourgeois economists; it was first put forward (apart from similar demands at the end of the 18th century) by the first *radical* followers of Ricardo, immediately after his death. In 1847 I wrote about this in my article against Proudhon: 'We understand that economists such as Mill' (the elder, not his son John Stuart who also repeated this in a somewhat modified form), 'Cherbuliez, Hilditch and others demand that rent should be handed over to the State in place of taxes. That is a frank expression of the hatred which the *industrial capitalist* bears towards the *landed proprietor*, who seems to him a useless thing, an excrescence upon the general body of bourgeois production.'[3]

We ourselves, as already mentioned, adopted this appropriation of land rent by the State as one of many other *transitional measures* which, as noted in the *Manifesto*, are and must be contradictory in themselves.

But the first person to draw the *socialist panacea* from this desideratum of the *radical* English bourgeois economists, to declare this procedure as the solution of the antagonisms contained in today's mode of production, was *Colins*, a Belgian-born one-time Napoleonic hussar officer from Paris who, in the last period of Guizot and the first of Napoleon le petit,[4] gave joy to the world with his thick volumes on his 'discovery', just as he made that other discovery that there is no God, but that there is an *'immortal'* human soul, and that the animals have 'no sensitivity'. For, you see, if they had any sensitivity, i.e. a soul, then we would be cannibals and a Kingdom of Righteousness on earth could never be founded. His 'anti-landownership theory', along with his soul-etc. theory, has been preached for years in the Parisian monthly *Philosophie de l'Avenir*[5] by his few remaining followers, mostly Belgians. They call themselves *'collectivistes rationnels'*[6] and sing the praises of Henry George. After them and along with them the Prussian banker and one-time lottery collector, Samter from East Prussia, a bone-head, has flogged this 'socialism' in a thick volume.

And these 'socialists' since Colins have this in common: they allow *wage labour* and hence also *capitalist production*, to continue, by attempting to convince themselves or the rest of the world that *all the faults* of capitalist production must vanish by themselves if land rent is transformed into tax paid to the State. So the whole thing is only an attempt, in socialist guise, to *save the rule of the capitalists* and in fact to *re-establish it* on an even wider basis than the present.

This cloven hoof, which is also a mule's hoof, is clearly seen poking out of the declamations of Henry George. With him it is even more unpardonable since he should have posed the question the other way about: how was it that, in the United States where the land was relatively – i.e. compared with civilised Europe – accessible to the large mass of the people and to a certain degree (again relatively) still is, the capitalist economy and the corresponding enslavement of the working class has developed *more quickly* and *more shamelessly* than in any other country?

On the other hand, George's book, and the impact it has made on you, is significant in that it is a first – if unsuccessful – attempt at liberation from orthodox political economy.

By the way, H. George seems to know nothing about the history of earlier *American Anti-Renters*, who were more practical than theoretical. Otherwise he is a talented writer (also talented at giving the Yankees a good advertisement), as can be seen from his article on California in the *Atlantic*. He is also possessed of an objectionable modesty and exagg- eration, which is the hallmark of all such panacea-mongers . . .

[1] H. George, *The Land Question etc* . . ., 3rd edition of *The Irish Land Question*, London.

[2] French: 'backward'.

[3] This quotation in French in original.

[4] Napoleon the Small, i.e. Louis Bonaparte.

[5] French: 'The Philosophy of the Future'.

[6] French: 'Rational Collectivists'.

1882

165. Engels to Bernstein *January 25[-31]*, 1882

. . . Bürkli's interest-bearing mortgage bills,[1] which are supposed to represent money, are even older than that original confused Old Hegelian Pole, Cieszkovsky. Similar plans for the greater happiness of the world were drawn up even at the time of the foundation of the Bank of England. Since Volume I of *Capital* has not yet opened the discussion on Credit (apart from the simple debt relationship), credit money *can* only be considered at best here in its simplest form (symbol of value etc.) and in relation to its subordinated money functions, but *interest-bearing* credit money cannot be discussed yet. So Bürkli is correct when he tells Schramm that all these passages from *Capital* do not relate to *his* particular paper money; and Schramm is correct when he shows Bürkli, with the help of *Capital*, that he has not the vaguest idea of the nature and function of money. But Bürkli's particular suggestion for money is not thus revealed as a nonsense; for this, apart from the general proof that this 'money' is incapable of fulfilling the basic functions of money, we require also the particular proof of the functions which such paper really can fulfil, particularly when Bürkli says: What has Marx got to do with it? I support Cieszkovsky – and Schramm's whole case against Bürkli collapses. It is fortunate that the *Sozialdemokrat* has not become involved in the whole mess. All this activity will probably subside by itself.

The fact that these crises are one of the most powerful levers in political upheavals has already been stated in the *Communist Manifesto* and is explained in the review section of the *Neue Rheinische Zeitung* up to and including 1848, but it is also explained that returning prosperity also breaks revolutions and lays the foundations for the victory of reaction. A detailed proof of this would have to take into consideration the interim crises, which are partly of a local and partly of a special nature; we are at present undergoing such an interim crisis which can be traced to pure stock-exchange swindles; until 1847 these were regular connecting links so that in my *Condition of the Working Class*, the cycle appears as five-yearly . . .

[1] K. Bürkli, *Democratic Bank Reform. Or: How Can the People Receive Cheaper Interest*, Zürich 1881.

166. Engels to Bernstein   *February 22, 1882*

. . . I suppose that Bürkli will permit every Zürich landowner to take out this kind of mortgage on his house and allow the receipt for this transaction to circulate as money. So then the mass of circulating money would be governed by the amount of the value of the property in question and not by the much smaller amount which suffices for circulation. So now we have:

1. Either bills which cannot be exchanged, and these will depreciate according to the law which Marx developed;

2. Or bills which can be exchanged, and then the amount which is surplus to circulation will return to the bank for exchange and will cease to be money, so that the bank will naturally have to invest capital.

Now, an interest-bearing money substitute – i.e. one which changes its value daily – is not suitable for circulation precisely because of this quality; firstly one must not agree the price of a commodity in real money, but rather the price of the bill. The people of Zürich would have to be worse businessmen than I thought if, if the bills were exchangeable, they did not all hasten to the bank at once to exchange them, but instead only used the old commode[1] non-interest-bearing money. Then the Central Bank would invest its own capital, and everything it could scrape together in mortgages and would do its best to procure new business capital.

But if the bills cannot be exchanged, these bills would immediately cease to be money. One would take metal or good money from the outside world, which is fortunately just a little bit bigger than the canton of Zürich, and would use that, since no one would accept these dull notes as money, for they – as you rightly say – would then be nothing but olde worlde mortgage deeds. And if the government were to insist on foisting them on the public as money, it would get its desserts . . .

¹ French: 'easy, comfortable'.

167. Engels to Bernstein   *March 10, 1882*

. . . *Bi-metallism*. The main point is that we – particularly after the terrible braggery of the main 'leaders' about the economic superiority of our Party as against the bourgeoisie, and for which these same gentlemen are quite ignorant – that we must guard against publishing such economic howlers which these same gentlemen unashamedly bandy about as soon as they think they can flatter a particular species of worker with them, or win an electoral victory or some other advantage. So because Saxony produces silver ore, people think they can be taken in by the dual currency swindle. In order to win a couple of voters, our Party would willingly disgrace itself eternally in that very area where its strength is *supposed* to lie!

But that is just like our Messrs Literati. Just like the bourgeois literati, they believe that they have the privilege of learning nothing and reasoning everything. They have scraped together a kind of literature for us which looks for colleagues in economic ignorance, half-baked utopianism and arrogance and which Bismarck does us the great pleasure of banning.

With dual currency today, it is not a question so much of dual currency in general as the particular dual currency in the relation: gold to silver at 15½:1. This difference must therefore be made.

Dual currency makes itself more impossible daily because the value-relation of gold and silver, at one time at least approximately constant and only slowly varying, now fluctuates daily and violently and in fact with the tendency to devalue silver as a result of a colossal increase in production, particularly in North America. The silver barons invent the story that gold is exhausted. But the cause of the change in value can be anything they want; the fact remains, and this is our first concern, that silver daily loses the ability to function as a measurement of value, while gold retains that ability.

The value relation of both is now approximately 17½:1. But the silver people want to impose the old relation of 15½:1 on the world once more, and this is just as impossible as maintaining machine-spun thread and cloth continually and generally at the same price as hand-spun thread and cloth. The mint does not determine the value of the coin, but only guarantees the weight and content to the recipient, so that it can never transmit the value of 17½ to 15½ pounds of silver.

All this is so clearly and exhaustively discussed in *Capital*, chapter on Money (3rd chapter, pp.72-120),[1] that nothing more need be said about it. For material relating to the latest fluctuations, see Soetbeer, *Edelmetall-Production und Werthverhältnis usw*, Gotha, Perthes 1879.[2] Soetbeer is the main authority in this field and the father of German coin reform – he preached the 'Mark' at ⅓ thaler even before 1840.

So: if silver is minted at 15½ pounds = 1 pound of gold, then it flows back into the State coffers, for everyone is trying to get rid of it. This is the experience of the United States with their silver dollar which was minted with the old content – only worth 90 cents – and equally Bismarck when he tried to re-circulate by force the silver thaler which had been withdrawn and replaced by gold.

Herr Bank President Dechend imagines that he can pay off Germany's foreign debts, through dual currency, in bad silver instead of fully-valued gold and that he can thereby avoid any gold crisis, which would of course be very commode[3] for the Reichsbank – if only it could happen. But this only goes to show that Herr Dechend proves himself to be totally incapable of being a bank president and to belong in the Debit Bank rather than in the Reichsbank.

The Prussian Junker would also be very happy if he could repay, or repay with interest, his mortgage debts (incurred à 15½:1) in silver à 17½:1. And since all this would take place in the domestic field, then this kind of cheating the creditor by the debtor would be quite feasible if – the nobleman could only find people to give him silver à 17½:1 so that he could pay off at 15½:1. For his own means would not permit him to pay. But he would also have to accept his silver at 15½:1, and so everything would remain the same for him.

As for German silver production, the yield of *German* ore annually decreases against the (Rhineland) yield from *South American* ore. In 1876, the total production in Germany was circa 280,000 pounds, of which South American ore accounted for 58,000, which has since risen sharply.

It is clear that the decline of silver to small change must depress the value of silver even more, for the use of silver for other purposes is minimal compared with its use as money and so it will not increase rapidly, because demonetisation would bring more silver on to the market.

One should never think that England will ever introduce a dual currency. No country with a gold currency can *now* reintroduce a dual currency for any length of time. *General* dual currency is already a general impossibility. If everyone agreed to set silver to 15½:1 today, then that would not alter the fact that it is only worth 17½:1, and absolutely nothing can be done about it. One could just as well agree that 2×2 are 5 ...

[1] See *Capital*, Vol.I, FLPH Moscow 1961, pp.94-145; Penguin ed, pp.188-244.
[2] A. Soetbeer, *The Production of Precious Metals and the Value Relation between Gold and Silver from the discovery of America to the Present Day*, Gotha 1879.
[3] French: 'handy, comfortable'.

168. Engels to Kautsky   *September 12, 1882*

... You ask me what English workers think of the colonial policy. Well, exactly the same as what they think of politics in general: the same as the bourgeois think. For there is no workers party here, there are only Conservatives and Liberal-Radicals, and the workers eat happily thanks to England's monopoly of the world market and colonies. In my opinion, the real colonies, that is, those countries occupied by a European population – Canada, the Cape, Australia – will all become independent; but the countries merely governed, and inhabited by natives – India, Algeria, the Dutch, Portuguese and Spanish territories – will have to be taken over rapidly by the proletariat and will have to be led towards independence as rapidly as possible. How all this will develop is difficult to say. India will perhaps have a revolution, in fact very probably, and since the self-liberating proletariat cannot conduct a colonial war, this revolution would have to be given free rein; this of course could not pass off without all kinds of destruction – but that is in any case inseparable from all revolutions. The same thing could be enacted elsewhere, for example in Algeria and Egypt, and *for us* that would certainly be the best thing. We will have enough to do at home. Once Europe is reorganised, and North America, then we shall have such a colossal power and offer such an example that the semi-civilised countries would of themselves follow in the wake; economic necessity alone would see to that. But the question of which social and political phases these countries would then have to pass through to achieve a socialist organisation for themselves, can, I believe, only be the subject for fairly idle speculation. Only one thing is certain: the victorious proletariat can never force any advance on any foreign people without undermining its own victory. Which actually does not exclude wars of defence of various kinds . . .

169.   Engels to Marx   *December 15, 1882*

. . . By the way, the general re-introduction of serfdom is one of the reasons why Germany could not develop any industry in the 17th and 18th centuries. In the first place, the *inverse* division of labour in the guilds, the opposite to that in manufacturing: instead of being divided within the workshop, it was divided *between guilds*. At this point emigration to the guild-free countryside took place in England. In Germany this was prevented by the transformation of the peasantry and the inhabitants of the farming market towns into serfs. But then the guilds finally broke up, as soon as competition in foreign manufacture made its appearance. I will leave aside the other reasons which contributed to holding back German manufacture . . .

1883

170. Engels to Bernstein

February 8, 1883

. . . Stock exchange tax. It has existed for many years in England, as a simple, everyday rubber stamp on the conveyancing document – ½ percent of the sum paid and 5 shillings clerical fee (there are few shares au porteur[1] here, and they do not qualify). So the only result of this is that the *real* stock exchange business is done in speculation for differences, where no real conveyancing takes place. So only the so-called 'solid capital investment' is affected. And even that is not so bad that stock-exchange speculators cannot by-pass it.

I am against it 1. because we must really only demand *direct* taxes and reject *all* indirect ones, so that the people know and feel what they are paying and so can tackle capital; 2. because we can never yield a single penny to *this* government.

The outcry against the stock exchange, as you rightly say, is petty-bourgeois. The exchange only alters the *distribution* of the surplus value which has *already been stolen* from the workers, and as such how this distribution takes place can only be of secondary relevance to the workers. But the exchange alters the distribution in the direction of centralisation, enormously accelerates the concentration of capital and is therefore just as revolutionary as the steam engine.

Also truly petty-bourgeois are those taxes with a moral purpose – with the exception of beer and schnapps. They are quite ridiculous here and thoroughly reactionary. If the American stock exchange had not created a colossal amount of capital, how could a great industry and a social movement ever be possible in the farming area there?

It would be very good if you could intervene in this. But with caution. The Stoeckers should not be given any room for manoeuvre here.

The third edition of *Capital*. It will probably still take some time, since Marx is still ill. His stay in Ventnor in continual rain was bad for him. The loss of his daughter has come on top of that. He has been so hoarse off and on for the past three weeks that he cannot speak much; nothing much can be done (but please do not say anything in the paper about it).

We would be grateful to you for the Rodbertus-Meyer book.[2] The man was once very close to discovering surplus value, but his Pomeranian estate prevented him . . .

Kautsky has sent me his pamphlet on American corn. Wonderful irony:[3] three years ago he said the population should be limited, because otherwise they would have nothing to eat; and now there is not enough population to eat up even the American produce! This is what comes of studying so-called 'questions' one after the other, with no connectedness. Thereby one naturally falls victim to that dialectics which – in spite of Dühring – is 'objectively inherent to things themselves' . . .

[1] 'A bearer share'.
[2] K. Rodbertus, *Letters and Socio-Political Essays*, 2 vols.
[3] See letter 160 above for a discussion on Kautsky's earlier views on food and population.

171. Engels to Bernstein   *February 10, 1883*

. . . To return to the question of stock exchange tax: we do not need to deny the 'immorality' and thievery of the stock exchange at all, we could even quite drastically describe it as the peak of capitalist competition, where property quite directly becomes theft, but then we would have to draw the conclusion that it is in no way in the interest of the proletariat to break this sharp point of modern economy, but rather to let it unfold quite freely so that even the dimmest of people can see where modern economy is leading. Moral indignation can be left to those who are covetous enough to go to the exchange without being stock-brockers themselves and then, as is normal, getting plundered. And then when stock exchange and 'solid business' get in the way of each other and when the landed junker, also trying to make some crisp paper for himself and is also inevitably fleeced, becomes the third party in the struggle among the three main sections of the exploiting class, then we, the fourth, will laugh . . .

172. Engels to Lavrov[1]   *April 2, 1883*

. . . I have found the manuscript of the 'Circulation of Capital' and of the 3rd book: 'The Structures of the Total Process'[2] – almost 1,000 pages in-folio. Up till now it has been impossible to tell if this manuscript can, in its present form, go straight to the printers. In any case, I shall have to copy it since it is a rough draft. Tomorrow I will at last have the time to spend several hours reviewing all the manuscripts which Mohr[3] has left us. In particular there is an outline of the dialectic which he always wanted to do. But he always kept the state of his work a secret; he knew that, once warned about anything he had ready, we would have bullied him until he agreed to publish it. All this is amongst ourselves, for I have no right to publish anything without Tussy, who is my literary co-executor . . .

[1] This letter in French in original.
[2] These titles in German in original.
[3] i.e. Marx.

173. Engels to Domela-Nieuwenhuis   *April 11, 1883*

. . . Marx left behind a thick manuscript for the second part of *Capital*,[1] which I must first read through (and what handwriting!), before I can tell how easily it can be printed and how much it must be supplemented by later notebooks. In any case, *the main material is there.* – Since I cannot say anything more definite, I ask you not to write anything in the press about it just now, for that would only lead to misunderstandings. Apart from that, Marx's youngest daughter Eleanor is literary co-executor with me, and I can do nothing without her, and ladies, as you know, stick to form . . .

[1] See Engels's foreword to Volume II of *Capital* for his description of the manuscript.

174.   Engels to Sorge

. . . The third edition of *Capital* is giving me the devil's own work. We have one copy in which Marx has made a note of the alterations required and the additions from the French edition, but the whole detailed work has still to be done. I have done up to the 'Accumulation', but this part involves almost a total revision of the whole theoretical section. Hence the responsibility. For the French translation is partly a dulled version of the German, and Marx would never have written German like that. And then the booksellers are putting on pressure. I cannot think of going on to Volume II without finishing this. There are at least four versions of the beginning in existence, M[arx] had set down to it so often only to be interrupted by illness when it came to the definitive revision. How the layout and the conclusion of the last one – which dates from 1878 – will concord with the first – which dates from 1870 – I cannot yet say . . .

If it had not been for the massive amount of American and Russian material (two cubic metres of Russian statistics alone), Volume II would have been printed long ago. These detailed studies kept him back for years. As usual, everything had to be complete and up to date, and now it has all come to nothing, except his notes, in which I hope to find many critical notes which can be used as footnotes for Volume II . . .

I have already read five sheets of final proofs of the third edition, the man promises to deliver three sheets per week . . .

175.   Engels to Bebel

I am making use of a moment of peace to write to you. In London with a deal of work, the many disturbances (three adults and two little children in one room!) and then the correction, the revision of a sample English translation and of a French popularisation of *Capital*,[1] just you try writing a letter!

I have corrected up to Sheet 21 of the third edition, which contains many additions, and the thing will appear by the end of the year. As soon as I am back, I will have to get down to Volume II, and that will be the devil's own work. Along with completely finished parts, others are purely outlined, all of them in rough copy with the exception of two chapters. The cited references are in no order, thrown together in heaps, just collected for later selection. And the handwriting is absolutely only legible to myself – and that with difficulty. You ask how it came about that I of all people could be kept in the dark about how ready the thing was? Quite simple: if I had known, I would have given him no respite night and day until it was quite finished and printed. And M[arx] knew that better than anyone else; he also knew that if the worst happened, as it now has, I would be able to publish the manuscript in his spirit, which is what he also told Tussy . . .

---

[1] G. Deville, *'Capital' by Karl Marx. Abridged and Accompanied by an Appendix on Scientific Socialism*, Paris 1883.

176.   Engels to Kautsky   *September 18, 1883*

. . . Generally, in all those scientific studies which cover such a broad area and massive amounts of material, anything significant can only be the fruit of many years of study. Individual new and correct views, such as appear in your articles, can be developed more readily; but to have an overview of the totality and to put it into a new order can only be done when the subject is plumbed to the depths. Otherwise books like *Capital* would be more numerous. So I am pleased to note that you deal with themes – for immediate written work – such as Biblical pre-history and colonisation, where something can still be done with less exhausting study and where the effect is still opportune. The colonisation article pleased me a great deal. Unfortunately you only used German material, which as usual is dully coloured and does not reflect the harshest glaring lights of tropical colonisation, nor the latest methods: colonisation in the interests of stock exchange swindles, as is now directly and officially practised by France in Tunisia and Tonkin. Here is a striking example of the South Seas slave trade: the attempted annexation of New Guinea etc. by Queensland was directly intended for the slave trade. On almost the same day as the annexation ship left for New Guinea, a Queensland ship, the 'Fanny', also went there and to the islands to the east in order to load up *labour*, but only returned with wounded and other unpleasant signs of battle, *without* labour. The *Daily News* reports this and remarks in an editorial that the English could scarcely accuse the French of such practices as long as they did the same! (Beginning of September) . . .

Incidentally Java provides the proof that the population has nowhere and never increased so rapidly as under the system of a not too oppressive labour bondage: 1755 – 2 million; 1826 – 5½ million; 1850 – 9 million; 1878 – 19 million; increased almost tenfold in 125 years – the only example approximating to Malthusian increases. Once they send the Dutch away the population will become fairly stable . . .

Volume II of *Capital* will still provide me with enough work. The greatest part of the manuscript dates from *before 1868* and is in places pure rough draft. The second will be a great disappointment to the Vulgar Socialists, for it contains almost exclusively strictly scientific, very fine studies on things which occur within the capitalist class itself, and so nothing from which to make catchwords and declamations . . .

1884

177. Engels to Lavrov[1]   *January 28, 1884*

    . . . As for this second volume, I am at last beginning to get a clear idea. For Book II, the circulation of capital, we have a version of the most important sections, dating from 1875 and later; that is, of the beginning and the end. There we shall only need footnotes for cited references. For the middle section there are no less than four versions dating from before 1870; that is the only difficulty. Book III: capitalist production in its totality,[2] exists in two versions from before 1869; later, there are only a few notes and a whole notebook of equations for calculating the many factors which determine the transformation of the rate of surplus value into the rate of profit. But the notes on books both on Russia and on the United States contain a whole mass of material and notes on land rent, and others relate to monetary capital, to credit, to paper money as an instrument of credit etc. I do not yet know how to make use of them for Book III; perhaps it will be better if I collect them in a separate publication; that is certainly what I shall do if incorporating them into *Capital* becomes too difficult. Above all, I want to have the book out as soon as possible, and then particularly that it should be a book by *Marx*.

    We expect copies of the 3rd edition of the 1st volume any day now, and we will send you one immediately they arrive.

    The Russian translations appearing in Geneva – the *Manifesto* etc. – gave me much pleasure.

I have just received a letter from two Poles, Krzyvizky and Sos-
novsky, asking me for our consent to a Polish translation of *Capital* –
naturally we gave it . . .

[1] This letter in French in original.
[2] Book III was not included in Vol.II but forms Vol.III of *Capital* under the title
'Capitalist Production as a Whole'.

178. Engels to Lavrov[1]   *February 5, 1884*

. . . Volume II – oh! if only you knew, my old friend, how hurried I
am with it! But six months have been lost because of my accursed illness.
And still I cannot seriously begin before mid- March; it will take me until
then to put all the books, papers, newpapers etc. in order – and I can
only work at that for a few hours during the day without tiring myself.
There is even more of a hurry because I am the *only person alive* who can
decipher this handwriting and these abbreviations of words and style. As
for publishing it in serial form, that depends partly on the editor and
partly on German legislation; up till now, I do not believe that it would
be at all effective with a book of this nature. I will attempt to do what
L[opatin] wants for the proof sheets. But now, about two months ago,
Vera Z[asulich] wrote asking me to leave the translation to her. I told her
that I would uphold Lopatin's earlier claim and that it was still too early
to discuss that; but that what could be discussed today would be the
possibility of publishing the translation in *Russia*. Do you think that
would be a possibility? Book II is purely scientific, dealing only with
questions *amongst bourgeois*; but III will contain passages which make me
doubt even the possibility of publishing them in Germany under the
emergency laws.

For the publication of the complete works of M[arx] there is the
same difficulty; and that is only one of the number of difficulties to be
overcome. I have around 60 sheets (each 16 printed pages) of old
manuscripts by M[arx] and myself between 1845 and 1848. One could
only give extracts of all this, but I will not be able to set down to it before I
have finished the manuscript of the 2nd volume of *Capital*. So there is
nothing else to be done except wait . . .

Deville has sent me his manuscript for revision. Since I was ill, I
limited myself to the theoretical part, where I found little to correct. But

the descriptive part was written too hastily; firstly, it is sometimes unintelligible for anyone who does not have the original, and then, very often, he gives M[arx]'s conclusions while remaining silent on the only situations in which these conclusions are valid; this sometimes gives a more or less false impression. I have called his attention to this, but he was in too much of a hurry to publish the book.

[1] This letter in French in original.

179. Engels to Bernstein

April 11, 1884

. . . In this Rodbertus affair, it is best that you wait until you have seen my introduction to the *Misère*;[1] you will certainly have no knowledge of the main, English points there (referring to *Misère* p . . .)[2] which make it is evident that the socialists' *use* of Ricardo's theory of value – the great hobby-horse of Rodbertus – was a well-known commonplace in England since 1820 in economics and since 1830 among socialists. I have already written to you, I believe, to say that I will prove just here that Marx was far from conceding the tiniest point to Rodbertus, but rather, even in the *Misère*, was able to criticise both the works already written and those unwritten by the said Rodbertus in advance and without knowing them. I think we would be best to wait with the attack until the *Misère* has come out in German, and then to get stuck into it. (I mean the main attack: some skirmishing is always good for provoking the Rodbertians.)

I am looking forward to your manuscript. Notabene, if the Hegelian expressions give you difficulties in the second section, then just leave spaces in the manuscript, and I will fill them in; in German we must use the correct school terminology, otherwise it will be incomprehensible.

Three copies of the third edition.[3] The enclosed *Dühring* gave me some headaches, whereupon I just put it aside, thinking that it had crept in through negligence. I never once thought that this was a hint for the second edition. That it is so gives me particular pleasure, all the more since I am now learning from different sides that the thing has had a quite unexpected (for me) effect, particularly in Russia. The tedium of a polemic with an insignificant opponent has thus not prevented the attempt to provide an encyclopaedic overview of our conception of the philosophical, natural-scientific and historical problems, from having some effect. I will just make stylistic changes and perhaps some additions in the natural-scientific section – the earlier publication in two parts was based on the way the thing appeared (as a separate print), otherwise it would have been completely nonsensical . . .

¹ *The Poverty of Philosophy*, originally written in French.
² There is a gap in the manuscript here – the reference is probably to *The Poverty of Philosophy* (1976), pp. 66-67.
³ Of Volume I of *Capital* (1883).

180. Engels to Kautsky   *April 26, 1884*

I made up my mind, as I told everybody here, to play a trick on Bismarck and write something (Morgan) which he simply could not ban. But even with the best will in the world – I could not do it. I simply *can* not write the chapter on monogamy and the concluding chapter on private property as the source of class conflict and as the instrument for the destruction of the old communal system in such a way that it keeps within the bounds of the Anti-Socialist Law.¹ As Luther said: The Devil take me, I cannot do otherwise.

The thing would also be meaningless if I only wished to make an 'objective' report on M[organ] and did not try to treat him critically, nor to make use of new results, nor to present our conceptions and the conclusions already gained. Our workers would get nothing from it. So – either good, and necessarily banned, or – villainous and permitted. I cannot do the latter.

Next week (Schorl[emmer] is here again until Monday) I will probably be finished: there will easily be four sheets or more. If you then *wish* – after reading it – to risk publishing it in the *N[eue] Z[eit]*, then do not blame me if blood and thunder descends upon your head. But if you are reasonable and do not want to risk the whole newspaper for the one article – then get the thing printed as a pamphlet, either in Zürich or as with *Die Frau*.² It is up to you.

I believe that the thing will have an especial importance for our overall conception. M[organ]'s results allow us to gain totally new points of view by supplying us with a factual basis in pre-history, which has been lacking up till now. Whatever doubts you may still have on individual pre-historical and 'primitive' aspects, the problem is largely solved by the 'gens' and pre-historical society explained. And so the thing must be treated seriously, closely examined, brought together in all its connections – but it must also be treated with *no heed to the Anti-Socialist Law*.

One main point is this: I must prove how brilliantly Fourier anticipated M[organ] in so very many things. Fourier's critique of civilisation only appeared in all its brilliance because of M[organ]. And this proof will need attention . . .

¹ In this letter, Engels describes his *The Origin of the Family, Private Property and the State* (1884), which involved the findings of L.H. Morgan.
² Reference to A. Bebel's *Die Frau und der Sozialismus* (Woman and Socialism), Zürich and Göttingen 1879.

181. Engels to Kautsky   *May 23, 1884*

. . . I now have *Capital* by Rodb[ertus].¹ There appears to be nothing in it. The man is an eternal repetition of the most meagre content.

The archive material is in my safe keeping and I am following it through conscientiously. As soon as I reach the concluding chapter and have organised various other things – books etc. – in the house, Volume II of *Capital* will be attacked – during the *day*, and in the *evening* I will first of all revise your *Misère de la Philosophie*² as well as making notes and introductions for it. This division is not only useful, but absolutely necessary, since M[arx]'s handwriting cannot be studied by artificial light for any length of time, unless one really wants to become blind. My critique of Rodb[ertus] will of course only limit itself mainly to the accusation of plagiarism, and all the other things – his social Utopias of Salvation, land rents, land credit, annulment of debts of landed gentry, etc. will only be mentioned in passing. So you will have enough material for seeing off this little Pomeranian exploiter of cottagers, who might perhaps have become a second-class economist if he had not been a Pomeranian. Since those Schlappes à la Thuringian Free Arse,³ who support us on one side and the professorial socialists on the other and who try to immune themselves against both sides, play the 'terrible Rodbertus' off against Marx now and try to raise even the Adolph Wagners and other Bismarckians to the status of prophets of Career Socialism, then we have absolutely no reason to spare these wonders invented by Rodbertus himself and heralded by Meyer (who knows nothing about economy and has his secret oracle in Rodbertus). The man has give us nothing economical, he has a deal of talent, but always remained a dilettante and above all an ignorant Pomeranian and arrogant Prussian. The most he has supplied is all kinds of nice and correct points of view, but he has never been able to make anything of them. How can a well-behaved fellow even think of being the evangelist of the careerists of Bismarckian socialism? This is the vengeance of history on this artificially flabby 'wonder' . . .

[1] K. Rodbertus-Yagetsov, *Capital. Fourth Social Letter to von Kirchmann* . . . Berlin 1884.
[2] This refers to the German translation (from French) of *The Poverty of Philosophy*, prepared by Bernstein and Kautsky, which was published in Stuttgart in 1885.
[3] A reference to the German reformist Max Quarck, whose pseudonym was 'Freiwald Thüringer' (Thuringian Free Forester) – Engels calls him 'Freiarsch Thüringer'.

182. Engels to Kautsky   *June 21, 1884*

. . . Book II of *Capital* will still give me some headaches, at least at the beginning, more than the I. But there are wonderfully beautiful investigations here, which will make people clear at last on the question of what money is and what capital is, and many other things . . .

183. Engels to Kautsky   *June 26, 1884*

The anti-Rodb[ertus] manuscript[1] will be returned tomorrow by registered post. I find but little to remark upon, I have made a few notes in pencil. Otherwise there is also the following:

1. Roman Law as the perfected law of *simple commodity production*, i.e. of pre-capitalist production which, however, usually includes the legal relations of the capitalist period. Which is precisely what our town-bourgeois *needed* for their elevation and what they did *not* find in the local prescriptive law.

On page 10 I have a number of objections. 1. Surplus value is only an exception with production by slaves and serfs; it should be called surplus *product*, which is mostly directly consumed but is not *turned into value*.

2. The question of the means of production is not quite right. In all societies based on a natural division of labour, the product, and so also to a certain degree the means of production – at least in part – governs the producers. In the Middle Ages, the land governed the peasant, who was only a part of the land, the craftsman's tool governed the guild-worker. Division of labour is the direct rule of the instrument of labour over the worker, if not in the capitalist sense.

A similar fault appears at the end of your section on the means of production.

1. You ought not to separate *agriculture* from political economy, and even less from *technology*, as you do on page 21 and 22. Crop rotation, artificial fertiliser, the steam engine, mechanised weaving-looms – are not to be separated from capitalist production, just as the tools of the primitives and the barbarians can be separated from *their* production. The tools of the primitive determine his society just as much as modern ones determine capitalist society. Your view is that production indeed determines the social institution *now*, but that this was not the case before capitalist production, because the tools had as yet committed no Original Sin.

As soon as you say means of production, you also say society, and society *co-determined* by these means of production. Means of production *as such*, outside society and without influence on it, cannot exist any more than capital *as such*, but we still have to prove how the means of production, which only had a very mild effect in earlier periods (including simple commodity production) compared with the present one, came to have the present despotic influence, and your proof seems to be lacking because it does not mention one of the poles: the creation of a class which did not have any means of production itself, and so had no means of existence and so had to partially sell itself.

As for the positive suggestions of Rodb[ertus], the thing to stress is his Proudhonism – he declares himself for Proudhon I who anticipated the French Proudhon. Constituted value, which Rodb[ertus] discovered as early as 1842, has to be established. These suggestions are pitiful echoes of the exchange bank of Bray and Proudhon. The worker is only supposed to have one quarter of the product, but that for certain! We can talk about that later.

Rest (physical) is doing me a deal of good, I am improving every day and this time I am effecting a real cure. The dictation of the II book of *Capital* is proceeding excellently. We are already at Section II – but

227

there are large gaps there. The editing is naturally provisory, but that will also be completed. I see the way forward, cela suffit.[2]

[1] Kautsky's article against Rodbertus's book *Capital*, which appeared in the social-democratic review *Neue Zeit* in 1884.
[2] French: 'that is enough'.

184. Engels to Bernstein   *August 1884*

. . . An index for *Capital* would be very desirable. But why not for the whole thing when it is ready? But that will probably happen next year, if I do not collapse, of which there is at present no prospect. Also, between ourselves, the *History of Theory* is mostly written.[1] The manuscript for the *Critique of Political Economy* of 1860 to 1862 contains, as I think I showed you here, circa 500 quarto pages. *Theories of Surplus Value*, in which incidentally there is a great deal to be deleted, since it has been treated differently in the meantime, but that is enough of that.

Lassalle has quoted Rodbertus on one occasion in his Schulze-Bastiat,[2] which would have earned him some healthy enmity from anyone else. That is, as the authority – or inventor – of a trifle. The *letters*[3] may indeed have contributed much to the Rodbertus cult. The main factor was the wish of the non-Communists to set up an equally non-communistic rival beside Marx, and also the unscientific confusion of people. For all those people who hang around the state-socialist border of our Party, express themselves sympathetically, but still want to avoid prosecution by the police, His Excellency Rodbertus is manna from heaven . . .

[1] Engels means the *Theories of Surplus Value*, intended as Vol.III of *Capital*.
[2] F. Lassalle, *Herr Bastiat-Schulze von Delitzsche, the Economic Julian, or: Capital and Labour*, Berlin 1864.
[3] K. Rodbertus, *Social Letters to von Kirchmann* Vols I-IV, Berlin 1850-1884.

185. Engels to Kautsky   *August 22, 1884*

. . . *Misère*.[1] The revision of the manuscript which I have is complete. Apart from a few simple misunderstandings of French niceties, which one really only properly understands in France itself, there was not much to be altered. Instead of translating 'rapports'[2] by 'Beziehungen',[3]

I usually put 'Verhältnis',[4] because the first is too vague and because M[arx] himself always translated the German 'Verhältnis' by 'rapport' and vice versa. In addition, in the example 'rapport de proportionalité',[5] the 'rapport' is *quantitative*, which can only then be translated by 'Verhältnis', because 'Beziehung' mostly has a qualitative meaning. I still have to make a few footnotes. I await your next manuscript. I can only look at passages referring to Hegel and Hegeliana in London, since I need editions of Hegel for that. I will do everything I can to finish it quickly. But at the same time, *Capital* Book II must also be completed, and there is still a damned large amount to do; and that, in *this* conflict, takes precedence! However, I will do everything I can. But when do you have to have the preface?[6] I will divide the reply to Rodbertus, one part in the preface to Book II of *Capital*, the other in the one for *Misère*. There is no alternative, since the things arrived simultaneously and the R[odbertus] accusation has been made so formally.[7] I must be polite in *Capital*, but with the preface to the *Misère* I am at liberty to speak from the heart . . .

[1] i.e. The German translation of *The Poverty of Philosophy*.
[2] French: 'relations'.
[3] German: 'connections, relationships, relations'.
[4] German: 'relation'.
[5] French: 'proportional relations'.
[6] Engels wrote the preface for the first German edition of *The Poverty of Philosophy*.
[7] Rodbertus had accused Marx of plagiarism in *Capital*.

186. Engels to Kautsky   *September 20, 1884*

Herewith the manuscripts by registered post.

In economic terms, your article on R[odbertus] was very good:[1] again, what I wish to dispute are your apodictic statements in fields where you yourself are not certain and where you lay yourself open to S[chramm] who has been skilled enough to attack.

This is particularly the case in the 'abstraction' which you have picked to pieces far too generally. The difference here is this:

Marx unites the available general content of things and relations in their most general expression of thought, so his abstraction only reflects the already existing content of things in a form of thought.

R[odbertus], on the other hand, invents a more or less incomplete expression of thought for himself and measures things against this concept, and they are supposed to behave according to it. He looks for the true, *eternal* content of things and of social relations, but their real content is essentially transient. Thus *true* capital. This is not the *present* realisation of the concept, but only an incomplete one. Instead of deducing the concept of capital from the present, indeed the only really existing, capital, he avails himself of the isolated man in order to move from present capital to true capital, and asks himself what might appear as capital in the production of the isolated man: namely, simple means of production. Thereby, true capital is unceremoniously lumped together with the means of production, which is either capital or not, according to circumstance. Thereby all the *bad* qualities, namely all the *real* qualities of capital, are removed from capital. Then he can demand that real capital should behave according to this concept, that is, should now only function as a simple social means of production, and be deprived of anything which makes it capital, and yet remain capital – indeed, precisely because of that, that it should become true capital . . .

[1] See footnote 1 to letter 183.

1885

187. Engels to Lavrov[1] *February 12, 1885*

. . . In the German translation of the *Misère* there are only a few explanatory footnotes by myself, but there is also an article on Proudhon by Marx of 1865 and his speech on free trade in 1847.

Volume II of *Capital* is at the printers; yesterday I corrected the 4th sheet. The rest of the manuscript will leave here in a fortnight. Volume III will be the most important; I will set down to it as soon as II is finished. – The English edition is being delayed since the two translators have too much to do elsewhere to set down to it zealously: I hope it will be finished before summer . . .

In the preface to Volume II of *Capital*, I come back to Rodbertus in order to prove that his objections to M[arx] are based on a completely incredible ignorance of classical political economy.

[1] This letter in French in original.

188. Engels to Becker *April 2, 1885*

. . . Volume II of *Capital* is two-thirds printed and appears in circa two months, III is well under way. This III, which contains the conclusive results, and indeed quite brilliant things, will finally overturn the whole of economic science and cause an enormous uproar . . .

189.   Engels to Danielson[1]   *June 3, 1885*

I have received your letter of the 24/6 May[2] and hope you will have received the sheets 21-26 forwarded to you 13th May. Today I forward 27-33, the conclusion. In a few days I hope to be able to send you the preface etc. From that preface you will see that the manuscript of Volume III has been written as early as 1864–1866 and thus before the period when the author, thanks to your kindness, became so intimately acquainted with the agricultural system of your country. I am at present working at the chapter on the rent of land and have so far not found any allusion to Russian conditions. As soon as the whole manuscript shall have been transcribed into a legible handwriting, I shall have to work it out by comparison with what other materials have been left by the author, and there are, for the chapter on rent, very voluminous extracts from the various statistical works he owed to you – but whether these will contain any critical notes that can be made use of for this volume, I cannot as yet tell. Whatever there is, shall be used most conscientiously. At all events the mere work of transcription will occupy me far into autumn, and as the manuscript is nearly 600 pages in folio, it may again have to be divided into two volumes.

The analysis of rent is theoretically so complete that you will necessarily find therein a good deal of interest for the special conditions of your country. Still this manuscript excludes the treatment of the pre-capitalistic forms of landed property; they are merely alluded to here and there for the sake of comparison.[3]

[1] This letter in English in the original.
[2] i.e. April 24 in the old Russian calendar and May 6 in the new.
[3] Engels had apparently not finished reading the manuscript at this point, since Section 6 of Volume III of *Capital* contains a chapter on pre-capitalistic forms of land rent (chapter 47).

190.   Engels to Sorge   *June 3, 1885*

. . . Volume II of *Capital* will now appear shortly; I am expecting the last clean-proof sheet of the preface where Rodbertus gets his deserts. Book III is proceeding splendidly, but will still take a long time – but there is no damage done, for Volume II must first be digested. Volume II will cause great disappointment, because it is so purely scientific and does not contain much agitational material. On the other hand, III will come like a thunderclap, because here the whole of capitalist production is dealt with in its interconnectedness and all of the official bourgeois economic science will be thrown overboard. But I am still going to have some trouble with this. Since New Year I have already dictated the final draft of over half and I think that I will be finished with this first task in about four months. But then comes the real editing, and that will not be easy, since the most important chapters are in a fair disorder – as far as the form is concerned. However, it will all work out, it only needs time. You understand that I must abandon everything else in order to finish, and so I must neglect my correspondence and there can be no talk of writing articles. But do me the pleasure of not putting anything in the *Socialist*[1] about what I have said about Volume III. That would only cause unpleasantness in Zürich and other places. I will say what is necessary for the public in the preface to Volume II . . .

[1] The New York organ of the National Executive of the Socialist Party of North America.

191.   Engels to Bebel   *June 22, 1885*

. . . Book III of *Capital* is for the most part dictated from the manuscript into legible handwriting. This first task will be almost ready in five or six weeks. Then comes the very difficult final editing, which will necessitate a great deal of work. But it is brilliant, will burst like a thunderstorm. I expect the first copies of Book II daily. You will receive one immediately.

192.   Engels to Danielson[1]   *August 8, 1885*

I have considered your proposal to write a special preface for the Russian edition,[2] but I do not see how I could do so in a satisfactory way.

If you consider that it will be better not to refer to Rodbertus[3] at all, then I would propose that you leave out the whole of the second part of the preface. As an exposition of the author's[4] place in the history of economical science, it is far too incomplete, unless justified by the special circumstances under which it was written, by the attacks of the Rodbertus clique. This clique is extremely influential in Germany, makes a deal of noise and will no doubt soon also be heard of in Russia. It is such a very cheap and convenient way of settling the whole question, to say that our author merely copied R[odbertus], that it is sure to be repeated everywhere where our author is read and discussed. But of all these matters you are the best judge, and so I leave the matter entirely in your own hands, the more so as I have not the remotest idea what your censorship would allow to pass and what not . . .

[1] This letter in English in the original.
[2] i.e. the Russian edition of Volume I of *Capital*.
[3] Danielson had suggested this because Rodbertus was little known in Russia. Engels puts forward the case for not omitting the references to him.
[4] i.e. Marx.

193. Engels to Danielson[1] *November 13, 1885*

. . . I had no doubt that the II volume would afford you the same pleasure as it has done to me. The developments it contains are indeed of such a superior order that the vulgar reader will not take the trouble to fathom them and to follow them out. This is actually the case in Germany, where all historical science, including political economy, has fallen so low that it can scarcely fall any lower. Our Kathedersozialisten[2] have never been much more, theoretically, than slightly philanthropic Vulgärökonomen,[3] and now they have sunk to the level of simple apologists of Bismarck's Staatssozialismus.[4] To them, the II volume will always remain a sealed book. It is a fine piece of what Hegel calls 'die Ironie der Weltgeschichte',[5] that German historical science, by the fact of the elevation of Germany to the position of the first European power, should be again reduced to the same vile state to which it was reduced by the deepest political degradation of Germany, after the Thirty Years' War. But such is the fact. And thus, German 'science' stares at this new volume without being able to understand it; only, a wholesome fear of the consequences prevents them from criticising it in public, and so, official economic literature observes a cautious silence with regard to it. The III volume will however compel them to speak out . . .

[1] This letter in English in the original.
[2] German: 'professorial socialists'.
[3] German: 'Vulgar Economists'.
[4] German: 'State Socialism'.
[4] German: 'the Irony of World History'.

1886

194. Engels to Sorge

April 29, 1886

. . . The manuscript[1] contains mostly the same things that M[arx] noted in his copy for the third edition. In other places which integrate insertions from the French edition, I do not commit myself unconditionally, because 1. the work for the third edition was much later and therefore more decisive, in my opinion, 2. M[arx] wanted to have many of the difficult passages for the intended American translation – which was outside his control – translated correctly from the French, simplified translation rather than incorrectly from the German, and this consideration is now void. In spite of this, I have been given many very useful hints which, in time, can be useful for the fourth German edition. As soon as I have finished with it, I will send it back to you by registered post . . .

I think the printing of the English translation of *Capital* Volume I is to begin in a fortnight or three weeks. I am not finished with the revision by a long chalk, but 300 pages are complete and another 100 nearly ready for printing . . .

---

[1] Marx had made a whole series of additions and amendments for the planned American translation of Volume I of *Capital* and even suggested using the French edition as the basis for the English translation. These notes by Marx form the manuscript discussed here.

195. Engels to Kelley-Vischnewetzky[1]   *August 13[-14], 1886*

. . . A very good bit of work would be a series of pamphlets stating in popular language the contents of *Das Kapital*. The theory of surplus value No.1; the history of the various forms of surplus value (co-operation, manufacture, modern industry) No.2; accumulation and the history of primitive accumulation No.3; the development of surplus value making in colonies (*last chapter*) No.4 – this would be especially instructive in America, as it would give the economical history of that country, from a land of independent peasants to a centre of modern industry, and might be completed by facts specially American . . .

[1] This letter in English in the original.

1887

196. Engels to Danielson[1]

. . . I think you will be doing a good work in showing to the public of your country the application of our author's[2] theory, to *their* circumstances. But perhaps you had better wait, as you say, until the completion of his work. The chapter on the rent of land, although written before he had studied Russian economic conditions, and written without reference thereto, will still be very necessary to you. The III volume will be taken in hand after clearing off some other accumulated work; with the exception of three Abschnitte,[3] the greater part is almost ready for press . . .

Up to the present no reviews of the English edition have appeared. The professional reviewers evidently do not know what to make of the book, and are afraid to burn their fingers.

[1] This letter in English in the original.
[2] i.e. Marx.
[3] German: 'sections'.

197. Engels to Sorge

March 10, 1887

. . . V[ischnewetzky] is not capable of translating the *Manifesto*. There is only one man who can do that, namely Sam Moore, and he is doing so just now; I already have the manuscript of the first section. But one should remember that the *Manifesto*, like almost all the smaller things by Marx and myself, are at present still too difficult for America to understand. The workers there are only now entering the movement, are still quite raw and enormously backward in theory because of their generally Anglo-Saxon and particularly American nature and imagination — here the lever must be placed directly under practice, and for that we need a whole new literature. I already suggested to V[ischnewetsky] earlier that the main points of *Capital* should be dealt with popularly in separate small pamphlets. Once the people are set on the right track, then the *Manifesto* cannot fail to have its effect; but now it would only influence a few . . .

1888

198. Engels to Danielson[1]

January 5, 1888

... I am afraid your land bank for the nobility will have about the same effect as the Prussian land banks have had. There the nobility took up loans under pretext of improving their estates, but really spent most of this money in keeping up their habitual style of living, in gambling, trips to Berlin and the provincial chefs-lieux etc.[2] For the nobility considered it their first duty *standesgemäss zu leben*,[3] and the first duty of the state seemed to them, to enable them to do so. And so, in spite of all banks, of all the enormous direct and indirect money-presents made to them by the state, the Prussian nobles are over head and ears indebted to the Jews, and no raising of the import duties on agricultural produce will save them ...

The peasants' bank too seems similar to the Prussian peasants' banks; and it is almost inconceivable how difficult it is for some people to see that all fresh sources of credit opened up to landed proprietors (small or large) must result in enslaving them to the victorious capitalists.

My eyes still require *des ménagements*,[4] but anyhow I hope in a short time, say next month, to be able to resume my work on the III volume; unfortunately I cannot as yet make any promises as to the time of finishing it.

The English translation has sold and is selling very well, indeed surprisingly well for a book of that size and class; the publisher is enchanted with his speculation. The critics are on the other hand very,

very much below the average low level. Only one good article in the *Athenaeum*; the rest either merely give extracts from the preface, or if trying to tackle the book itself, are unutterably poor. The fashionable theory just now here is that of Stanley Jevons, according to which value is determined by *utility*, id est *Tauschwert = Gebrauchswert*,[5] and on the other hand by the limit of supply (id est the cost of production), which is merely a confused and circuitous way of saying that value is determined by supply and demand. Vulgar economy everywhere! The second great literary organ here, the *Academy*, has not yet spoken.

The sale of the German edition I and II volume goes on very well. There are a great many articles written about the book and its theories, an extract or rather independent reproduction in *Karl M[arx] Ökonomische Lehren* von K[arl] Kautsky,[6] not bad, though not always quite correct; I will send it you. Then a miserable apostate Jew Georg Adler, Privatdozent[7] in Breslau, has written a big book, the title of which I forgot, to prove M[arx] wrong, but it is simply a scurrilous and ridiculous pamphlet by which the author wants to call attention – the attention of the ministry and bourgeoisie – on himself and his importance. I have asked all my friends *not* to notice it. Indeed if any miserable impotent fellow wants to *faire de la réclame*[8] for himself he attacks our author . . .

[1] This letter in English in the original.
[2] French: 'main towns'.
[3] German: 'to live according to their station'.
[4] French: 'some rest, treatment'.
[5] German: 'Exchange-value = use-value'.
[6] *Karl Marx's Economic Doctrines*, by Karl Kautsky.
[7] German: 'private tutor'.
[8] French: 'to advertise'.

199. Engels to Schmidt   *October 8, 1888*

. . . I am very curious to hear about your work.[1] Apart from you, Lexis also tried to resolve the question which I am bound to return to in the preface to Volume III of *Capital*. I am not at all astounded that you have finally arrived at the Marxist viewpoint in the course of your studies, for I believe that anyone who approaches the matter objectively and fundamentally will do the same. Even today it still gives many a professor enough trouble to keep silent about the necessary and inherent conclusion when, as usual, they are exploiting Marx; and others, as the extract from our Thucydides[2] – which you used – shows, fall back on pure childishness in order to make any kind of reply!

If my eyes last out, as I hope they do – my American trip did me an extraordinary amount of good – then Volume III will be ready for printing this winter and will burst on this society like a bomb during the New Year. I have stopped all my other tasks, or delayed them, in order to finish this off, for it is a most pressing job. The larger part is now almost ready for printing, but two or three sections out of seven require some mighty revision, particularly the first, of which there are two versions.

America I found very interesting; indeed, one should see this country with one's own eyes, for its history does not go back beyond commodity production and because it is the beloved country of capitalist production. Our normal conceptions of it are as false as those of a German schoolboy on France . . .

---

[1] C.Schmidt, *The Average Rate of Profit on the Basis of Marx's Law of Value*. Stuttgart 1889.
[2] Marx and Engels called the vulgar economist Wilhelm Roscher the 'German Thucydides' – Thucydides (460-400 BC) was a Greek historian whose style of writing was often excessively flowery and obscure, and who studied 'social evils'.

200. Engels to Danielson[1] *October 15, 1888*

I was prevented from replying to your kind letters of January 8/20 and June 3/15 – as also to a great many other letters – first by a weakness of my eyes which made it impossible for me to write at my desk for more than two hours a day and thus necessitated an almost complete neglect of work and correspondence, and second by a journey to America during August and September from which I am only just returned. My eyes are better, but as I now shall take in hand Volume III and finish it, I must still be careful not to overwork them and consequently my friends must excuse me, if my letters are not too long and not too frequent.

The disquisitions in your first letter on the relation between rate of surplus value and rate of profit are highly interesting and no doubt of great value for grouping statistics; but it is not in this way that our author attacks the problem. You suppose in your formula that every manufacturer keeps all the surplus value which he, in the first hand, appropriates. Now upon that supposition, merchants' capital and bankers' capital would be impossible, because they would not make any profit. The profit of a manufacturer therefore cannot represent *all* the surplus value he has extracted from his workmen.

On the other hand, your formula *may* serve to calculate approximately the composition of different capitals in different industries, under the rule of a common and equal rate of profit. I say *may*, because I have not at this moment materials at hand from which to verify the theoretical formula established by you.

You wonder why in England political economy is in such a pitiful state. It is the same everywhere; even classical economy, nay, even the most vulgar free trade Hausierburschen[2] are looked upon with contempt by the still more vulgar 'superior' beings, who fill the university chairs of economy. That is the fault of our author, to a great extent; he has taught people to see the dangerous consequences of classical economy; they find that *no* science at all, on this field at least, is the safer side of the question. And they have so well succeeded in blinding the ordinary philistines, that there are at the present moment four people in London, calling themselves 'Socialists', who claim to have refuted our author completely by opposing to his theory that of – Stanley Jevons! . . .

I have read with great interest your physiological observations upon exhaustion by prolonged labour time and the quantity of potential energy in the shape of food required to replace the exhaustion. To the statement of Ranke quoted by you I have to make a slight exception: if the 1,000,000 kilogrammetres in food merely replaces the amount of heat and mechanical work done, it will still be insufficient, for it does not then replace the wear and tear of muscle and nerve; for that not only heat-producing food is required, but *albumen*, and this cannot be measured in kilogrammetres alone, as the animal body is incapable of building it up from the elements.

I do not know the two books of Ed[ward] Young and Phil[ips] Bevan, but there must be some mistake in the statement, that spinners and weavers in the cotton industry in America receive $90 to 120 a year. That represents $2 a week= 8/- sterling, but in reality equal, in purchasing power, to less than 5/- in England. From all I have heard, the wages of spinners and weavers in America are nominally higher but in reality only fully equal to those in England, that would make them about $5 to 6 a week, corresponding to 12/- to 16/- in England. Remember that spinners and weavers now are all women or boys of 15 to 18 years. As to Kautsky's statement, he made the mistake of treating dollars as if they were pounds sterling; in order to reduce them to marks, he multiplied by 20 instead of by 5, thus obtaining fourfold the correct amount. The figures from the census (Compendium of the 10th census of the US, 1880, Washington 1883; p.1124, specific Cotton Manufacture) are:

Operatives and officers..174,659
deduct clerks, managers etc...2,115

172,544 operatives

Men (over 16 years) 59,685
boys (under 16 years) 15,107
women (over 15 years)..84,539
girls (under 15 years)..13,213

172,544;
total wages $42,040,510

or $243.06 per head per annum, which agrees with my estimate given above, as what the men get more will be made up by what girls and boys get less.

To prove to you to what depth of degradation economical science has fallen, Lujo Brentano has published a lecture on *Die Klassiche Nationalökonomie* (Leipzig 1888), in which he proclaims: General or theoretical economy is worth nothing, but special or practical economy is everything. Like natural science (!) we must limit ourselves to the *description* of facts; and such descriptions are of infinitely higher value than all a priori deductions. 'Like natural science!' That is *impayable* in the century of Darwin, of Mayer, Joule and Clausius, of evolution and the transformation of energy! . . .

[1] This letter in English in original.
[2] German: 'hawkers'.

1889

201. Engels to Kautsky

January 28, 1889

Today I have a suggestion to make to you, which has the blessing of Ede, Gina and Tussy.

Even in the most favourable circumstances, I predict that I will still have to go easy on my eyes for a very long time yet in order to rectify them. So the possibility of dictating the manuscript of Book IV of *Capital*[1] to anyone myself is excluded at least for a few years.

On the other hand, I must see to it that not only this, but also the other manuscripts by Marx remain usable even without me. This would only be possible if I could drum these hieroglyphics into the head of someone who could take my place if necessary and in any case assist me with the publication. And for this I can only use you and Ede. So I suggest firstly that we three do it.

Now, Book IV is the first that must be considered, and Ede is too involved with the editing of the *Sozialdemokrat* and the many hindrances and cliques in the shop here. But I think that you, with so much free time, could, with some whip-cracking and practice and with the help of your wife, translate the circa 750 pages of the original (of which a good part will probably be a reiteration of Book III) in perhaps two years, and make a readable manuscript of it. If you could but get to grips with the handwriting, you could then dictate to your wife, and then the thing will proceed quickly . . .

Ede is also burning with curiosity to be initiated into the hieroglyphics; I already have other manuscripts for him and will drum the thing into him as well, but naturally I told him that I can only pay one person, and he was very understanding about it. In the final analysis, we are talking about doing a complete edition later – something which may not be during my lifetime – of Marx's and my things; and precisely on this score I would like to make some provision. I have mentioned this to Tussy as well and we can expect every possible support from her. As soon as I have taught you two to understand Marx's handwriting without difficulty, a great weight will be lifted from my shoulders, and I can spare my eyes for a time without neglecting a basic duty, for then the manuscripts are no longer a book of seven seals for at least two people.

Until now, apart from little Eleanor, only the Edes and the Avelings know of my plan, and if you agree to it, no one apart from you need know anything of the details of the matter. And perhaps Louise will find some suitable task as well.

So consider the matter, and if you agree then come here as soon as possible . . .

[1] i.e. *Theories of Surplus Value*.

202.   Engels to Danielson[1]   *July 4, 1889*

. . . The III volume has lain fallow for the last three months in consequence of various unavoidable circumstances,[2] and as the summer season is always a very idle time, I am afraid I shall not be able to do much at it before September or October. The section on banks and credit offers considerable difficulties. The leading principles are announced clearly enough, but the whole context is such that it presupposes the reader to be well acquainted with the chief works of literature on the subject such as Tooke and Fullarton,[3] and as this is not the case generally, it will require a deal of explanatory notes, etc. . . .

The last section, 'on rent of land' will, as far as I recollect, require but formal revision, so that, the bank and credit section once finished (it is ⅓ of the whole), the last third (rent and the different classes of revenue) will not take long. But as this closing volume is such a splendid and totally unanswerable work, I considered myself bound to bring it out in a shape in which the whole line of argument stands forth clearly and in bold relief. And with the state of this manuscript – a mere first sketch, often interrupted, and left incomplete – that is not so very easy . . .

[1] This letter in English in original.

[2] Engels talks about the state of the manuscripts left by Marx in other letters – to Danielson (April 23, 1885, November 9, 1886), to Becker (May 22, 1883, June 20, 1884) and to Bebel (November 6, 1892) – which are not included in this collection.

[3] T. Tooke, *An Inquiry into the Currency Principle*, 1844; J. Fullarton, *On the Regulation of Currencies* (2nd ed.), 1845.

203.   Engels to Kautsky   *September 15, 1889*

. . . I have been able to do nothing on Volume III since February because of this damned congress, and now I am prevented by the necessity of a fourth edition of Volume I and I must first deal with that. It is no great labour, but when one is only allowed to work at a desk for three hours per day, it drags a bit. And then the two months of night and fog are coming . . .

Your articles on the miners of Thuringia[1] are the best things you have ever done, a real study which exhausts the decisive points, and that with a simple investigation of the facts, not, as with your story about population or the prehistoric family, just intended to confirm a previously-held opinion. This work sheds light on an essential part of German history; there are one or two gaps here and there in the chain of argument, but that is not of any importance. For the first time I became clear (something that I learned from Soetbeer only indistinctly and vaguely)[2] on how very much the gold and silver production in Germany (and in Hungary, whose precious metals were taken all over the West via Germany) was the last decisive moment which placed Germany economically at the head of Europe from 1470 to 1530, and so at the centre of the first bourgeois revolution in religious guise, the so-called Reformation. The *final* moment in the sense that it came on top of the relatively high development of guild-craft and transit trade and so gave Germany the advantage over Italy, France and England . . .

[1] A series of articles by K. Kautsky in *Neue Zeit* of 1889: 'The Miners and the Peasant War (1525), particularly in Thuringia'.

[2] A. Soetbeer, *The Production of Precious Metals, etc.*, Gotha 1879.

...tary stock exchange dealings of some Jay Gould or a Vanderbilt etc. – dealings which are totally alien to the particular railway and its interests qua² a means of communication. And even here in England, we have seen decades of struggles between different railway companies over the border areas between any two – struggles which devoured enormous sums of money, not in the interest of production and transport, but simply for a rivalry which was usually only intended to facilitate stock-exchange deals by the money dealers owning the shares.

I have already answered your question on 'historical materialism' as such, with these few hints at my conception of the relation of production to commodity trade, and of the two to monetary trade. The question is best understood from the standpoint of the division of labour. Society creates certain common functions which it cannot dispense with. The people mentioned here form a new branch of the division of labour *within society*. This gives them particular interests, even ones opposed to those of their mandators, they become independent of them, and – the State comes into being. And now a similar thing occurs as in commodity trade and later in monetary trade. The newly independent power has to follow the movement of production in general, but also, thanks to its inherent relative independence (that is, an independence once gained and then slowly developed), has an effect on the conditions and processes of production. This is an interaction of two unequal forces: between, on the one hand, the economic movement, and, on the other, the new political power which strives for the utmost independence and which, once instituted, is endowed with self-movement; generally speaking, the economic power asserts itself, but it must also suffer the reaction of the political movement which it itself engendered, and which has the potential for relative independence – the movement on the one hand, of the State power, and on the other of the simultaneously created Opposition. Just as the movement of the industrial market is generally, (and under the above conditions) reflected in the money market – and naturally *inverted* – so the struggle of the opposing classes which existed beforehand is reflected in the struggle between government and opposition, but also invertedly, no longer directly, but indirectly, not as a class struggle but as a struggle for political principles, and so inverted that it would take thousands of years to get to the bottom of it.

The effect of the State power on economic development can be one of three types: it can proceed in the same direction, in which case

collapses after a while in any great modern people; or it can bloc..
economic development in a particular direction and prescribe another
direction – this case comes down to one of the first two. But it is clear that
in cases II and III, the political power can cause great damage to
economic development and can create a massive wastage of energy and
material.

Now there is also the case of the conquest and brutal annihilation of
economic resources, which, under certain conditions in previous eras,
could destroy a whole local and national economic development. Today
this case has mostly quite opposite effects, at least among great peoples:
in the long run, the vanquished sometimes gain more economically,
politically and morally than the victors.

It is the same in Jus:[3] as long as the new division of labour is
necessary and creates professional lawyers, a new independent area of
activity is opened up which, even with all its general dependence on
production and trade, still has the particular ability to react upon those
areas. In a modern State, law must not only correspond to the general
economic situation and express it, but must also be an expression which
is *coherent in itself*, and which does not offend itself by inner contradictions. And in order to achieve this, the reflection of the economic
relations becomes more and more distorted. And this is all the more valid
when a law book more rarely represents the stark, undiluted, unfalsified
expression of the dictatorship of one class: for that would even offend
against the 'concept of law'. The pure and logical concept of law of the
revolutionary bourgeoisie of 1792 and 1796 has already been falsified on
all sides in the 'Code Napoléon', and as long as it is embodied in it, it
must become weaker daily on account of the increasing power of the
proletariat. And this does not prevent the 'Code Napoléon' from being
the law book which forms the basis of all new codifications in all parts of
the world. The development of 'law' thus mostly consists in the attempt
to put to one side the contradictions arising from the direct translation of
economic relations into legal principles and to create a harmonious legal
system, and then the influence and force of the further economic
development breaks through this system continually and enmeshes it in
new contradictions (I am principally talking about civil law here).

The reflection of economic relations as the principles of law is
equally necessarily one which stands on its head: it proceeds without
entering the consciousness of the person involved; the lawyer imagines

he can operate with a priori phrases, while these are really only reflections of the economy – and everything is standing on its head. And it seems to me to be natural that this inversion, which, as long as it is not recognised, constitutes the thing we call an *ideological viewpoint*, for its part also has repercussions on the economic basis and can modify it within certain limits. The basis of the law of inheritance, assuming an equal stage of development of the family, is an economic one. In spite of this, it will be difficult to prove that in England, for example, the absolute freedom to draw up a will, or in France its severe restriction, only has economic causes in every detail. But, in a very significant way, both have an effect on the economy by influencing the distribution of wealth.

As for the even more airy-fairy ideological spheres religion and philosophy, etc., these come from a prehistoric stock, existing in and a legacy of the historical period, of – what we would today call idiocy. At the basis of these various false pictures of nature, of the qualities of Man himself, of spirits, magic forces etc., there is usually only a negative economic factor; the low economic development of the prehistoric period has as its extension, and partially as its precondition or even as its cause, the false images of nature. And even if economic necessity were the mainspring of a progressive recognition of nature and became so to an increasing degree, it would still be pedantic to attempt to find economic causes for all these prehistoric idiocies. The history of the sciences is the history of the gradual displacement of this idiocy, or rather of its replacement by new, but always less absurd, idiocy. The people who attend to this again belong to particular spheres of the division of labour and imagine themselves to be occupied with a totally independent area. And insofar as they form an independent group within the social divisions of labour, so far also their productions, and their errors, have repercussions on the whole social development, even on the economic aspect. But in all this, they themselves also live under the governing influence of economic development. In philosophy, for example, this can best be shown in the bourgeois period. Hobbes was the first modern materialist (in the 18th century sense), but was an absolutist at a time when the absolute monarchy was at its zenith throughout all Europe and in England was entering a struggle with the people. In religion, as in politics, Locke was a son of class compromise and 1688. The English deists and their more logical successors, the French materialists, were the true philosophers of the bourgeoisie, the French even being those of the bourgeois revolution. The German philistine is always present in German philosophy from Kant to Hegel – now positively, now negatively. But philosophy of every period as a specific area of the division of labour, has as its precondition a specific body of thought handed down by its forebears from which it takes its point of departure. And as a result, economically backward countries can play first fiddle in philosophy: France in the 18th century as against England, on whose philosophy the French base themselves, and later Germany as against both. But in both France and Germany, philosophy, like the general flourishing of literature in that period, was also the result of an economic upsurge. I am sure about the final supremacy of economic development in these areas too, but it takes place in conditions set by the individual area itself: in philosophy, for example, by the intervention of economic influences (which usually only act in political etc. guise) on the existing philosophical material which the predecessors provided. Here economy creates nothing a novo,[4] but it determines the manner of transformation and development of the existing body of thought, in a mostly indirect fashion, since the political, legal and moral repercussions have the greatest direct influence on philosophy.

I have said everything necessary on religion in the last section on Feuerbach.

So if Barth considers that we deny each and every repercussion of the political etc. reflections of the economic movement on this movement itself, then he is simply tilting at windmills. He should just look at Marx's *Eighteenth Brumaire*, where the discussion is almost exclusively about the *particular* role which is played by political struggles and events, naturally within their *general* dependence on economic movements. Or at *Capital*, in the section, for example, on the working day, where legislation – which is indeed a political act – has such a drastic effect. Or at the section on the history of the bourgeoisie (chapter 24).[5] Or why do we struggle for the political dictatorship of the proletariat if the political power is economically impotent? Power (i.e. State power) is also an economic force!

But I have no time to criticise the book[6] at present. Volume III must first be published, and in any case I believe that Bernstein, for example, could deal with this quite well.

What all these gentlemen lack is the dialectic. They always see only a cause here, an effect there. They simply do not see that this is a hollow abstraction, that, in the real world, such metaphysical polar opposites only exist in crises, that the whole great course of history proceeds in the form of interaction – even if it is interaction between unequal forces, of which the economic movement is by far the strongest, most basic and most decisive, that nothing is absolute here and all is relative – and Hegel just does not exist for them . . .

[1] A. Soetbeer *The Production of Precious Metals etc.*, Gotha 1879.

[2] Latin: 'as'.

[3] Latin: 'law'.

[4] Latin: 'from the beginning, anew'.

[5] *Capital*, Vol. I, chapters 26–32.

[6] P. Barth, *The Philosophy of History of Hegel and the Hegelians until Marx and Hartmann.*

1891

205. Engels to Sorge

. . . I now have three pamphlets to finish, reprints of 1. *Civil War in France*, the Address of the General Council of the Commune. I will have this reprinted in a *revised* edition, along with the two statements of the General Council on the Franco-German war, which are topical today more than ever. Then an introduction by myself. 2. *Wage Labour and Capital* by Marx, which I must elevate to the stage reached by *Capital*, because otherwise it would provoke confusion among workers – on account of the imperfect manner of expression (for example, 'sale of labour' instead of 'labour power' etc.) and so an introduction is also necessary. 3. *The Development of Socialism* by myself, which I will try to make somewhat more popular where at all possible . . .

206. Engels to Kautsky

March 17, 1891

. . . And then *Wage Labour and Capital* was written in the pre-surplus-value terminology, and that must be changed for propaganda with 10,000 copies. So I must translate it into modern speech and precede it with a justification . . .

207. Engels to Oppenheim

. . . You touch on a few difficult topics which cannot be discussed exhaustively in one short letter. Certainly, it would be a progressive step if the workers' co-operatives could negotiate pay with the bosses directly and in the name of all. Here in England this has been a goal for almost fifty years, but the capitalists know their advantage too well to even nibble at it, unless forced. In the great dock strike of 1889, it was achieved, and both earlier and later it was achieved temporarily; but at the first opportunity the gentlemen emancipate themselves once more from this 'insufferable tyranny' by the co-operatives and declare it impermissible that a third, uncalled for, party should become involved in the patriarchal relationship between themselves and their workers. It is the old story: in times of good business, demand for labour forces the gentlemen to do some fair dealing, in bad times they use the surplus supply of labour to cancel all these concessions. But on the whole, the resistance of the workers and their growing organisation in such a way that the general situation – the average – rises slightly so that no crisis sets the workers back for any length to a position *below* or even *at* the null point, the *lowest* point of the previous crisis. But it is difficult to say what will happen if we ever experience a long, chronic, *general* industrial crisis of five to six years.

The employment of surplus workers by the State or by local authorities, and the nationalisation of the food trade, are points which, in my opinion, would have to be discussed more than they are in your letter. Not only *trade*, but also the potential *production* of the food in the country, would have to be involved. For how else can the surplus be employed? They are surplus precisely because there is no market for their produce. But here we arrive at the expropriation of the landowners, and that is a good stretch further than the present German or Austrian State would go. And then we cannot hope for anything like that from either one or the other. How it proceeds and what will result if the Junkers expropriate the Junkers can be seen here in England where, in every possible medieval form, a much more modern State system is in operation than anywhere right or left of the Erzgebirge.[1] That is precisely the sore point: as long as the possessing classes remain at the helm, any nationalisation is not an abolition but only an alteration in the form of exploitation; in the French, American and Swiss republics no less than in the monarchist Central and despotic Eastern Europe. And, in order to remove the possessing classes from the helm, we first need a revolution in the heads of the working masses, as is now – if relatively slowly – happening; and in order to achieve this, we need a still faster tempo in the revolution in methods of production, more machinery, more concentration of workers, more ruination of peasants and the petty bourgeoisie, more tangibility and more massivity in the inevitable results of modern big industry.

In proportion as this economic revolution is completed swifter and incisively, so measures will necessarily appear – apparently intended to alleviate sudden defects which have grown large and unbearable – whose results will undermine the roots of previous modes of production, and the working masses will gain a voice through the general franchise. *Which* particular measures will be the first depends on local and temporary conditions and cannot be predicted generally. But – this is my opinion – truly liberating steps would only be possible if the economic revolution brought the large mass of workers to a realisation of their situation, and thus paved the way to political power. The other classes could only ever patch something together or invent it. And this process of clearing workers' heads now advances rapidly day by day, and in five to ten years, divers parliaments will look quite different.

Work on Volume III will be resumed as soon as the accursed minor tasks and the endless correspondence with all the people abroad gives me time. But then I will make a revolution and close up shop and not let myself be disturbed. I hope to finish this year, I am hard pressed, and I *must* finish it . . .

[1] Mountains between south-east Germany and Czechoslovakia.

208. Engels to Schmidt

July 1, 1891

. . . I have your two letters of March 5 and June 18 in front of me. You would do best to leave your work on the credit system and the money market unfinished until Volume III appears, for you will find much that is new here and still more that has not been studied yet in this matter – new tasks along with new solutions. As soon as the summer vacation is over, Volume III will be absolutely finished. Your second plan on the transitional stages for a communist society merits reflection, but I would advise you: Nonum prematur in annum;[1] this is the most difficult question to discuss, because the conditions continually change.

For example, each new trust alters them, and within a decade, the points of attack are completely displaced . . .

¹ Latin: 'do not hurry, but take great care' (literally: 'it must be finished within nine years').

209. Engels to Danielson¹   *October 29[-31], 1891*

. . . The 'Züchtung von Millionären',² as Bismarck puts it, seems indeed to go on in your country with giant steps. Such profits as your official statistics show, are unheard of nowadays in English, French or German textile manufactories. 10, 15, at the outside 20 per cent average profits, and 25 to 30 per cent in very very exceptional years of prosperity, are considered *good*. It was only in the childhood of modern industry that establishments with the very latest and best machinery, producing their goods with considerably less labour than was at the time socially necessary, were able to secure such rates of profit. At present, such profits are made only on lucky speculative undertakings with new inventions, that is to say on one undertaking out of a hundred, the rest mostly being dead failures.

The only country where similar, or approximately similar profits are nowadays possible in staple industries, is the United States, America. There the protective tariff after the Civil War, and now the MacKinley Tariff, have had similar results, and the profits must be, are, enormous. The fact that this state of things depends entirely on tariff legislation, which may be altered from one day to another, is sufficient to prevent any large investment of *foreign* capital (large, in proportion to the quantity of domestic capital invested) in these industries, and thus to keep out the principal source of competition and lowering of profits.

Your description of the changes produced by this extension of modern industry in the life of the mass of the people, of the ruin of their home industry for the *direct consumption of the producers*, and by and by also of the home industry carried on for the capitalist purchaser, reminds me vividly of the chapter of our author on the 'Herstellung des innern Markts'³ and of what took place in most places of Central and Western Europe from 1820 to 1840. This change, of course, with you has different effects to some extent. The French and German peasant proprieror dies hard, he lingers for two or three generations in the hands of the usurer before he is perfectly ripe for being sold out of his land and house; at least in the districts where modern industry has not penetrated. In Germany the peasantry are kept above water by all sorts of domestic industries — pipes, toys, baskets, etc. — carried for account of capitalists; their spare time being of no value to them after they have tilled their little fields, they consider every copeck they receive for extra work as so much gain; hence the ruinously low wages and the inconceivable cheapness of such industrial products in Germany.

With you, there is the resistance of the *obshtshina*[4] to be overcome (although I should say that that must be giving way considerably in the constant struggle with modern capitalism), there is the resource of farming land from the large proprietors which you describe, in your letter of May 1st — a means of securing surplus value to the proprietor but also of continuing a lingering existence to the peasant *as a peasant*; and the kulaki too, as far as I can see, on the whole prefer keeping the peasant in their clutches as a *sujet à exploitation*,[5] to ruining him once and for all and getting his land transferred to them. So that it strikes me, the Russian peasant, where he is not wanted as a workman for the factory or town, will also die hard, will take a good deal of killing before he does die.

The enormous profits secured by the youthful bourgeoisie in Russia, and the dependence of these profits on a good crop (harvest) so well exposed by you, explain many things otherwise obscure. Thus what should I make out of this morning's statement in the Odessa correspondence of a London paper: the Russian commercial classes seem to be possessed of the one idea, that war is the only real panacea for the ever increasing depression and distrust from which all Russian industries are now suffering — what should I make of it and how explain it but for this complete dependence of a tariff-made industry on the home market and on the harvest of the agricultural districts on which depends the purchasing power of its only customers! And if this market fails, what seems more natural to naive people than its extension by a successful war?

Very interesting are your notes on the apparent contradiction that, with you, a good harvest does *not* necessarily mean a lowering of the price of corn. When we study the real economical relations in various countries and at various stages of civilisation, how singularly erroneous and deficient appear the rationalistic generalisations of the 18th century — good old Adam Smith who took the conditions of Edinburgh and the Lothians as the normal ones, of the universe! Well, Pushkin already knew that:

. . . i pochyemu
Nye nuzhno zolota yemu,
Kogda postoy produkt imeyet.
Otyets ponyat' yego nye mog
I zyemli otdaval v zalog.[6]

Yours very sincerely,

P.W. Rosher

Next Monday I begin again with volume III – and hope not to discontinue until complete.

This letter has been delayed until today 31st October in consequence of interruption.

[1] This letter in English in original.
[2] German: 'The breeding of millionaires'.
[3] German: 'The creation of the home market'.
[4] Peasant village community.
[5] French: 'object of exploitation'.
[6] '. . . Of gold

what has he any use,

whose wealth consists of nature's produce.

His son the father failed to understand

and mortgaged every acre of his land.' From Pushkin's *Eugen Onegin*.

210. Engels to Schmidt   *November 1, 1891*

. . . The inversion of Hegel's dialectics is based on its pretensions to being a 'self-development of thought' and so the dialectic of things is only its reflection, whereas the dialectic in our heads is in fact only the reflection of the real development which takes place in the natural and human-historical world, in accordance with dialectical forms.

Just compare Marx's study of the development from commodity into capital with Hegel's development of being to essence, and you will see a very good parallel; here the concrete development, resulting from facts, there the abstract construction, in which the most brilliant thoughts and often very important negations, such as that of quality into quantity and vice versa, are presented as an apparent self-development of one concept from another, negations of which one could easily have invented a dozen others . . .

211. Engels to Kautsky

December 3, 1891

Your letter of October 30 has been left unanswered for a long time, for which Volume III is to blame; I am sweating over it again. Just now I have reached the most difficult part, the last chapters (some six or eight) on money capital, banks, credit etc., and there, once started, I must stay without interruption, and look through the literature again, and in short be quite au fait, so that – probably – I can finally leave it all as it is, but can also be quite sure that I have not committed a blunder either positively or negatively . . .

The latest studies which have superseded Marx's chapter on the historical tendency of capitalist accumulation are in any case done by Geiser, who passes for a truly scientific authority in Breslau. But it is impossible to allow Liebknecht, in embarrassment (for he obviously did not know that the sentences were taken from *Capital*), to blurt out the first best 'rubbish!' – as he is wont to say – which entered his head . . .

212. Engels to Kautsky

December 27, 1891

. . . You will understand that – since Volume III must be resumed again as soon as possible, and then finished *without interruption* – I can only look fleetingly through your manuscript, but what I can do will be done with pleasure.

The nova[1] on exchange-value and value in the third edition of *Capital* originate in hand-written additions by Marx, unfortunately only a few, and these were developed under severe difficulties in illness; Marx searched at length for the correct expression, and corrected a great deal . . .

---

[1] Latin: 'new things'.

1892

... Many thanks for your article contra Wolf.[1] But it forced me to read Wolf's opus as well, a thing I once quietly placed in a cupboard against worse times. Since the man is of the opinion that the German language is only destined to conceal his own lack of thought, it was to a certain extent a real task to read the rubbish: however, one can soon detect the vacuity of it all. You have presented the main points clearly and quite correctly, and it was very good that you set aside all the minor issues; these are only really intended to trap the reader and divert his attention from the main errors. I had already deduced that the man is a genius when it comes to economic stupidity, from an article in the *Neue Freie Presse*, where he tried to confuse the mind of the Viennese bourgeois even more than it already is. But this time he actually exceeded my expectations.

Let us reduce his argument to mathematical expressions: C_1, C_2, two total capitals whose variable components respectively $= V_1$, V_2, and their *masses* of surplus value respectively $= S_1$, S_2. At an equal rate of profit for both (profit and surplus value being omitted for just now), we have:

$$C_1 : C_2 \;=\; S_1 : S_2, \quad \text{so} \quad \frac{C_1}{S_1} = \frac{C_2}{S_2}.$$

Now, we must determine the rates of surplus value necessitated by this condition, by multiplying the one side of the equation by $\dfrac{V_1}{V} = 1$, and the other by $\dfrac{V_2}{V_2} = 1$; thus:

$$\frac{C_1\,V_1}{S_1\,V_1} = \frac{C_2\,V_2}{S_2\,V_2} = \frac{C_1}{V_1} \times \frac{V_1}{S_1} = \frac{C_2}{V_2} \times \frac{V_2}{S_2}\,.$$

If we bring the respective factors to the other side of the equation, where the fraction is inverted, we then have:

$$\frac{C_1}{V_1} \times \frac{S_2}{V_2} = \frac{C_2}{V_2} \times \frac{S_1}{V_1} \quad \text{or} \quad \frac{C_1}{V_1} : \frac{C_2}{V_2} = \frac{S_1}{V_1} : \frac{S_2}{V_2}\,,$$

or else the rates of surplus value, in order to produce Wolf's equal rates of profit, must behave like the respective total capitals divided by their respective variable components. If they do not do this, then Wolf's equal rates of profit are out of the window. But the economic fact which Herr Wolf had to prove was that they 1. *could* do this and 2. *always had* to do this. Instead of this, he presents us with a deduction which *contains* the thesis which has to be proved as a *pre-condition*. For the equation for rates of surplus value is, as it now stands, only another form of the equation for equal rates of profit.

Example: $C_1 = 100, \quad V_1 = 40, \quad S_1 = 10$

$\phantom{\text{Example: }}C_2 = 100, \quad V_2 = 10, \quad S_2 = 10$

$$\frac{C_1}{V_1} : \frac{C_2}{V_2} = \frac{S_1}{V_1} : \frac{S_2}{V_2}$$

$$\frac{100}{40} : \frac{100}{10} = \frac{10}{40} : \frac{10}{10} \qquad \text{Correct.}$$

Now, I truly believe that you are going too far in maintaining the existence of the unconditional equality of rates of surplus value for the total large-scale production. The economic levers which determine the equality of rates of profit are, I think, much stronger and more immediate than those which act upon the equalisation of rates of surplus value. However, the *tendency* is there and the differences are practically insignificant, and finally all economic laws are only expressions of the tendencies which gradually assert themselves in conflict with each other.

When the preface to Volume III appears, Herr Wolf will be in ecstasies . . .

---

[1] Engels describes the articles by Schmidt and Wolf in the preface to Volume III of *Capital*.

214. Engels to Bebel *March 8, 1892*

. . . This business of unemployment may yet become worse next year. The protective tariff system has had precisely the same results as free trade: swamping of the markets of the individual nations, and almost everywhere at that – only not so badly here as where you are. But even here, where we have survived two or three small creeping crises since 1867, there at last seems to be an acute crisis in the offing. The colossal cotton harvests of the last two or three years (up to 9 million bales per year) have depressed prices to the worst level of the crisis of 1846 and so colossally affected production that manufacturers here have to over-produce because the American planters have over-produced! Thereby they lose a heap of money, because, with the falling prices of raw material, the product spun from expensive cotton is always already devalued before it reaches the market. *That is also the reason for the cries for help from the spinners in Germany and Alsace*; but they keep quiet about it in the Reichstag. In other branches of industry as well, there is not much more happening, railway revenues and exports of industrial products have dropped off decidedly in the last fifteen months, so that next winter it could be ugly again here. We can scarcely expect an improvement in continental protective tariff states, trade agreements could bring some temporary relief, but that will be cancelled out again within a year. And if next winter begins with the same rumpus, on a larger scale, in Paris, Berlin, Vienna, Rome, Madrid, and the same echo reverberates from London and New York, it could become more serious. But then the good thing is that, in Paris and London at least, there are town councils which recognise their dependence on their worker-electors *only too well*, and which will oppose the demands feasible today – employment in public works, short working hours, wages according to the demands of the trade unions – even less when they see in them the only and best means for protecting the masses against the worse socialist – *really* socialist – heresies. Then we shall see whether the Berlin and Viennese town

councils, which were elected according to class and electoral qual-
ification, will have to follow their example nolentes volentes . . .[1]

[1] Latin: 'willy nilly'.

215. Engels to Danielson[1]   *March 15, 1892*

. . . You are passing indeed through a momentous period for your
country, the full importance of which can hardly be over-estimated.
From your letters it seems to me that you look upon the present
neuroshai[2] not as an accident, but as the necessary result, as one of the
unavoidable concomitants of the economic development entered upon
by Russia since 1861. And that is my opinion too, as far as one can judge
from a distance. With the year 1861 Russia entered upon the development, on a scale worthy of a great nation, of modern industry. The
conviction ripened that nowadays no country can take a befitting rank
among civilised nations without possessing steam-driven industrial
machinery and providing, to a great extent at least, for its own wants of
manufactured goods. And upon that conviction Russia has acted, and
acted with great energy. That she surrounded herself with a rampart of
protective duties, was but too natural, English competition forced that
policy upon almost every great country, even Germany, where *une grande
industrie*[3] had successfully developed under *almost absolute free trade*, joined
the chorus and turned protectionist, merely to accelerate the process of
what Bismarck called die Züchtung von Millionären.[4] And if Germany
entered upon this course even without any necessity, who can blame
Russia for doing what to her *was* a necessity, as soon as the new
industrial course was once determined upon?

To some extent your present situation appears to me to find a
parallel in that of France under Louis XIV. There, too, manufactures
were placed in a condition of vitality by Colbert's protective system; and
within 20 or 30 years, it was found out, that a national manufacturing
industry, under the circumstances then existing, can be created only at
the expense of the peasantry. The Naturalwirtschaft[5] of the peasants was
broken up and supplanted by the Geldwirtschaft,[6] the home market was
created and, at the same time, nearly destroyed again, at least for the
time, by this process and the unprecedented violence with which
economic necessity enforced itself, and by the increased taxation in

money, and in men, necessitated, then, by the introduction of standing armies by conscription, as it is nowadays necessitated by the introduction of the Prussian military system of universal army service. And when at last a crop or two failed, then arose that universal state of discomfort all over the country which we find depicted in Boisguillebert and Marshal Vauban.

But there is one immense difference: the difference between old 'Manufaktur' and modern 'grande industrie' which (in the action upon the peasant, the agricultural producer on a small scale and with its own means of production) is as the difference between the old smooth-bore flint-musket of 1680 and the modern repeating rifle, calibre 7.50 millimetres, of 1892. And moreover, whereas in 1680 agriculture on a small scale was still the normal mode of production, and large estate-farming could only be a *rising* exception, but always an exception, large farming with machinery is now the rule and becomes more and more the only possible mode of agricultural production. So that the peasant today appears to be doomed.

You remember what our author said in the letter on Zhukovsky – that if the line entered upon in 1861 was persevered in, the peasants' obscina must go to ruin. That seems to me to be in course of fulfilment just now. The moment seems getting near, at least in some districts, where the whole of the old social institutions of Russian peasant life not only lose their value to the individual peasant, but become a fetter, exactly as they have done in former times in Western Europe. I am afraid we shall have to treat the *obshtshina* [7] as a dream of the past, and reckon, in future, with a capitalist Russia. No doubt a great chance is thus being lost, but against economic facts there is no help. The only curious thing is that the very men in Russia who never tire of defending the invaluable superiority of Russian primitive institutions as compared with those of the rotten Occident, are doing their very best to destroy those primitive institutions and to replace them by those of the rotten Occident!

But if the Russian peasant is doomed to be transformed into a proletarian, industrial or agricultural, the *pomeshtchik* [8] does appear to be doomed too. From what I gather, this class is even more in debt than the peasants, and has to sell out gradually. And between the two seem to step in a new class of landowners, village *kulak* [9] or town-bourgeois – the fathers of, perhaps, a future Russian landed aristocracy??

The failure of last year's crop has brought all this out into glaring daylight. And I am quite of your opinion that the causes are entirely social. As to deforestation, that is as essentially, as is the ruin of the peasants, a vital condition of bourgeois society. No European 'civilised' country but has felt it, and America,* and no doubt Russia too, feels it at this moment. Thus deforestation, in my eyes, is essentially a social factor as well as a social result. But it is also a very common pretext for interested parties, to devolve the blame for economic mishaps upon a cause which apparently nobody can be made responsible for.

The failure of the crop, in my opinion, has only made *patent* what was there already *latent*. But it has terribly accelerated the velocity of the process going on. The peasant, at seed-time this spring, will be infinitely weaker than he was at seed-time last autumn. And he will be called upon to recover strength under far more unfavourable circumstances. A pauper, over head and ears in debt, no cattle, what can he do – even in the places where he has got through the winter without having to leave his land? It therefore seems to me that it will take years before this calamity is completely overcome, and that when that point is reached, Russia will be a very different country from what she was even on 1st January 1891. And we will have to console ourselves with the idea that all this in the end must serve the cause of human progress . . .

[1] This letter in English in original.
[2] Russian: 'bad harvest'.
[3] French: 'big industry'.
[4] German: 'the breeding of millionaires'.
[5] German: 'natural economy'.
[6] German: 'money economy'.
[7] Russian: 'peasant village community'.
[8] Russian: 'estate owner'.
[9] Russian: 'rich peasants'.

* In America, I have seen it myself four years ago. There great efforts are made to counteract its effects and redress the mistake.

216. Engels to Kautsky *March 30, 1892*

Yesterday evening I sent the corrected preface back and added two lines to the 2nd edition.[1] I think that will suffice. The old preface still serves one purpose: to prevent the resuscitation of the Rodbertus swindle, which, like all such fashionable articles, has the tendency to recur periodically. Admittedly, it took effect extraordinarily rapidly. But it is not my fault that the great men played against us are fellows who can be destroyed in two prefaces. This apart, the economic deductions contained therein still benefit the Germans; the helplessness of many of our people in economic polemic is peculiar, but scarcely satisfying.

. . . A propos, I have *not* looked through the proofs of Marx's article on Pr[oudhon]² from the Berlin *Sozialdemokrat*, I had no time . . .

¹ In 1884, Engels wrote the preface to the 1st edition of Marx's *The Poverty of Philosophy*. In 1892, he revised the preface and added a few lines on the 2nd edition.
² Karl Marx, *On P.J. Proudhon*, dating from 1865. Engels attached this article to the German edition of *The Poverty of Philosophy*.

217. Engels to Danielson¹   *June 18, 1892*

. . . The fact I especially wanted to lay stress upon, is that the *neuroshai*,² to use the official expression, of last year, is not an isolated and accidental occurrence, but a necessary consequence of the whole development since the close of the Crimean War; that it is a result of the passage from communal agriculture and domestic patriarchal industry to modern industry; and that it seems to me, that this transformation must in the long run endanger the existence of the agricultural *obshtshina*³ and introduce the capitalist system in agriculture too.

I conclude from your letters that, as to these facts themselves, you are agreed with me; as to the question whether we like them or not, that is another thing, and whether we do like them or not, the facts will continue to exist all the same. The more we leave our likings and dislikings out of the question, the better we shall be able to judge of the facts themselves and of their consequences.

There can be no doubt, but that the present sudden growth of modern '*grosse Industrie*' in Russland⁴ has been caused by artificial means, prohibitive duties, state subventions etc. The same has taken place in France, where the prohibitive system has existed ever since Colbert, in Spain, in Italy, and, since 1878, even in Germany; although that country had almost completed its industrial transformation when, in 1878, the protective duties were introduced in order to enable the capitalists to compel their inland customers to pay them such high prices as would enable them to sell abroad for less than cost price. And America has done exactly the same, in order to shorten the period during which American manufacturers would not be in a position to compete on equal terms with England. That America, France, Germany and Austria will be enabled to arrive at conditions where they can successfully fight English competition in the open market of the world at least in a number of important articles, of that I have no doubt. Already now France, America and Germany have broken the industrial monopoly of England to a certain extent, which is felt here very much. Will Russia be able to attain the same position? Of that I have my doubts, as Russia, like Italy, suffers from the absence of coal in industrially favourable localities, and moreover, as you develop so well in yours of 12/24 March, has quite different historical conditions to contend with. But then we have the other question to answer: Could Russia, in the year 1890, have existed and held its own in the world, as a purely agricultural country, living upon the export of her corn and buying foreign industrial products with it? And there I believe we can safely reply: *no*. A nation of 100 millions that plays an important part in the history of the world, could not, under the present economic and industrial conditions, continue in the state in which Russia was up to the Crimean War. The introduction of steam engines and working machinery, the attempt to manufacture textile and metal products by modern means of production, at least for home consumption, *must* have been made sooner or later, but at all events at *some* period between 1856 and 1880. Had it not been made, your domestic patriarchal industry would have been destroyed all the same by English machine competition, and the end would have been – India, a country economically subject to the great Central Workshop, England. And even India has reacted by protective duties against English cotton-goods; and all the rest of the British colonies, no sooner had they obtained self-government, than they protected their home manufactures against the overwhelming competition of the mother country. English interested writers cannot make it out, that their own free trade example should be repudiated everywhere, and protective duties set up in return. Of course, they *dare* not see, that this, now almost universal, protective system is a – more or less intelligent and in some cases absolutely stupid – means of self-defence against this very English Free Trade, which brought the English manufacturing monopoly to its greatest height. (Stupid for instance in the case of Germany which had become a great industrial country under free trade and where protection is extended to agricultural produce and raw materials, thus raising cost of industrial production!) I do not consider this universal recurrence to protection as a mere accident, but as a reaction against the unbearable industrial monopoly of England; the *form* of this reaction, as I said, may be inadequate and even worse, but the historical necessity of such a reaction seems to me clear and evident.

All governments, be they ever so absolute, are *en dernier lieu*[5] but the executors of the economic necessities of the national situation. They may do this in various ways, good, bad and indifferent; they may accelerate or retard the economic development and its political and juridical consequences, but in the long run they must follow it. Whether the means by which the industrial revolution has been carried out in Russia, have been the best for the purpose, is a question by itself which it would lead too far to discuss. For my purpose it is sufficient if I can prove that this industrial revolution, in itself, was unavoidable.

What you say about the necessary accompaniments of such tremendous economic changes, is quite correct, but it applies more or less to all countries that have gone or are going through the same process. Exhaustion of the soil – *vide*[6] America; deforestation – *vide* England, France and at the present moment Germany and America; change of climate, drying up of rivers is probably greater in Russia than anywhere else on account of the level nature of the country that supplies these enormous rivers with water, and the absence of an Alpine snow-reservoir such as feeds the Rhine, Danube, Rhône and Po. The destruction of the old conditions of agriculture, the gradual transition to capitalistic farming on large farms, are processes which are completed in England and East Germany and now proceeding everywhere else. And it seems to me evident that la grande industrie en Russie tuera la commune agricole,[7] unless other great changes occur which may preserve the *obshtshina*. The question is, will there be time for such a change in public opinion in Russia, as will make it possible to graft modern industry and modern agriculture upon the *obshtshina*, and at the same time to modify the latter in such a way that it may become a fit and proper instrument for the organisation of this modern production and for the transformation of such production from a capitalistic to a socialised form? You will admit that to even think of carrying out such a change, a tremendous progress has first to be made by the public opinion of your country. Will there be time to effect this, before capitalistic production, aided by the effects of the present crisis, undermines the *obshtshina* too deeply? I have no doubt whatever that in a good many districts the *obshtshina* has recovered from the blow it received in 1861 (as described by V.V.).[8] But will it be able to resist the incessant blows dealt to it by the industrial transformation, by rampant capitalism, by the destruction of domestic industry, by the absence of communal rights of pasture and woods, by the transformation of the peasants' Naturalwirtschaft into Geldwirtschaft, by the growing wealth and power of *Kulaki* and *miroyedi*?[9]

I have to thank you too for the books you were kind enough to send me, especially Kablukov and Karyshev. At the present moment I am so overworked that I have not been able, for six months, to read through one single book in any language; I keep your books for my time of rest in August. What you say about Kablukov seems to me perfectly correct, as far as I can follow it without reading the book itself. The agricultural labourer who has no land of his own, and no hired land, finds employment for only a portion of the year, and if he is paid *for this work only*, must starve the whole unemployed time, unless he has other kinds of work to do during that time; but modern capitalist production takes every chance of such work from him. This difficulty is got over as far as possible, in the following way in Western and Central Europe: 1. The farming capitalist or landowner keeps a portion of the labourers, all the year round, on his farm and feeds them as much as possible with its products, so as to spend but little actual money. This is done to a great extent in North East Germany, in a lesser degree here in England, where however the climate admits of a good deal of agricultural work being carried on in winter. Moreover, in *capitalist farming*, there is a good deal of work to be done on a farm even in winter. – 2. Whatever is still required to keep the agricultural labourers alive, and only just alive, during winter, is often enough procured by the work of the women and children in a fresh kind of domestic industry (see *Capital*, I volume, chapter 13, 8d). This is the case in the South and West of England, and for the small peasantry, in Ireland and Germany. Of course, while the transformation is proceeding, the disastrous effects of the separation of agriculture from domestic patriarchal manufacture are most striking, and that is the case with you just now . . .

[1] This letter in English in the original.
[2] Russian: 'bad harvest'.
[3] Russian: 'peasant village community'.
[4] German: '*big industry* in Russia'.
[5] French: 'in the final analysis'.
[6] Latin: 'see'.
[7] French: 'big industry in Russia will kill off the agricultural community'.
[8] V.V.= V.P. Voronzov.
[9] Russian: 'exploiters, usurers'.

218. Engels to Schmidt *September 12, 1892*

. . . I am curious to hear more about your studies on the rate of profit. Fireman did not send me Fireman's article.[1] Is that edition to be had separately? If so, I will order one for myself if you will give me the exact details of volume and title of the article. To reprint the section on the rate of profit, particularly in advance, is absolutely impossible; you know that, with Marx, everything is so connected that nothing can be taken outside its context. Besides, if I remain in good health and am *left in peace*, I will finish Volume III this winter – but please do not breathe a word of this, I know how often I can be interrupted – and then the poor professorial souls will have comfort on that score, but then immediately have so much discomfort.

You will find an article by myself on the Marxian concept of history in the next edition of *Neue Zeit*; it has already appeared in English here.[2]

The Germans can be of absolutely no use in matters of money and credit. Marx himself cruelly mocked Knies years ago.[3] The two most useful English things are Tooke, *An Inquiry Into the Currency Principle*, 1844, and Fullarton, *On the Regulation of Currencies*, 2nd edition 1845, both only to be found in second-hand bookshops. All that has to be said on money *qua money*[4] is in Volume I of *Capital*. In III, naturally, there is a lot on credit and credit money, and it is precisely this section which is giving me the most difficulty.

Rogers's *Economical Interpretation of History* is in many respects a very educative book, but extremely shallow in theoretical terms. There is naturally no question of a conception à la Marx.

I took great pleasure in your essay in the *Neue Zeit*[5] – it came propitiously here, since the Jevons-Mengerians are waxing horribly fat in the Fabian Society and look down with endless disgust on the far out-of-date Marx. If there were a review here to publish it, I would get it translated by Aveling – under my supervision, and with your permission. But *now* that would probably be difficult – there is no such review! . . .

---

[1] P. Fireman, *Critique of the Marxian Theory of Value*. Engels describes it in the preface to Vol.III of *Capital*.

[2] *On Historical Materialism* – written as an introduction to the English edition of *The Development of Socialism, Utopian and Scientific*. An abridged version appeared in *Neue Zeit*, Vol.II, Part I (1892/93).

[3] See letter 152 above.

⁴ Latin: 'as money'.
⁵ C. Schmidt, 'The "Psychological" Movement in Recent Political Economy', in: *Neue Zeit*, Vol.11, Part II (1891/92)

219. Engels to Danielson[1]   *September 22, 1892*

So far, then, we agree upon this one point, that Russia, in 1892, could not exist as a purely agricultural country, that her agricultural production must be complemented by industrial production.

Now I maintain that industrial production nowadays means grande industrie, steam, electricity, self-acting mules, powerlooms, finally machines that produce machinery. From the day Russia introduced railways, the introduction of these modern means of production was a foregone conclusion. You *must* be able to repair your own locomotives, wagons, railways, and that can only be done cheaply if you are able to *construct* those things at home, that you intend to repair. From the moment warfare became a branch of grande industrie (ironclad ships, rifled artillery, quick firing and repeating cannon, repeating rifles, steelarmed bullets, smokeless powder etc.), la grande industrie without which all these things cannot be made, became a political necessity. All these things cannot be had without a highly developed metal manufacture. And that manufacture cannot be had without a corresponding development in all other branches of manufacture, especially textile.

I quite agree with you in fixing the beginning of the new industrial era of your country about 1861. It was the hopeless struggle of a nation with primitive forms of production against nations with modern production, which characterised the Crimean War. The Russian people understood this perfectly; hence their transition to modern forms, a transition rendered irrevocable by the Emancipation Act of 1861.

This necessity of the transition from the primitive methods of production that prevailed in 1854, to the modern methods that are now beginning to prevail – this necessity once conceded, it becomes a secondary question whether the hothouse process of fostering the industrial revolution by protective and prohibitive duties was advantageous or even necessary, or otherwise.

This industrial hothouse atmosphere renders the process acute, which otherwise might have retained a more chronic form. It crams into twenty years a development, which otherwise might have taken sixty or more years. But it does not affect the nature of the process itself, which, as you say, dates from 1861.

One thing is certain: If Russia really required, and was determined to have, a grande industrie of her own, she could not have it at all, except under *some* degree of protection, and this you admit. From this point of view too, then, the question of protection is one of *degree* only, not principle; the principle was unavoidable.

Another thing is certain: if Russia required after the Crimean War a grande industrie of her own, she could have it in one form only: the *capitalistic form*. And along with that form, she was obliged to take over all the consequences which accompany capitalistic grande industrie in all other countries.

Now I cannot see that the results of the industrial revolution which is taking place in Russia under our eyes, are in any way different from what they are, or have been, in England, Germany, America. In America conditions of agriculture and landed property are different, and this *does* make some difference.

You complain of the slow increase of hands employed in textile industry, when compared with the increase of quantity of production. The same is taking place everywhere also. Otherwise, whence our redundant 'industrial reserve'? (*Capital*, chapter 23, section 3 and 4.)

You prove the gradual replacing of men's work by that of women and children. (*Capital*, chapter 13, section 3,a.)

You complain that the machine-made goods supersede the products of domestic industry and thus destroy a supplementary production, without which the peasant cannot live. But we have here an absolutely necessary consequence of capitalistic grande industrie: the creation of the home market (*Capital*, chapter 24, section 5), and which has taken place in Germany during my lifetime and under my eyes. Even what you say, that the introduction of cotton goods destroys not only the domestic spinning and weaving of the peasants, but also their *flax cultures*, has been seen in Germany between 1820 and now. And as far as this side of the question: the destruction of home industry and the branches of agriculture subservient to it – as far as this is concerned, the real question for you seems to me this: that the Russians had to decide whether *their own* grande industrie was to destroy their domestic manufacture, or whether *the import of English goods* was to accomplish this. *With* protection, the *Russians* effected it, *without* protection, the *English*. That seems to me perfectly evident.

Your calculation that the sum of the textile products of grande industrie and of domestic industry does not increase, but remains the same and even diminishes, is not only quite correct, but would not be correct if it came to another result. So long as Russian manufacture is confined to the home market, its products can only cover home consumption. And that can only slowly increase, and, as it seems to me, ought even to decrease under present Russian conditions.

For it is one of the necessary corollaries of grande industrie, that it *destroys* its own home market by the very process by which it *creates* it. It creates it by destroying the basis of the domestic industry of the peasantry. But without domestic industry the peasantry cannot live. They are ruined, *as peasants*; their purchasing power is reduced to a minimum, and until they, *as proletarians*, have settled down into new conditions of existence, they will furnish a very poor market for the newly-arisen factories.

Capitalist production, being a transitory economical phase, is full of internal contradictions which develop and become evident in proportion as it develops. This tendency to destroy its own market at the same time it creates it, is one of them. Another is the *besvychodnoye polosheniye*[2] to which it leads, and which is developed sooner in a country *without* a foreign market, like Russia, than in countries which more or less are capable of competing on the open world market. This situation without an apparent issue finds its issue, for the latter countries, in commercial revulsions, in the forcible opening of new markets. But even then the cul-de-sac stares one in the face. Look at England. The last new market which could bring on a temporary revival of prosperity by its being thrown open to English commerce, is China. Therefore English capital insists upon constructing Chinese railways. But Chinese railways mean the destruction of the whole basis of Chinese small agriculture and domestic industry, and, as there will not even be the counterpoise of a Chinese grande industrie, hundreds of millions of people will be placed in the impossibility of living. The consequence will be a wholesale emigration, such as the world has not yet seen, a flooding of America, Asia and Europe by the hated Chinaman, a competition for work with the American, Australian and European workman on the basis of the Chinese standard of life, the lowest of all – and if the system of production has not been changed in Europe before that time, it will have to be changed then.

Capitalistic production works its own ruin, and you may be sure it will do so in Russia too. It may, and if it lasts long enough, it will surely produce a fundamental agrarian revolution – I mean a revolution in the condition of landed property, which will ruin both the *pomeshtshiki*[3] and the *mushiki*[4] and replace them by a new class of large landed proprietors drawn from the *kulaki*[5] of the villages and the bourgeois speculators of the towns. At all events, I am sure the conservative people, who have introduced capitalism into Russia, will be one day terribly astonished at the consequences of their own doings.

[1] This letter in English in original.
[2] Russian: 'hopeless situation'.
[3] Russian: 'estate owners'.
[4] Russian: 'peasants'.
[5] Russian: 'rich peasants, kulaks'.

1893

220. Engels to Bebel

January 24, 1893

... I am very curious to see the stenographic copy of Singer's speech on the Stock Exchange; it read very well in *Vorwärts*. But one point is easily passed over in this connection by all our people: the Stock Exchange is an institution where the bourgeoisie do not exploit the workers, but *each other*; surplus value changing hands in the Stock Exchange is already *in existence*, a product of *past* exploitation of workers. Only when this process is completed can it serve Stock Exchange swindles. The Stock Exchange primarily interests us indirectly, just as its influence, its effect on capitalist exploitation of the workers, is felt only indirectly, in a roundabout way. To demand that workers should become directly interested in and wax indignant on the fleecing of the Junkers, manufacturers and petty-bourgeois in the Stock Exchange, is to ask workers to reach for arms to protect their own direct exploiters, who are in possession of the surplus value thieved from these self-same workers. No thanks! But the most noble fruit of bourgeois society, as the hearth of extreme corruption, as the hothouse of the Panama and other scandals[1] – and also as an excellent means for the concentration of capitals, for the displacement and dissolution of the last rags of natural interconnections in bourgeois society, and simultaneously for the destruction of all orthodox morality, for their perversion into their opposites – as an incomparable means of destruction, as the mightiest accelerator in the impending revolution – in this historical sense, the Stock Exchange also interests us directly . . .

[1] The Panama scandal – a reference to the collapse of the limited company set up in 1879 to build the Panama Canal. In 1888, it failed and the succeeding investigation revealed large-scale corruption and speculation among French MPs and journalists.

221. Engels to Shmuilov   *February 7, 1893*

. . . Marx developed the theory of surplus value in the fifties by himself and quietly, and used all his power to resist publishing anything on it before he was completely sure of it in all details. Hence the non-appearance of the second and following numbers of *A Contribution to the Critique of Political Economy* . . .

222. Engels to Danielson[1]   *February 24, 1893*

Pardon my long silence. It was not voluntary. I have to make an effort – a supreme effort to finish Volume III this winter and spring. In order to attain that, I have to forbid myself all extra work and even all correspondence that is not absolutely necessary. Otherwise nothing would have detained me from continuing with you the discussion of our highly interesting and important problem. I have now finished – all but a few formal matters – the *redaction* of section V (banks and credit), the most difficult of all, both from the state of the subject and *from the state of the manuscript*. Now remain but two sections – ⅓ of the whole –, of these the one – rent of land – is upon a very difficult subject too, but as far as I recollect the manuscript is far more finished than that of section V. So that I still hope to be able to complete my task in the allotted time. The great difficulty was to get three to five months absolute freedom from all interruption, so as to devote the whole time to section V, and that is now fortunately done. In working, I have often thought of the immense pleasure this volume will give to you, when it appears; I shall send you advance sheets as I did for volume II . . .

[1] This letter in English in the original.

223. Engels to R. Meyer

July 19, 1893

... But the main objection which you raise[1] is that agricultural work cannot be done by industrial workers and that a shortening of the working day to a uniform length for the whole year in agriculture is not possible. But you have misunderstood Bebel the turner.

As for the question of working time, nothing prevents us from employing as many workers as necessary at sowing and harvest times and every time when a rapid deployment of labour power is required. If the working day were eight hours, then one could employ two or even three shifts per day; even if everyone only worked two hours daily – at this special work – then eight, nine or ten shifts could be used in succession, as soon as we had the people who were trained in such work. And that, and nothing else, is what Bebel said. In industry also, we will not be so limited in increasing the number of spindles that are used, say, in two hours in a spinning mill, so that the requirements of every spindle are fulfilled in two hours labour. But the spindle could then be used for ten to twelve hours, and workers employed for two hours, and a shift could be changed every two hours.

As for your objection concerning the poorer towns which are ruined for the length of their existence for agricultural work – that may well be quite true. I gladly confess my inability to plough, sow, mow, or even pick potatoes, but fortunately Germany has such a colossal rural population that a national management could easily reduce everyone's labour time and still retain the surplus force. If one were to transform all of Germany into farms of 2,000 to 3,000 'Morgen'[2] – more or less, according to natural conditions – one could then introduce machine work and all the modern improvements: for do we not have more than enough skilled workers among the peasant population? But now the farm work does not suffice to employ this population for a whole year. Great masses would lie around idle for lengthy periods if they were not employed in industry. And equally, our industrial workers would languish physically if they were not given an opportunity to work in fresh air and particularly in farming. All right, the present adult generation might not be suited for this. But if the young men and girls spend a few years in succession, in summer when there is something to do, in the country – how many college terms would they then need to cram in order to graduate in ploughing, harvesting etc? You surely do not claim that one may only spend one's life doing one thing, that one must work oneself into a state of stupidity like our peasants, until one has learned something useful about agriculture? And this, and nothing else, is what I read in Bebel's book: '. . . production itself, like the spiritual and physical education of men, can only be developed to its highest stage if the old division of town and country, agriculture and industry is eliminated'.

As for the question of the viability of large estates as against small-holdings, in my opinion it simply comes down to the fact that the large estate gradually creates the small-holding, and the latter again, just as much and just as necessarily, creates the former. Just as unlimited competition brings about monopoly, and the latter again brings about the former. This circulation, however, is unavoidably connected with crises, acute and chronic sufferings and the periodic ruin of whole layers of society, and equally with a colossal waste of means of production and products; and since we are now fortunate enough to be able to dispense with Messrs Large-Estate-Owners and no less with the peasant owners, and since agricultural production, no less than industry, has reached a stage of development which, in our opinion, not only permits but even demands the wholesale takeover of the land by society, then we have to break out of the circulus vitiosus.[3] For this purpose, large estates and large manorial estates give us a better starting point than the small peasant holdings, just as large factories in industry are more suitable than small workshops. And the political reflection of this is that the farming proletariat of large estates can become social democrats just as much as the urban proletariat, as soon as the latter press them hard, while the ruined peasant and the urban craftsman only turn to social democracy after a diversion into anti-semitism.

The suggestion that the manorial gentry engendered by feudalism – lord or squire – should ever learn to farm as bourgeois, and to look to his first allegiance like the latter, and capitalise a part of the surplus value created annually, contradicts all the experiences of all ex-feudal countries. I am quite willing to believe that the gentlemen, by necessity, must thieve for themselves many of the appurtenances of the standard of living expected of them; but it has never once happened that they learn to live within their incomes and lay beyond something for a rainy day,[4] and I have yet to see it for myself; at most exceptionally, but certainly not as a class as such. These people have lived for two hundred years from state aid alone, and that alone has tided them over every crisis.

[1] Against A. Bebel's *Die Frau und der Sozialismus* (Woman and Socialism).

[2] 1 Morgen = ⅔ acre.

[3] Latin: 'vicious circle'.

[4] From 'to live within . . . rainy day' in English in original.

224. Engels to Sorge

December 2, 1893

. . . The abolition of the Law on the Purchase of Silver[1] has saved America from a severe money crisis and will accelerate industrial recovery. But I do not know if it might not have been better if this crash had actually occurred. The phrase about cheap money seems to sit deep in the bones of your Western peasants. Firstly, they imagine that if there were a great deal of means of circulation on the land, then the bank rate would have to fall; but here they confuse means of circulation with disposable money capital, and Volume III will present very enlightening things on this.[2] But secondly it suits all debtors to run up debts at first in good currency and later to repay them in depreciated currency. Therefore the debt-ridden Prussian Junkers also cry out for a dual currency which would make a disguised Solonic repayment possible.[3] Now if the United States could have waited with their silver reform until the consequences of the idiocy had rebounded on the peasantry as well, then that would have penetrated many a thick head.

The tariff reform, however slowly it is applied, still seems to have caused a kind of panic among the manufacturers in New England. I hear – privately and from newspapers – news of numerous redundancies among the workers. But that will sort itself out as soon as the law, and hence the uncertainty, is sorted out. I am convinced that America can boldly take up competition with England in all the main branches of industry . . .

[1] In 1893, the US Congress voted to abolish the 1890 law which limited the annual purchase of silver to 54 million ounces.

[2] See Volume III, chapters 22, 26, 28.

[3] Solon (640-560 BC), a legislator in Athens, ended civil strife by announcing the cancellation of debts, the ending of serfdom and modification to the laws of Draco (Draconian laws).

1894

Engels to Starkenburg[1]   *January 25, 1894*

Here is the answer to your questions!

1. By economic conditions, which we regard as the determining basis of the history of society, we mean the manner and way in which men in a specific society produce their means of subsistence and exchange these products amongst themselves (insofar as a division of labour exists). Thus the *entire technology* of production and of transport is included in this. In our conception, this technology also determines the manner and mode of exchange and hence the distribution of products and so, after the dissolution of the gentile society, the division into classes, and hence the relations of lordship and vassalage, and hence the State, politics, Law etc. In addition, included in economic relations is the *geographical basis* on which these take place and also the actually transmitted remnants of earlier economic stages of development which have persisted, often only as tradition or *vis inertiae*,[2] and naturally the environment which surrounds this society on the outside.

If, as you say, technology is largely dependent on the state of science, then science is even more dependent on the *state* and *requirements* of technology. If society has a technical requirement, then this will advance science more than ten universities put together. The whole of hydrostatics (Torricelli etc.) was engendered by the need to regulate the mountain rivers of Italy in the 16th and 17th centuries. We only learned anything rational about electricity after its technical applications were discovered. But in Germany it is unfortunately the custom to write the history of science as if it had fallen from heaven.

2. We regard economic conditions as the ultimate determinant of historical development. But nationality itself is an economic factor. However, here we must not overlook two points:

a) Political, legal, philosophical, religious, literary, artistic etc. development is based on economic development. But they all react upon each other and also upon the economic basis. It is not the case that the economic basis is *cause*, *is solely active* and everything else is only a passive effect. Rather, there is an interaction which takes place upon the basis of the economic necessity which ultimately asserts itself. The State, for instance, exercises an influence through protective tariffs, free trade, good or bad fiscal systems, and even the deathly debility and impotence of the German philistine which resulted from the economic misery of Germany between 1648 and 1830, which are expressed firstly in Pietism and then in sentimentality and cringing servility to the princes and nobility – even that was not without economic effect. That was one of the greatest obstacles to recovery and it was not removed until the revolutionary and Napoleonic wars made the chronic misery an acute one. The economic situation, therefore, does not have an automatic effect, as people here and there try comfortably to imagine, but men make their own history; they do so however in a specific environment which conditions them, on the basis of already existing actual relations in which the economic relations – however much these themselves are influenced by the other political and ideological relations – are ultimately the decisive ones and form the one continuous thread which alone leads to understanding.

b) Men make their own history, but until now they have not done so with a collective will according to a collective plan or even in a clearly defined society. Their aspirations collide, and all such societies are therefore governed by *necessity*, whose complement and form of appearance is *accident*. The necessity which exerts itself here in every accident is again ultimately an economic necessity. And now we must deal with the so-called Great Men. That such and such a man and precisely that man is thrown up at a particular time in a particular country is, of course, pure chance. But if one eliminates him there is still a need for a substitute, and this substitute will be found, *tant bien que mal*,[3] but he will be found in the long run. That Napoleon, precisely that very Corsican, became the military dictator whom the French Republic required when it was exhausted by its own warfare, was accident; but the fact that, if a Napoleon had not been forthcoming, another would have taken his place, is shown by the fact that a man was always found as soon as he became necessary: Caesar, Augustus, Cromwell, etc. If Marx discovered the materialist conception of history, then Thierry, Mignet, Guizot and all the English historians up to 1850 show that this conception was emerging, and Morgan's discovery of the same proves that the times were ripe for it and that it just *had* to be discovered.

So with all the other chances and apparent chances of history. The further the particular field which we are investigating is removed from the economic field, and the closer it approaches the purely abstract ideological sphere, the more we shall find that it will show accidents in its development and the more its curve will run in a zigzag. But if you take the average axis of the curve, you will find that this axis will run more and more nearly parallel to the axis of economic development the longer the period considered and the wider the field dealt with.

In Germany the greatest obstacle to a correct understanding is the irresponsible neglect of economic history by literature. It is so difficult, not only to rid oneself of the conceptions of history drummed into one at school, but even more to collect all the material necessary for doing so. For instance, who has even read old G[ustave] von Gülich, whose dry collection of material still contains so much stuff for the explanation of countless political facts!

By the way, the fine example given by Marx in his *Eighteenth Brumaire* should, I think, provide a fairly good answer to your queries, precisely because it is a practical example. And I also think that the *Anti-Dühring* I, chapters 9-11 and II, chapters 2-4, and III, 1 or the introduction, and then the last section of *Feuerbach* have already touched on most of the points.

Please do not weigh each word of the above like grains of gold, but keep the general connection in mind; I regret that I have not the time to be as exact in my wording here as I should be in the case of publication . . .

[1] Starkenburg was also known as 'Borgius'.
[2] Latin: 'inertial force, inertia'.
[3] French: 'for better or worse, good or bad'.

226. Engels to Kautsky

. . . The war between China and Japan signals the end of the old China,[1] the complete, if gradual, revolution of the whole economic basis, extending to the replacement of the old connection between agriculture and industry on the land by big industry, railways etc., and hence the mass emigration of Chinese coolies to Europe, and so for us an acceleration of the debacle and a heightening of the collision leading to crisis. This is another case of the splendid irony of history: only China remains for capitalist production to conquer, and, by finally achieving this stage, makes it impossible for capitalism to exist in its fatherland . . .

[1] See also Engels's letter to Sorge of November 10, 1894, in Marx and Engels *Selected Correspondence*, Moscow 1975, pp.449-51 (No.257).

1895

227. Engels to Plekhanov[1] *February 26, 1895*

. . . I will not have the time to read the critique in *Russkoye Bogatstvo* concerning my book.[2] I have already seen enough on the subject in the volume of January 1894.[3] As for Danielson, I fear there is nothing to be done with him. I sent him, *by letter*, the Russian affairs column under the title of 'International News from the "People's State"', and in particular the 1894[4] appendix which was written, *in part*, directly with him in mind. He received it, but, as you see, it is useless. There is no way of discussing with the generation of Russians to which he belongs, which always believes in the spontaneo-communist mission which distinguishes these Russians, the true *Svyataya Russi*,[5] from other profane peoples.

For the rest, in a country like yours where modern big industry is propped up on the primitive peasant community, and where all the intermediary phases of civilisation are represented simultaneously, in a country which besides is surrounded more or less efficiently by an intellectual Chinese Wall erected by despotism, one should not be astonished if combinations of the most bizarre and impossible ideas emerge. Look at that poor devil Flerovsky, who imagines that tables and beds think but have no memory. This is a phase through which the country has to pass. Little by little, with the growth of towns, the isolation of talented people will disappear and with it these mental aberrations which are caused by isolation, by the disconnectedness of sporadic knowledge of those odd thinkers, and with those *Narodniki*,[6] by the despair at seeing their hopes fade. In fact, a Narodnik ex-terrorist will end up quite logically as a Tsarist.

In order to get involved in this polemic, I would have to read a whole literature, and then follow the polemic and reply to it. But this would take up all my time for a year; and the only useful result would probably be that I know Russian much better than now; but I am being asked to do the same for Italy, with reference to the illustrious Loria. And I am already overwhelmed with work!. . .

[1] This letter in French in original.
[2] i.e. A review of Engels's *The Origin of the Family, Private Property and the State*, by L. Sak – who was hostile to Marxism.
[3] Reference to N. Mikhailovsky's *Literature and Life*.
[4] Engels's appendix to his article 'Social News from Russia'.
[5] Russian: 'Holy Russia'.
[6] Populists.

228. Engels to Schmidt   *March 12, 1895*

. . . I believe that your letter provides some explanation of why you have been diverted when dealing with the rate of profit.[1] There I find the same tendency to go off into details, for we must blame the eclectic method of philosophising which has caused so much damage in German universities since 1848 and which loses all perspective and too often ends in rather aimless and fruitless speculation on particular points. Now, of the classical philosophers it was precisely Kant whom you chiefly studied formerly, and owing to the position of German philosophising in Kant's time and owing to his opposition to Wolf's pedantic Leibnitzianism, Kant was more or less forced to make some apparent concessions in form to this Wolfian speculation. This is how I explain your tendency, which is also apparent in your appendix on the law of value in your letter, to become so tied up with details without always, it would appear, paying attention to the interconnection as a whole, that you degrade the law of value to a fiction, a necessary fiction, somewhat in the way that Kant turned the existence of God into a postulate of the practical reason.

The objections which you raise about the law of value apply to *all* concepts, considered from the standpoint of reality. The identity of thinking and being, if I might express myself in a Hegelian manner, everywhere coincides with your example of the circle and the polygon.

Or else the two of them, the concept of a thing and its reality, run side by side like two asymptotes, always approaching each other but never meeting. This difference between the two is the very difference which prevents the concept from being reality directly and immediately and prevents reality from being its own concept immediately. Because a concept has the essential nature of the concept and does not therefore prima facie[2] coincide with reality, from which it had to be abstracted in the first place, it is nevertheless more than a fiction, unless you declare all the results of thought to be fictions because reality corresponds to them only very circuitously, and even then only approaching it asymptotically.

Is the case of the rate of profit any different? At any particular moment it exists only approximately. If for once it were to be realised in two establishments down to the last jot and dot, if both yielded *exactly the same rate of profit* in a given year, then that would be a complete accident, for in reality the rates of profit differ from business to business and from year to year according to the different circumstances, and the general rate only exists as an average of many businesses and a number of years. But if we were to demand that the rate of profit – say 14.876934 . . . down the hundredth decimal place should be exactly the same in every business and in every year, under threat of degradation to fiction, then we would grossly misunderstand the nature of the rate of profit and of economic laws in general – none of them have any reality except as an approximation, a tendency, an average, and not as *immediate* reality. This is partly due to the fact that their action collides with the simultaneous action of other laws, and partly because of their nature as concepts.

Or take the law of wages, the realisation of the value of labour power, which is realised only as an average, and not always even that, and which varies in every locality, even in every branch of industry, according to the usual standard of living. Or take the land rent, which represents a surplus profit over and above the general rate, resulting from a monopolised force of nature. In this case, too, there is by no means a direct coincidence of real surplus profit and real rent, but only approximately, on the average.

It is exactly the same with the law of value and the distribution of the surplus value according to the rate of profit.

1. Both attain their most complete approximate realisation only with the prerequisite that capitalist production has been completely established everywhere, that is, when society has been reduced to the

modern classes of landowners, capitalists (industrialists and merchants) and workers – all intermediate stages having been eliminated. This condition does not obtain yet even in England and will never exist as long as we do not let it.

2. Profit, including rent, consists of various components:

a) profit from swindling – which is cancelled in the algebraic formula;

b) profit from the increased value of stocks (for example, the remainder of the last harvest when the next one has failed). This *should* theoretically also balance out eventually, as long as it has not already been cancelled by falls in the value of other commodities, either by the capitalist buyers having to contribute what the capitalist sellers gain, or, with the means of subsistence of the workers, by eventual increases in wages. The most essential of these increases in value, however, are *not permanent*, so the balancing only occurs as an average over the years, and is totally incomplete, notoriously at the expense of the workers; they produce more surplus value because their labour power is not paid in its entirety;

c) the total sum of surplus value, from which however that part is deducted which is *presented as a gift to the buyer*, particularly in crises in which the surplus production is reduced to its real content of socially necessary labour.

From this of course it naturally follows that the total profit and the total surplus value can only coincide approximately. But if you consider that both the total surplus value and the total capital are not constant, but rather variable amounts which change from day to day, then every other coincidence of the profit rate through $\frac{\Sigma S}{\Sigma(c+v)}$ other than that of an approximating series, and any coincidence of total price and total value other than one which constantly tends towards unity and yet perpetually moves away from it again, appears an utter impossibility. In other words, the unity of concept and appearance manifests itself as an essentially infinite process, and that is just what it is, in this case as in all others.

Did feudalism ever correspond to its concept? Founded in the kingdom of the West Franks, developed in Normandy by the Norwegian conquerors, continued by the French Normans in England and in southern Italy, it came closest to its concept – in the ephemeral kingdom of Jerusalem, which left behind in the 'Assises de Jerusalem'[3] the most classic expression of the feudal order. Was this order a fiction because it achieved a shortlived existence in Palestine alone, and even that, for the most part, on paper only?

Or are the concepts which prevail in the natural sciences fictions because they by no means always coincide with reality? From the moment we accept the theory of evolution, all our concepts of organic life correspond only approximately to reality. There would otherwise be no alteration; on that day when concept and reality in the organic world coincide then all development will cease. The concept 'fish' includes life in water and breathing through gills: so how could you get from fish to amphibian without breaking through this concept? And it has been broken through, for we know of a whole series of fish which have developed their air bladders further, into lungs, and can breathe air. How could you get from the egg-laying reptile to the mammal, which gives birth to living young, without bringing one or both concepts into conflict with reality? And in reality we have in the monotremata a whole sub-class of egg-laying mammals – I have seen the eggs of the duck-billed platypus in Manchester in 1843 and in arrogant small-mindedness mocked this stupidity – as if a mammal could lay eggs: and now it has been proven! So do not treat the concept of value in the same way as I treated the duck-bill and later had to beg its pardon! . . .

[1] A reference to C. Schmidt's work *The Average Rate of Profit on the Basis of the Marxian Law of Value*, Stuttgart 1889.

[2] Latin: 'at first sight'

[3] A collection of laws of the Kingdom Of Jerusalem (1100–1187), set down in the 13th century.

229. Engels to Viktor Adler   *March 16, 1895*

. . . Since you wish to plough through *Capital* II and III while you are behind bars, I will give you few tips to make it easier.

Volume II, Section I. Read chapter 1 thoroughly, then you can take it easier with chapters 2 and 3; chapter 4 again more exactly as a summary; 5 and 6 are easy and especially 6 which deals with secondary matters.

Section II, chapters 7 to 9 are important. 10 and 11 are especially important. Similarly 12, 13, 14. 15, 16, 17 on the contrary are only for cursory reading at first.

Section III. This is a quite excellent presentation of the entire circulation of commodities and money in capitalist society (the first since the days of the Physiocrats) – excellent in content, but fearfully heavy in form because 1. it is patched together from two treatments of the problems by two different methods, and 2. because treatment No.2 was completed forcibly during a period of illness in which the brain was suffering from chronic insomnia. This section I would keep until the *very end, after the first reading* of Volume III. And this could be dispensed with at first for your work.

Then Volume III.

Important here: in Section I, chapters 1 to 4; less important for the *general* connectedness, on the other hand, and so not requiring much time at first, are chapters 5, 6, 7.

Section II. *Very important*; chapters 8, 9, 10. Chapters 11 and 12 can be skimmed through.

Section III. *Very important*, everything, 13 to 15.

Section IV. Also very important, but also easy to read – 16 to 20.

Section V. Very important – chapters 21 to 27. Less so chapter 28. Important chapter 29. On the whole not important for your purposes chapters 30 to 32; important in so far as they deal with paper money etc., chapters 33 and 34; important on the international rate of exchange; chapter 35, very *interesting for you* and easy to read, 36.

Section VI. Land rent, 37 and 38 important. Less so, but still to be taken in 39 and 40. More to be passed over, 41 to 43 (Differential rate II, particular cases). 44 to 47 again important and mostly also easy to read.

Section VII is very fine, but unfortunately only a torso and also with strong traces of sleeplessness.

Thus, if you go through the main things thoroughly according to this and the less important ones only superficially to begin with (it is best first to re-read the main things in Volume I), then you will gain an overview of the whole and then the sections you have passed over will be more easily worked through . . .

230. Engels to Schmidt

April 6, 1895

I am very grateful for your tenacity in the question of 'fiction'. Here indeed there is a difficulty, which I superseded only as a result of your insistence on 'fiction'. The solution is in III, pages 154 to 157, but not clearly developed or emphasised, and this last circumstance suggests to me that I can write a short article for *Neue Zeit*[1] on this point, with reference to Sombart and your objection. However I still have a second point in which I would like to extend Volume III by considering certain alterations in economic relations since 1865 in order to harmonise them with today's conditions.[2]

But in order to develop that point on the effectiveness and validity of the law of value, the thing would be simplified for me if you allowed me to refer not only to the 'Hypothesis' of your *Centralblatt* article,[3] but also to the 'fiction' in your two letters or one or two passages from them for a closer definition of what you mean in the 'Hypothesis' of your article. So please re-read the passage cited above and tell me then whether you will allow me to state that the passages are taken from letters to me from Dr Conrad Schmidt. If you were convinced by the Marxian position that the law of value for commodity production is something more than a necessary fiction, and if we were then of the same opinion, I would naturally renounce this gladly . . .

[1] Engels's 'Extension and Addition to Volume III of *Capital*. I. Law of Value and Rate of Profit'. In *Neue Zeit*, Vol.14, Part I (1895-96). See *Capital* Vol.III, FLPH Moscow 1959, pp.868-83.

[2] As above: 'II. The Stock Exchange'. Both these articles are printed as appendices to Volume III of *Capital*, FLPH Mosocw 1959, pp. 868-86.

[3] C. Schmidt's 'The Third Volume of Capital'. In *Sozialpolitisches Centralblatt*, Vol.4, Part 22 (February 25, 1895).

231. Engels to S. Bauer   *April 10, 1895*

I give you my best thanks for your kind despatch of the facsimile of Quesnay's *Tableau*[1] and your monograph on it, which I have just read with great interest. You emphasise with justification that, since Baudeau, no one has understood this important piece of economic work, until Marx, who was of course the first to bring the Physiocrats back out of the gloom to which they had been exiled by the later successes of the English school. If I am still permitted to publish Book IV of *Capital* you will find still more detailed recognition of Quesnay's services and those of his pupils.

[1] See the table given with letter 59 above.

232. Engels to R. Fischer

April 15, 1895

. . . It is as I feared with the essays from the old *Rheinische Zeitung*: the copyright law has lapsed and we can only salvage our right of ownership by swift action. So it is quite in order for you to announce that the articles will be printed by you, or else annotated and introduced by myself. Perhaps under the title:

Karl Marx's Early Literary Works. Three Essays from the (first) 'Rheinische Zeitung', 1842. I. The Rhineland Provincial Parliament on the Freedom of the Press. II. Ditto on the Law on the Theft of Wood. III. The Condition of the Vine Growers in the Mosel. Edited and Introduced by F. Engels.

I am not entirely happy with the title; if possible you should search around for a definite title. As for the article on the Mosel, I am certain of the thing to the extent of what I always heard from Marx, precisely through his concern with the Law on the Theft of Wood, and with the condition of the Mosel peasants, that he was directed towards economic relations by mere politics and so came to socialism . . .

233. Engels to Kautsky

May 21, 1895

. . . Meanwhile I am about to send you some work for the *N[eue Z[eit]* which will please you: 'Supplement and Addenda to *Capital*, Volume III, No. 1: "Law of Value and Rate of Profit", a Reply to the Objections of Sombart and C[onrad] Schmidt'. Later I shall send No.2: the role of the stock market, which has altered very considerably since Marx wrote on it in 1865. More will follow according to requirements and time. The first article would have been finished if my mind had been free.

As regards your book,[1] I can say that it improves the more I get into it. Plato and Early Christianity are still inadequately treated according to the original plan. The medieval sects are much better, and even crescendo.[2] The best are the Taborites, Münzer, the Anabaptists. Very many important economic analyses of political events, although they are parallelled by commonplaces where there were gaps in your study. I have learned a great deal from the book; it is an indispensable preliminary study for my new revision of the *Peasant War*. The two main mistakes are these: 1. a very sketchy examination of the development and role of the declassed, almost pariah-like elements which were bound to appear whenever a town was formed, and which constituted the lowest stratum of the population of every medieval town, outside the Markgenossenschaft[3] free from feudal dependence and the craft guild. This is difficult, but it is the *main basis*, for, by degrees, as the feudal ties were loosened, this became the *pre*-proletariat, which made the revolution in 1789 in the faubourgs[4] of Paris, which absorbed all the outcasts of feudal and guild society. You talk of proletarians, but this expression is ambiguous, and bring in the weavers whose importance you describe quite correctly – but only *after* declassed journeymen weavers came to exist outside the guilds, and only *in so far as* there were such can they be regarded as 'proletariat'. Here there is still some room for improvement.

2. You have not fully understood Germany's position in the world market, in so far as it is possible to speak of it, or Germany's international economic position at the end of the 15th century. This position *alone* explains why the bourgeois-plebeian movement in its religious form, which was defeated in England, in the Netherlands and Bohemia, could achieve a *limited* success in Germany in the 16th century: the success of its *religious form*, whereas the success of the bourgeois content was reserved for the following century and for the countries which lay on the route for the new world markets: Holland and England. This is a lengthy subject, which I hope to deal with in extenso in the *Peasant War* – if only I were already at it!

Stylistically you sometimes use the editorial style and sometimes the professorial – in order to remain popular. That should be avoided. And then please, for my sake, will you not always apply the pun to Janssen which U[lrich] v[on] Hutten used about the *'obscuri viri'*?[5] The joke is of course that it means *both*: obscure and ignorant, and that is what Hutten *meant* to say.

But that is only incidental. You and Ede, you have both dealt with a completely new subject, and that is never perfect at the first attempt. You can congratulate yourself on having finished a book which can be read, now, when *only*, as it were, a first draft is available. But now you are both bound not to let the field opened lie fallow, but to investigate further, so that in a few years you can complete a new study which fulfils all its claims . . .

---

[1] This is Kautsky's book *Die Vorläufer des neueren Sozialismus* (The Antecedents of Modern Socialism), Vol.I, Parts 1-2, Stuttgart 1895. This was written in collaboration with Eduard Bernstein. An English translation of this section is *Communism in Central Europe in the Time of the Reformation*, London 1897.

[2] Latin: 'increasingly so'.
[3] German medieval village community.
[4] French: 'suburbs'.
[5] This is a reference to the anonymous satirical pamphlets by the early 16th century Humanists (Ulrich von Hutten etc.), *Epistolae obscurorum virorum* (The Letters of Obscure/ Ignorant Men). These were published supposedly as the ignorant reply by the Church to a Humanist manifesto *Clarorum Virorum Epistolae* (Letters from Famous/Lucid Men). The pun was that the letters were both ignorant and from insignificant backwoods clerics.

234. Engels to Turati[1] *June 28, 1895*

A resumé of the three volumes of *Capital* is one of the most difficult tasks which any writer can undertake. In my opinion, there are no more than half a dozen men in Europe who are capable of undertaking it. Amongst other indispensable conditions, one would have to know bourgeois political economy inside out and be a master of the German language. Now you say that your Labriolino[2] is not too strong on this last point, while his articles in *Critica Soziale* prove that he would be better off understanding Volume I properly before trying to make an independent study of the entire work. I do not have any legal right to prevent him, but I must wash my hands of him completely . . .

[1] This letter in French in original.
[2] Lit: 'little Labriola' – Arturo Labriola.

Index of Names

ADLER, Georg (1863–1908) – German bourgeois economist, reformist. 240

ADLER, Viktor (1852–1918) — Founder and leader of the Austrian Social Democrats, influential representative of reformism in the Second International; became a Centrist during the First World War. 289

ANNENKOV, Pavel Vasilyevich (1812–1887) – Russian journalist and literary critic, moderate liberal; knew Marx personally. 6

A.P.C. – see Pulszki.

ATTWOOD, Thomas (1783–1856) – Birmingham banker, politician and economist, bourgeois radical. 59, 65

AUGUSTUS OCTAVIANUS (63 BC–14 AD) – First Emperor of Rome. 283

AVELING, Edward (1851–1898) – English Socialist, author and doctor, came to Marxism through Engels; a member of the Socialist League. Married Marx's youngest daughter Eleanor. 245, 271

BABBAGE, Charles (1792–1871) – English mathematician and engineer, economist. 52, 54

BAKUNIN, Mikhail Alexandrovich (1814–1876) – One of the theoreticians and leaders of Anarchism, opponent of Marxism. 50

BARTH, Paul (1858–1922) – Bourgeois German publicist, opponent of Marxism. 253

BASTIAT, Frederic (1801–1850) – French Vulgar Economist, preached 'the harmony of interests between labour and capital'; supporter of free trade. 50, 60, 146-8, 228

BAUDEAU, Abbé Nicolas (1730–1792) – French politician and economist, Physiocrat. 291

BAUER, Bruno (1809–1882) – German theologian and publicist, one of the leaders of the 'Young Hegelians'. 128

BAUER, Stephan (b. 1865) – Swiss bourgeois economist. 291

BAYER, Karl Robert von (pseudonym Byr) (1825–1902) – German novelist, also published military writings. 180

BEBEL, August (1840–1913) – Marxist, co-founder of the German SPD, friend of Marx and Engels. 218, 233, 263, 276, 278, 279

BECKER, Johann Philipp (1809–1886) – Brush-maker, involved in the revolutionary movement since 1830 in Germany. Took part in 1848 revolution and the 1849 uprising in south Germany. One of the organisers of the German section of the International Working Men's Association in Switzerland and editor of its journal *Der Vorbote*; friend of Marx and Engels. 101, 231

Engels's house after the death of Marx. 245

DE PAEPE, Cesar (1842–1890) – Belgian doctor and publicist, one of the founders of the Belgian socialist movement, member of the International Working Men's Association, supporter of Marx. 164

DEVILLE, Gabriel (b.1854) – French socialist, author of a popular description of *Capital* Volume I; later turned away from the socialist movement. 222

DOLLFUS, Jean (1800–1887) – Manufacturer in Mulhouse, Alsace; rented houses to the workers in his factory. 129

DOMELA-NIEUWENHUIS, Ferdinand (1822–1889) – Founder of the Dutch social-democratic party; later became an anarchist. 198, 217

DÜHRING, Eugen (1833–1921) – Bourgeois philosopher and Vulgar Economist, representative of petty-bourgeois socialism. 124-7, 168, 184-5, 216, 223

DUNCKER, Franz Gustav (1822–1888) – German publisher, democrat, founder of the Hirsch-Duncker Trade Unions which were intended to place the workers movement under the control of the bourgeoisie. Friend of Lassalle. 64-6, 68-9, 81, 99, 104, 105, 151

EDE see Bernstein.

EISERMANN – German carpenter, lived in Paris, a 'True' socialist. 5

ELEANOR see Marx, Eleanor.

ENGEL, Johann Jakob (1741–1802) – German writer and literary historian, member of the Prussian Academy of Science. 86

ERMEN, Gottfried – Main shareholder of the firm 'Ermen and Engels' in Manchester. 103, 141, 142

ERMEN, Henry – Nephew of Gottfried Ermen. 141, 142

d'ESTER, Karl Ludwig (1811–1859) – Doctor in Cologne, member of the Communist League, took part in the south German uprising of 1849 and was a member of the Revolutionary Government; later lived in exile. 1

EULER, Leonhard (1707–1783) – Mathematician, physicist and astronomer; from 1766, lived in Russia and died there. 200

FALLMERAYER, Jakob Philipp (1790–1861) – Historian and traveller. 127

FAUCHER, Julius (1820–1878) – German Vulgar Economist, Left Hegelian, 'Free Trader'. 119, 146, 147

FECHNER, Gustav Theodor (1801–1887) – German physicist and idealist. 168

FEUERBACH, Ludwig (1804–1872) – German materialist and atheist. Most important German materialist philosopher before Marx. Ideologist of the radical democrats before 1848–49. In 1870 joined the SPD. 173, 252, 283

FIELDEN, John (1784–1849) – English manufacturer and radical politician, fought for the Ten Hours Law. 129

FIREMAN, Peter (b.1863) – Russian chemist and economist, emigrated to America. 271

FIRKS, Feodor Ivanovich, Baron (Schedo-Ferroti) (1812–1872) – Baltic estate owner, reactionary writer, opponent of the emancipation of the peasantry. 152

FISCHER, Richard (1855–1926) – German social democrat, one of the editors of *Vorwärts*; later became a Centrist. 232

FLEROVSKY see Bervi.

FOSTER, John Leslie (d.1842) – Irish judge and economist. 154

FOURIER, François Marie Charles (1772–1837) – French Utopian socialist. 6, 15, 225

FRAAS, Karl Nikolaus (1810–1875) – German botanist and agriculturist, professor at the University of Munich. 124, 127, 130

FRANKLIN, Benjamin (1706–1790) – North American politician, physicist and economist. Fought for the independence of the United States of

HESS, Moses (1812–1875) – Co-founder and contributor to the *Neue Rheinische Zeitung*, supporter of 'True' socialism, later a follower of Lassalle. 3, 121, 150

HILDITCH, Richard – English advocate and economist. 207

HOBBES, Thomas (1588–1679) – English materialist philosopher, supporter of the absolute monarchy. 74, 180, 251

HOFMANN, August Wilhelm (1818–1892) – German chemist. 105

HOFSTETTEN, Johann Baptist (d.1887) – Follower of Lassalle, co-editor of the *Sozialdemokrat*. 123

HUME, David (1711–1776) – Scottish philosopher and economist, developed the quantity theory of money in the struggle against mercantilism. 65, 68, 185

HUTTEN, Ulrich von (1488–1523) – Poet, humanist; fought against the Roman Catholic clergy up to and during the German Reformation; a leader of the German Imperial nobility during their uprising in 1522. 293, 294

HUXLEY, Thomas Henry (1825–1895) – English naturalist. Friend and supporter of Darwin. 82

ITZIG see Lassalle.

JACLARD, Charles Victor (1843–1903) – French publicist, follower of Blanc, member of the International Working Men's Association. Fought in the Paris Commune. 165

JAMES I (1566–1625) – King from 1603 to 1625. 162

JANSON, Julius Eduardovich (1835–1892) – Russian liberal economist and statistician. Professor at the University of St Petersburg. 203

JANSSEN, Johannes (1829–1891) – German historian. 293

JEVONS, William Stanley (1835–1882) – English philosopher and economist, defended a subjective theory of value. 240, 242, 271

JOHNSTON, Alexander (1804–1871) – Compiled the first atlas of physical geography. 31

JOHNSTON, James Finley Weir (1790–1855) – Agriculturalist, professor in Durham, author of a series of works on agricultural chemistry and geology. 31, 160

JONES, Richard (1790–1855) – English economist. 33

JOULE, James Prescott (1818–1889) – English physicist. 243

KABLUKOV, Nikolai Alexeievich (1849–1919) – Russian economist and statistician, liberal populist, professor at the University of Moscow. 203, 270

KANT, Immanuel (1724–1804) – Founder of German classical philosophy. 252, 286

KARISCHEV, Nikolai Alexandrovich (1855–1905) – Russian economist, statistician and publicist, liberal populist. 270

KAUFMANN, Illarion Ignatievich (1848–1916) – Russian economist and statistician, professor at the University of St Petersburg. 187, 197

KAUTSKY, Karl (1854–1938) – Leader of the German SPD, editor of their paper *Die Neue Zeit*. Began as a Marxist, but became openly revisionist in the 1890s. 199, 213, 216, 219, 224-6, 228, 229, 240, 243, 244, 246, 254, 260, 266, 284, 292

KAUTSKY, Louise – Austrian Socialist, Engels's secretary from 1890 onwards. 245

KELLEY-WISCHNEWETZKY, Florence (1860–1932) – Member of the Socialist Party of the USA, later a bourgeois reformist. Translated Engels's *The Condition of the Working Class in England* into English. 236-8

KLINGS, Karl – Worker from Solingen in Germany, leading member of the General German Workers Association. 93

KNIES, Karl (1821–1898) – One of the founders of the German reactionary historical school of political economy. 186, 271

KNOWLES, Alfred – Salesman in Manchester. Friend of Engels. 96

Index of Subjects